SURVIVING

Life with a Maternal Bully

SURVIVING: LIFE WITH A MATERNAL BULLY
Copyright 2015 Glenda Taylor

ISBN-13: 978-1514237885

ISBN 10: 1514237881

Credits

Cover design and book layout @NewGalleryPublishing.com
Cover center photo © Elle1 courtesy Shutterstock.com
Front cover background courtesy GraphicStock.com
Editing @MichaeleLockhart.com

Interior is set in Palatino Linotype. Chapter titles and headers are set in COPPERPLATE GOTHIC LIGHT.

All interior photographs are from the author's private collection.

SURVIVING: LIFE WITH A MATERNAL BULLY is available for immediate download as an Ebook on Amazon.com, for Kindle e-readers, and on Smashwords.com for all other e-readers.

The print edition of SURVIVING: LIFE WITH A MATERNAL BULLY is available on Amazon.com.

SURVIVING

Life with a Maternal Bully

Glenda Taylor

And a woman who held a babe against her bosom said, Speak to us of Children. And he said:

Your children are not your children.
They are the sons and daughters of Life's longing for itself.
They come through you but not from you,
And though they are with you yet they belong not to you.

You may give them your love but not your thoughts,
For they have their own thoughts.
You may house their bodies but not their souls,
For their souls dwell in the house of tomorrow,
which you cannot visit, not even in your dreams.

You may strive to be like them,
but seek not to make them like you,
For life goes not backward nor tarries with yesterday.
You are the bows from which your children as living arrows are sent forth.
The archer sees the mark upon the path of the infinite,
and He bends you with His might that His arrows may go swift and far.

Let your bending in the archer's hand be for gladness;
For even as he loves the arrow that flies,
so He loves also the bow that is stable.
Kahil Gibran, *The Prophet*

Children love their parents.

As they grow older, they judge them.

Sometimes they forgive them.

Oscar Wilde

Bullying, like racism,

is learned in the home,

practiced in the playground,

and perfected throughout life.

The Author

A cute kid

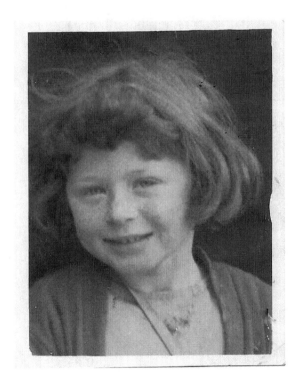

Me, about four years old

CONTENTS

ACKNOWLEDGEMENTS

1

BEGINNINGS

WHY WOULD ANY CHILD want to kill a parent? How could any child even consider killing a parent who supposedly had loved, nurtured, and protected its offspring? People listening to the nightly news would probably shrink back in their chairs, hands clasped over their mouths, horrified to learn that a child had turned into a killer.

That child could have been me.

Around the age of twelve, I began to think of my mother as Vera, not as Mum. I felt no connection to her. How could I? We had nothing in common. We looked nothing alike; we had no shared roots. She was as foreign to me as I was to her. It would have been foolish to expect love and comfort from a stranger. I grew to dislike Vera and refused to accept her as my mother.

As my story unfolds, perhaps the reader will understand why my emotions were often like an elastic band, stretched taut, ready to fly loose at any time. During our final confrontation, either Vera backed down or I might have swung from the end of a noose. "The child who killed her mother" could have been my epitaph.

Instead, I put an ocean between us.

My first eighteen years of life were stormy. I was given up for adoption by my biological mother in 1943, and a couple who were unable to have children adopted me. I suppose I would have imagined my adoptive mother would nurture, love and support me. She would praise me when I was successful, and be my cheering squad when I needed encouragement to reach a goal. My mother would tell me frequently that she loved me. She would hug and comfort me when I was hurt or had a bad dream and lift my spirits when I was down. I needed a mother who was affectionate and sensitive. My expectations proved unrealistic.

Vera was none of those things. Her focus appeared to be on duty, responsibility, and criticism. She had limited patience and felt she needed corporal punishment to discipline and control me. She seemed incapable of showing affection, offering a kind word, or a pat on the back. William Shakespeare had been right when he penned: "Expectation is the root of all heartache."

Over time, I withdrew from her emotionally and learned to keep my distance. Living in a home where I did not feel loved or wanted aroused feelings of helplessness, anger, and depression. The years dragged on and I learned to stifle my feelings. I had to survive.

When I was ten, I became cheeky and started to speak up when I felt under attack by Vera or unfairly berated. However, my defensive strategies backfired. When Vera's temper flared, my "speaking up" only increased the intensity of her wrath. A few seconds later, I would feel the sharp sting of her hand; she would bash my head against a concrete wall, or she would whack the back of my legs with the boiler stick.

Was I an easy child to raise? According to Vera, no, I was not. As an adult, I read several books about the difficulties of raising adopted children and the inability of many to attach emotionally with their adoptive mothers. Nurtured and secured for nine months in their biological mother's womb, they were in a safe environment, in tune with the rhythm of her body, recognizing the sound of her voice, and lulled to sleep by her breathing. Once born, adopted children are given to another woman, someone who is an alien. Could her smell, sound, and touch not match what the child has known for nine months? It might be traumatic. Who really knows?

Often, some adopted children can be difficult to communicate with, especially those adopted after infancy; some "act out" more than biological children. Adoptive parents needed to know this. However, in 1943, I doubt such things were discussed. Looking at the big picture, the adopted child has to come to grips with his or her reality and move on, accepting responsibility for his or her path in life. With loving, supporting parenting, the path will be smoother. With harsh or neglectful parenting, the outcome will vary.

As a pre-teenager, around age twelve, my only negative traits, at least that I remember, were that I could be outspoken and stubborn. I disliked hearing the word "No" and cringed from Vera's harsh criticism.

At the age of eleven, I recall Vera taking me into town to meet some woman.

"Glenda! Get washed and dressed. We have an appointment in town at eleven o'clock."

I was surprised. "Where're we going?"

"You'll know when we get there." Vera fumbled in her handbag. "Have you seen my wallet? Oh, no, here it is. I need someone to drill some sense into you, young lady."

I intuitively guessed it was a counselor for youngsters because Vera often accused me of being a "difficult child."

We arrived at a dark, dingy office building in the center of Bristol. Vera grasped my hand, and we stepped through the front door. Ahead of us, long, wooden benches lined the back wall. Facing us at the entrance was a blackboard with listings in white chalk of the office numbers for companies that leased space in the building.

Vera checked the board. "We need to find Room 124." She looked to her left and then to her right. "I think it's this way." We turned and headed down the corridor.

Vera knocked at Room 124 and we entered. A tall, thin woman dressed in a black skirt and pink twin-set stepped from her office to meet us. "How do you do, Mrs. Taylor? I'm Miss Jones." They shook hands. "And this must be Glenda, right?"

"Yes, this is my daughter." Vera sighed. "The one we spoke about."

Miss Jones pointed to the nearest chair. "You sit there, dear. When my conversation with your mum is over, I'll come and get you, all right?" She ushered Vera into her office.

Just before closing the door behind her, Vera wagged a finger at me. "Don't move until I return. Understood?"

I nodded. The wooden, high-backed chair in the waiting

room was uncomfortable. I didn't have a book with me, and there were no magazines in sight. I was bored. However, I followed Vera's instructions and didn't budge from the chair. I probably sat there for an hour, worrying and wondering what would happen when it was my turn to meet alone with the "pink twin-set."

The door to the inner sanctum finally opened. Out stepped Vera, with what looked to me like a self-righteous smile spread across her face. Miss Jones motioned for me to follow her. I clambered down from the chair and traipsed behind her into her office. She directed me to sit in the chair opposite her desk. The chair was rather high, leaving my legs free to swing back and forth.

Settled in her chair, Miss Jones leaned her elbows on the desk, her chin resting on her hands, and stared at me. "Well, now, Glenda. Your mother is worried. Did you know that?"

I shook my head.

"She tells me that she's having problems with you." Miss Jones paused. "She also tells me that you've become quite a handful. Why do you think that is, dear?"

"I don't know." I started swinging my legs. "I don't think I'm a handful. I'm just a kid."

A smirk crossed Miss Jones's face. "That's not what your mother says."

I fidgeted and squirmed on the tall chair. "Well, she's wrong."

"How is she wrong, dear?"

Pouting, I stared at her. "She's mean to me."

A frown furrowed Miss Jones's brow. "I'm sure she doesn't intend to be mean to you. Perhaps she's just trying to discipline you when you're naughty."

I blinked away tears that were threatening to betray my vulnerability. "She thinks I'm naughty all the time. And I'm not." I raised my voice. "She's just mean."

Miss Jones leaned back in her chair; her voice was slightly harsh. "That's not a nice thing to say about your mother."

"She's not nice to me." A tear escaped and slid down my cheek. I quickly brushed it away. "She doesn't love me."

"What a silly thing to say." Miss Jones smiled, leaned forward, arms on the desk, her hands interlocked. "All mothers love their children, you silly girl. You just need to be better behaved, and she'll love you more."

I pressed my back further against the chair, avoided eye contact with Miss Jones, looked down at my hands, and played with my fingers. She didn't get it, and I didn't know what else to say.

After thirty minutes of Miss Jones analyzing my alleged imperfections, presumably as told to her by Vera, and recommending ways I could change my behavior, she called Vera back into the room. I was not surprised when I overheard her whisper: "I understand your concerns. Your daughter can be difficult. She definitely has a mind of her own."

The rest of the conversation was a low buzz, like bees protecting a hive. Miss Jones guided Vera to a corner of the room where they continued to whisper, but the specifics were too faint to hear.

"Thank you for your time, Miss Jones." Vera walked toward me, pulling on her gloves. "Let's hope Glenda has learned something today, something that will improve her behavior." She grabbed my hand, and I climbed down from the chair.

"Come on, young lady. Let's go."

We left the dark, ugly building and made our way to the

bus stop to catch the Number 5 bus that would take us home.

We never again spoke of our visit to Miss Jones, and Dad never mentioned it. For years, I wondered why Vera pegged me as a "difficult child." Was it because I stood up for myself? Was it because I questioned her parental authority? I never figured it out.

I saw myself as a summer breeze wafting through Vera's life, not a tornado wreaking destruction. I was baffled. What did it take to please her? I did my chores, never skipped school, and got good grades. I never touched alcohol or experimented with drugs, and I continued to climb trees—and not chase boys—until I was sixteen. Teenage pregnancy was never an issue. I remained a virgin until age eighteen.

Finally, I figured it out: I could *never* satisfy Vera.

I was living with a woman who had demonstrated that she was emotionally distant, cold, and erratic. She did not believe in giving children privacy or respect. Her attitude quickly taught me to keep things to myself, and I became prickly and secretive.

Early on, I recognized a timid, sensitive side to my nature, which I learned to hide. It would be a mistake to show any vulnerability. I did not trust Vera and was loath to share information with her or reveal any dreams or fears. I never knew whether my shared inner thoughts would return to me as ridicule or become her idle gossip with neighbors over the garden fence.

I felt like an emotional prisoner in my home, frequently reminded by Vera that I should be grateful to her and my dad for adopting me. After all, I was "a bastard" who my biological mother "threw away." I was lucky to live in a home with respectable people. Time would teach me to tune out Vera's cruel remarks, but not before her words had seared deep wounds into my psyche.

I was always an avid reader, a pleasure I shared with my dad. My favorite book as a child was *Jane Eyre:* I thought Vera fit the role of Aunt Reed to perfection!

When I began to blossom into an attractive young woman, serious confrontations arose between Vera and me that revealed her jealous nature, although she would have denied this to her grave. There were times when I used this knowledge intentionally to make Vera look bad in my dad's eyes. I was no innocent in vying for Dad's attention to shift Vera into second place, a position she loathed.

If Vera possessed a sensitive, emotional side, these qualities remained hidden, at least to me. Her approach to motherhood was harsh and practical. Maybe because her previous experience with children was helping to raise her three brothers, she had no idea how to raise a daughter. I wondered whether Vera believed duty and responsibility were the only requirements for raising a child. Perhaps that was her idea of love.

Sifting through long ago, locked-away memories, I recalled hearing from family members that Vera's home environment had been turbulent. Her parents had had a rocky relationship, argued constantly, money was tight, and there were four children to feed and clothe. When Vera's sister Molly was born, the Smith family could not afford to feed a fifth mouth. Grandma Edith's sister, Elsie, was barren and had always longed for a child, so Edith gave Molly to Elsie. Since Edith's family was scrambling for daily financial survival, Vera quit school early so she could help care for her three brothers. As the eldest, Vera assumed duty and responsibility at a young age.

From a practical point of view, Vera taught me many skills. By the time I was fourteen, I could clean a house, cook and bake, and wash and iron. Most importantly, I could differentiate between needs and wants and manage money.

Learning to feel gratitude for these skills took many years of evolution. Decades later, I thanked her for these gifts.

I would run errands for the neighbors and, as a thank you, I would receive six pence. I can still hear my mother's voice: "Save thruppence and spend thruppence."

"Why? I want to spend it all!"

"You need to get into the habit of saving, young lady. Save threepence and spend threepence. 'Nuff said."

One day she was instructing me to change my bedding and clean my room. I was thirteen, and I followed her instructions. She came upstairs to inspect my room and promptly lifted up the comforter and looked under the bed. "Did you mop under here?"

"No."

"And why not?"

"Why would I? Nobody looks under my bed."

"I do. So get to it."

I bent down to mop under the bed. That was one of the few times I saw a smile flicker across Vera's face when she turned and walked away.

She was a stern taskmaster. Much later, I understood why. She wanted me to be independent. She made sure that I continued my schooling for an additional year to fine-tune my shorthand and typing skills. As Vera said, "If you can type, you can eat."

Her prediction proved accurate.

I have regretted that we were unable to connect as mother and daughter. A little humor and trust on both sides would have made a huge difference. Our relationship may never have devolved into such a desolate landscape of craggy boulders, a landscape over which we stumbled and sustained injuries that lasted a lifetime.

In 1987, everything changed. Dad died and left Vera alone. To my amazement, feelings of compassion engulfed me. It wasn't love for a mother, but compassion for a human being who was in pain and feeling lost. For Vera's sake, it was time to acknowledge her as my mother and return to calling her "Mum."

2
DEPARTURES
1985

FLIGHT 283, BOUND FOR THE UNITED KINGDOM, is now boarding at gate twenty-six. First class passengers must check their tickets...." The crisp tones of the flight attendant filled the departure lounge at the Phoenix airport.

An elderly gentleman in neatly pressed khaki pants and a brown, tweed sports jacket stood slowly and turned to face the woman seated beside him. Still slightly bent, he replaced his dark green trilby on his head, covering a monk's ring of wispy white hair, and smiled his encouragement to his wife as he extended his right arm.

Relying on her husband's arm to steady herself, the woman stood and tentatively took two steps forward, rocking slightly before gaining her balance. She smoothed real or imagined creases from her dark blue skirt and then patted her thin, white hair several times, making sure every strand was in place. Satisfied that all was in order, she leaned forward to pick up one of the three packages on the floor beside her chair.

The man intervened. "It's okay, I'll get them."

"Are you sure?"

"'Course I'm sure." Smiling tenderly, he reached down to retrieve the packages. "Here, you carry this small one. It's your Indian jewelry, remember?"

She grinned and held out her hand. "Oh, yes, I don't want to lose that."

"I'll carry the other two. Okay, here we go."

Arm in arm, they moved slowly toward the gate to board the flight that would return them to their home in England. Their thirty-day visit with their daughter in Arizona, whom they had not seen for seven years, was over.

———

The passengers were Alf and Vera Taylor, my adoptive parents. When I observed their frailty and need for each other, the anger and resentment that had festered in my heart for many years began to splinter.

They arrived in Arizona in early May1985. I had set out for the airport, my stomach in knots. *What am I going to say to these people? They're practically strangers*? I parked in front of British Airways and walked into the airport. Checking the board for incoming flights, I saw that my parents' plane had already landed. I scurried up the ramp and spotted two elderly people ahead, surrounded by luggage, sitting alone on a bench.

Drawing closer, I was stunned to realize that this frail couple was my adoptive parents. Mum was seventy years old, her hair capped snow-white. Dad, at age seventy-eight, who had always been a little chubby due to his fondness for sweets, was now thin and gaunt. Both stood up, awkward and stiff, as I came nearer. Mum's arm was tucked into Dad's, probably for security; both seemed to have shrunk at least two inches. I could tell from their expressions that they were not sure what type of welcome they would receive from their adopted daughter.

Something was happening to me that morning. Something inside overrode my stubborn reluctance to forgive. When faced with adoptive parents that were aging and fragile, despite our turbulent history, I crumbled. I discovered the beginnings of compassion for the parents that never really knew me and that I had never known.

I had arrived in their lives, a baby of six weeks, given up at birth by my biological mother needing to be loved and cherished. "Love" and "cherish" were unfamiliar concepts to Vera; duty and responsibility she understood.

It was time to retrace my steps and try to gain an understanding of my life as an adopted child, constantly shadowed by feelings of abandonment by my biological mother and living like an alien in a harsh and abusive adoptive home. After eighteen torturous years with Vera, to reach the beginning stages of forgiveness was a relief.

Looking back and waving goodbye to my parents, tears clouded my vision. I felt a strong premonition that my Dad would be gone in two years.

3
LOSS
1987

SUMMER TEMPERATURES IN ARIZONA can reach 115° degrees. When working in the yard, my flesh would feel scorched, like a pizza baking in a wood burning oven and perspiration would drip from my body.

One Saturday morning, in early summer of June 1987, I was in the kitchen, sipping my first cup of coffee and not quite awake. The phone rang, and I reached for the receiver. "Hello?"

"It's Mum. Your Dad's had a heart attack." She gulped a sob before she continued. "He's in the Bristol Infirmary. Scared me half to death. Fell down he did, right in front of the Post Office. It was awful. I had to have strangers help me get him home...."

Sorting out the details through Mum's jangled emotions was a challenge, but I managed to get the phone number of the hospital and the number of Dad's ward.

I told her, "I'm going to hang up and call the hospital. Let's hope the phone lines between Phoenix and the U.K. are not swamped. I'll call you right back. So stay put, okay?"

Mum took a few deep breaths between sobs. "All right. Don't be long."

I quickly dialed the number, thankful to hear: "Bristol Infirmary, may I help you?"

"Yes, please connect me with Ward 3. I need to speak to my father, Alfred Taylor. I'm calling from the States."

"Right you are, dear. One moment." The double trill of the phone echoed twice before I heard Dad's voice, somewhat feeble, but alert. "Hello?"

"Hi, Dad, it's me! How are you?"

I could hear the sunshine in his voice. "Glenda! Oh, it's so nice to hear your voice. I'm doing okay. Had quite a turn though." He groaned. "Whoa... and scared your mother. Scared me too. There we were, outside the post office, when I came over real queer. Had this awful pain in my chest. Took me to my knees. Not sure how I got home, but your Mum says that some kind people helped her get me back to the house."

"It's so good to speak with you, Dad." I was gladdened and reassured for the moment. "Can you transfer me to the Charge Nurse, so I can get a medical update? You know, for Mum. I said I'd call her right back, after I spoke with you."

"Course I can. Here we go."

Seconds passed before I heard clipped British tones, tinged with kindness. "Hello, my dear. This is Nurse Foster. I'm sure you want to know about your father. He's doing well, considering. We're finding it hard to keep him in bed though, but I think we've finally convinced him it's the best place. He should be able to return home in the next few days."

Relieved, I asked to be transferred back to my Dad. A few clicks later, Dad was on the line. We joked back and forth. He chuckled when he assured me that he was not chasing the nurses around the ward. Frankly, I wished he was, although for him, it would have been out of character.

"They don't even like me getting out of bed to go to the bathroom," he complained. "They want me to use those awful bedpans. I hate 'em but I have to do as they say. Should be going home in a couple of days. Be nice to sleep in my own bed. Can't sleep here, too damned noisy."

He sounded optimistic, and that made me happy.

"I'm going to call Mum with a progress report and tell her to expect you home shortly. She's worried sick. When you feel up to it, please call your favorite daughter and let her know how you're doing. Promise?"

"Course I will. Send my love to your mum. Thanks so much for calling me. You made my day."

I hung up and quickly dialed home. "Mum, I've talked to Dad and the Charge Nurse. She says he's doing fine, and Dad sounds chipper. They think he'll be released in a couple of days. Make sure he calls me when he gets home, okay?"

"All right." Vera sighed. "I don't know whether I'm coming or going. I'll be glad when this is all over. I don't know what to do with myself, being worried about your Dad and all." She sounded like a puppet without a puppeteer.

I offered more soothing comments and finally said, "Get some rest; he'll be home soon." We hung up.

I wondered at the ease of connection for my telephone calls between the hospital and my parents' home in Bristol, England. For international calls to go through without a hitch on a weekend was nearly a miracle.

In Arizona, June is one of the hottest months of the year. Dad was doing okay, so I needed to take care of the yard work before the heat became unbearable. I watered the plants and trees, filled the dogs' bowls, and made tracks to the garage to start loading the washing machine. My mind was racing, cluttered with memories of my relationship with Dad.

I recalled a gift that I had sent him several years earlier, a particularly special piece of jewelry, as it turned out.

Browsing trays of Native American jewelry in a family-owned jewelry store in Wickenburg, Arizona, I had admired an exquisite Zuni sterling silver ring inlaid with green turquoise.

"Do you have it in a smaller size?"

"No, I'm sorry we don't."

Rarely did I wear rings on my middle finger so I started to wander toward another display case when I thought of my father. Immediately, my mother's voice resonated in my head.

"Years ago I bought him a ring. He lost it. Bought him cuff links, he lost those too. God only knows how," she said. "Don't buy him anything these days; he never takes care of anything I buy him."

Although indoctrinated with Vera's pessimism for years, I chose to ignore her words and purchased the ring, knowing instinctively that it would fit my Dad, and he would not lose it. The following day I carefully packaged the ring and popped it in the mail.

About two weeks later Dad called, delighted with the ring, "It fits me perfectly." Of course it did.

The Arizona seasons tumbled one into the other and, periodically, I would read comments in Vera's letters, surprised that the ring remained snug on Dad's finger.

Recalling this incident was comforting. I had sent my Dad something to remind him of me, the little girl he had adopted and adored. When Vera's need to be Number One forced me aside as the years progressed, only then did my relationship with my Dad become fractured.

Unlike Dad's other articles of jewelry, including cuff links, which had inexplicably vanished, he did not lose the ring. I always harbored the hope that my Dad considered the ring precious because it came from me.

The sound of the phone ringing in the kitchen dragged me back to the present. *Damn! Another interruption! I'll never get this load of washing done without dissolving into a lake of sweat.*

"Glenda, it's Mum." Agonized and wounded words followed between her tears. "What shall I do? Your dad just died."

Over the line, I heard her sobbing.

"After he talked with you, he took a nap. When he woke up and reached for the bell cord, that's when it happened." She blew her nose. "He had a massive heart attack. They couldn't revive him. They tried, but it was too late."

I stopped breathing. *How could this be?* I'd just talked to him. He sounded chipper and quite strong. I didn't understand.

Hearing the torture and pain in my mother's voice, I tried to muster words of comfort but, like a toddler whose mouth is stuffed with peanut butter, I could not spit them out. Despite the heat, I shivered, trying to absorb the shattering news, listening to the distress in my mother's voice.

She suddenly said, "I'm going to hang up now. Have to call the relatives. So much to do. All on my own and no help."

I stammered a few words, but Mum was in her private world, planning what she needed to do. "I'll call you in a couple of days." The phone clicked silent.

I stood in the kitchen, staring out the window, but saw nothing. For years, I'd kept Dad on the sidelines because I felt rejected by him, but that had changed when he came to visit in 1985.

Where were my tears? Why couldn't I cry?

In the distance, the whine of the washing machine alerted me the load was ready for the dryer. Mechanically, I walked through the house to the garage. I lifted the lid of the washer, and then the tears finally began to flow. I cried for all the times I failed to tell him I loved him. I cried for all the wasted years because my anger toward him was too strong to forgive.

He once told me that he and Mum loved each other and arguing was their way of communicating. Their intense arguments always made me cringe. Now, I would have given anything to hear Dad loudly defend his position against his wife's attacks.

4
MOVING ON
1989

OUR SUNDAY MORNING PHONE RITUAL, Mum's and mine, began two years after Dad's death. At the age of seventy-two, Vera sold the family home in Bristol and moved into Chestnut Close, a snug one-bedroom apartment in an assisted living complex located in Stockwood on the outskirts of town.

Mum had sent me photographs of the two-story complex and the surrounding gardens. After researching several possibilities, it appeared to me that she had made an excellent selection: large windows with delicate white netting drapes allowed residents a private yet expansive view of well maintained grounds. Trees with luxuriant foliage generously offered shade to the complex. Honeysuckle hugged walls and fences and manicured lawns edged with rose bushes and other flowering shrubs were in abundance.

At first, our phone conversations were once a month. Mum was undoubtedly like the other residents. She would tell me how much she was reveling in her freedom from domestic responsibilities and enjoying the activities organized by the manager of the complex. There were bus tours around the British Isles, European cruises, parties, luncheons, and even the occasional date. One of her dates, after escorting her home from a birthday party, had once asked to "come in for a cup of tea".

"Cheeky monkey! I told him walking me home doesn't get you in the front door."

On another occasion, Mum talked about a new resident who had "taken a shine to her." He told her that he was lonely since his wife died and would like to get married again. He asked Mum whether she, too, was lonely.

"I have no intention of getting married again," she'd told him. "I'm through with cooking meals every day and washing a man's underpants. If you're looking for a wife, then you need to look in another direction because I'm not interested."

When I heard this, I knew that Mum had flipped her impulse control button to "off". Not surprisingly, she related that the fellow had followed her advice and pursued other matrimonial possibilities, which, according to her, seemed endless in an assisted living environment. Lonely widows missing male companionship, or seeking another mate, besieged widowers with casseroles or baked goods. It appeared to be a universal theme, but Mum had not signed on for this contest.

When Mum reached eighty-two she slowed down considerably. After ten years of freedom from marital and societal expectations, she would spend more time socializing with people in the complex who matched her pace.

She formed a close friendship with a younger woman who lived three doors away. Mum never told me her name, but I was happy to hear about the new friend because, during our eighteen years together, I met just one of Mum's friends, Gwen, and I suspected that she was Mum's only friend.

Blessed with an irreverent, dry sense of humor, Gwen would deliberately deliver one-liners and then place one hand over her mouth in mock repentance, mischief twinkling in her eyes. I connected instantly with Gwen the moment we met. She was usually upbeat and occasional good company for Mum when Dad worked nights. Her presence also deflected the constant tension between Mum and me. A sense of relaxation would envelop the house for the next couple of days and calm Mum's volatile nature.

Mum frequently told me that she had baked a Victoria sponge to take to her new friend's house the next day for tea. She loved to bake and the Victoria sponge cake was at the top of her recipe repertoire. This particular English sponge appeared in the movie *Calendar Girls.* The Yorkshire branch of the Women's Institute, the largest women's volunteer organization in the United Kingdom, held a competition for the best homemade sponge. Chris, played by Helen Mirren in the movie, entered a Victoria sponge that she'd bought from Marks & Spencer, and she won the competition.

Mum was a member for several years. And yes, it's true. If you can't bake, no worries. You can buy an excellent Victoria sponge at Marks & Spencer, a large department store in England where I had frequently shopped for lingerie and woolen sweaters and cardigans.

One Sunday morning, during one of our phone chats, Mum sounded distracted. "You don't sound yourself," I said. "Anything wrong?"

She choked back a sob. "My friend talked with her doctor yesterday." Mum sniffed and took a deep breath. "He says she has colon cancer. Can you believe that? She's only in her early sixties."

Six months later, her friend died.

Mum was distraught. "People die here all the time. I expected that, living in an old people's home. But this was so quick. I miss her. She was a good person. Never gossiped about anyone and now she's gone. Like your father. Here one day and then—*poof!*—no more. Nobody else here I want as a friend. Backstabbing bunch of nosy bitches. I'll just keep myself to myself."

For someone who made few friends this was a great loss. It was the second time Mum had lost someone she valued. The first was my father.

Dad was not particularly social: he didn't drink, play the ponies, or shoot pool, so his opportunities to form male friendships were limited to the fellows on the job. Other than Gwen, Mum and Dad lived in a world where outsiders rarely penetrated their private space. My parents seemed to communicate and understand each other, but were reticent to engage with others unless they were family.

After the loss of her friend, Mum was spending more and more time alone. She was eighty-two and no longer able to participate in many of the activities at the complex due to age-related health issues. Once I realized this, I started calling her every Sunday morning.

Several times I had suggested that she move to the States and live with me. Her response was always the same: "I'll think about it."

Vera Taylor, Chestnut Close, after Dad died

5
ROOMMATES?
1989

I HAD BEEN WILLING to give it a shot. Admittedly, it was a long shot. I'd hoped that because Mum and I were older, more mature, and she was alone, moving to Oregon or Washington and setting up house together might be an option. The climate was similar to England, and I could always find work as a paralegal, mediator, or legal secretary.

However, I wondered whether, over time, Mum would get lonely, lacking a partner to share the minutia of daily life. Surely, senior citizen groups were plentiful in the northwestern states. Mum could have made new friends, but *would* she? Except for during their dancing heyday, Mum and Dad had kept to themselves. Would she make an effort to go out and meet people, or would she rely on me as her sole companion?

Finally, Mum answered my question. She saw things differently.

"I don't think you and I can live together. Couldn't before, doubt much has changed. We are who we are, but I appreciate you asking. Besides, I don't want to uproot myself. I'd rather stay where I am, in a familiar place. If I moved, I would miss my brothers too much."

The issue was settled.

In retrospect, her refusal was a blessing. What was I thinking? The words had jumped from my mouth before my brain had a chance to clamp down on my tongue. Yes, my offer was genuine. It poured from my heart in response to the realization that Mum was alone. She'd never been alone her entire life. She was the eldest of five when she married Dad, and went straight from her parents' home to the home she shared with him for nearly fifty years.

Had Mum accepted my offer, I fear my daily routine would have required alcohol and valium to maintain civility, sociability, and equilibrium.

Vera and I were very different people. She enjoyed nattering with Dad or the neighbors, rehashing the events of the day whether they were hers or had come from others. Politics, history, literature, or world events were never topics of discussion during dinner.

Occasionally, Dad would mention something he'd read in the newspaper, and Vera would brush him aside. "Well, it's nothing to do with us. Why should we care?"

I was the first-born and only child, and therefore I always preferred the company of adults to children. I enjoyed competitive sports with my schoolmates or the neighborhood kids, but the satisfaction I felt from curling up in bed with a good book far outweighed the need for social discourse with my peers.

For the five years prior to Vera's death, I had several vivid, disconcerting dreams in which she would ask me to return to England.

"Now that your dad's gone, I have no one to talk to. It gets lonely cooking for one. My brothers all live in other parts of the country. I don't see them as often as I'd like. Don't you think it's time you came home?"

I would sit up in bed, sweating. The dream was always the same. After listening to her plea, I would refuse to return to England.

"Mum, you just don't get it. I sweated my butt off, often six days a week, sometimes working two jobs, for nearly twenty-five years to establish a professional career in the States, earn a decent salary, and shed the cloak of secretarial servitude. You pushed me into secretarial work. It was not my choice—it was what you wanted me to do. I'm not willing to return to England and give up what I've worked so hard to gain."

These dreams were very unsettling but, thankfully, the topic never came up in our weekly phone chats. They remained in the realm of dreams or, often, nightmares.

In retrospect, I need to acknowledge that my secretarial skills were extremely helpful. In my mid-forties, I finally found my niche. For twenty years, I served as a civil servant, ten years for the State of Arizona and ten years for Pima County. As it turned out, I would later discover that my biological mother's career had also been as a civil servant. I was born to be *of service*—a problem solver, an investigator, and a mediator—but not a *servant*, someone discouraged from using her brain.

6

BUILDING A RELATIONSHIP
1989–2007

IT WAS TIME TO CALL and check in on Mum. In one hand, I was carrying a mug of steaming coffee as I headed over to the phone next to the couch. In the other hand, there was a generous shot of bourbon laced with a little ginger ale in a crystal goblet. Nestled in the pocket of my shorts, menthol cigarettes and a jazzy-colored lighter were anticipating a connection.

If Vera was having a good day, the java would boost our conversation. If she was miffed at someone or about something, which would not be unusual, and started repeating herself as seniors tend to do, I'd summon the army of bourbon to forestall yawning or, worse, impatience. I sat on the couch, took a cigarette and the lighter from my pocket, and lit up. I inhaled deeply, dialed Mum's number, exhaled, and waited.

"Hello?"

"Hi, Mum! How are you?"

There was a pause. "Who's this then?"

"It's me, your only kid. Remember me?"

There was a moment of silence.

"Oh, Glenda, you're early. I wasn't expecting your call for another ten minutes."

"If you're busy, I can call back."

"No, no, that's all right. Let me get settled in the chair…. So, how are you?"

The outside world faded as I focused all my attention on my mother. How was she feeling? Did the latest medication ease her discomfort? Had she seen my Aunt Molly or heard from my Aunt Alma? How was Barbara, her friend and neighbor next door? What was the latest gossip about the elderly, suspected femme fatal who had moved into one of the downstairs flats a few weeks back and triggered heart palpitations amongst the male residents?

For twenty minutes, Mum and I swapped stories. Our lives, like arthritic joints, locked into routines with minimal drama, and each of us had adjusted to the slower pace of our respective worlds.

"Have you gone anywhere exciting lately?" I asked.

"No, don't get out much these days. Don't have the energy or the desire, truth be told."

"Are you still sewing?"

"Sometimes, if my arthritis is not too bad."

"Do you have any medication for the arthritis?"

"Nothing that works. The doctor gave me some cream to rub into my fingers, but the pain persists, so I don't use it." She sighed. "That's what happens when you get old. Mother had arthritis, so…. I suppose it's genetic. She passed it on to me."

"Do you have any new sewing projects in the works?"

"No, not right now, but I am embroidering a runner for my sideboard. I've always enjoyed embroidering, and it seems easier on the joints than sewing. All that pushing and pulling heavy fabrics through needles or through the sewing machine makes my joints ache."

"Have you heard from Molly or Alma?"

Mum grunted. "Your Aunt Molly was over here for tea a week or so back." A heavy sigh came over the phone line. "Typical Molly. Sits down all afternoon. Expects me to wait on her hand and foot. Never offers to help with the dishes. I don't know why I bother having her over here. Always complaining about her lot in life."

Mum rambled on for a minute or two until she ran out of breath. I wondered why, as she and her sister grew older, Aunt Molly had become an irritant to Mum. My great aunt and uncle—not my grandmother—raised Molly, so Mum and Molly spent very little time with each other. I decided not to pry; it wasn't any of my business.

"Well, what have you been doing with yourself?" Mum asked. "How much longer before you can retire?"

"I have to work four more years, but I like my job so that's not a problem."

"Hmm…. Must say you've done well for yourself." She paused. "Don't know how you did it, going from a secretary to a professional position. You couldn't have done that over here."

"That's why I left England. There was much more op-portunity for me here in the States, even if it took me twenty years!"

"Is that why you never came home?"

I hesitated. This was a loaded question. I never told Mum that since Dad died, I'd had several dreams of her asking me to return home because she was lonely. One advantage of com-municating by phone is that facial expressions remain hidden from the other party.

I deeply inhaled the cigarette smoke, watching the fire turn paper and tobacco into ash, and then flicked the ash into an ashtray. "Yes," I finally said. "I've worked too hard for too long to escape secretarial work and move into a professional position." *Did Mum not realize that for years I needed an ocean between us?*

Three or four seconds passed in silence.

Faster than a flea hopping from a Boxer to a Doberman, Mum changed topics. "How are the dogs?"

"Good. I go to the kennel every Sunday morning to do turnout. You know, clean out the cages, change the rugs, check those that need medical attention, and exercise and feed the greyhounds. It takes me and Griseldes, my turnout partner, about two hours to care for fifteen dogs."

I heard what sounded like a snap of impatience come across the line.

"That's a lot of work if you're not getting paid."

I took a large sip of the bourbon and ginger; the less said the better. Mum never quite grasped the concept of volunteering.

"What happened to cats? You always loved cats. Did you get another one after you put your tabby to sleep?"

I paused, remembering my big grey cat, Monster. "No, no more cats for me. Unfortunately, I've become allergic to cat dander. I sneeze constantly if I'm in someone's home longer than an hour where there's a cat." Monster had been my fur buddy for nineteen years. We had been so in tune that it was difficult to dwell on my beloved cat: I still missed the boy.

"I had to switch to dogs around the time you and Dad visited me in Phoenix. I'll always love cats because they're smart, independent, and low maintenance. But... I have to breathe too."

"True, shame though. Do you have a greyhound now? You know, fostering?" Mum was always curious about my devotion to retired racing greyhounds.

"Yes, I do. He's a black and white male called Anson. A real sweet boy."

Volunteering to help these gentle, sensitive dogs find solid adopters after they no longer brought home the winning purse from the racetrack, consumed most of my leisure time. From the comfort of my air-conditioned home I wrote grants, and over four years I generated close to $50,000 that was used for the dogs' veterinary needs. I could make a difference for these sweet souls that the racing industry had released from servitude. Based on my eight years of experience rescuing retired racing greyhounds, I'd learned that greyhounds were considered mere commodities, and many were unceremoniously discarded once they were no longer profitable.

"So," Mum asked, "how many dogs do you have living with you?"

"Three, plus one foster."

"Good heavens. I don't know how you do it. Working long hours and then having to take care of four dogs. You must be barmy!"

I laughed. "Yeah, I'm probably barmy, but I like having the dogs around. They're all well-behaved. They have their own doggie door so they can run and play in the back yard. And we go for an early walk every morning."

"How long are you going to keep the foster dog?"

"Until he finds a permanent home. That can be any time or it may take a few months. We have to find him a suitable adopter who will love him to bits."

"Seems to me that fostering is expensive," Mum said.

"Those dogs are big, they must eat a lot."

"Not really. I feed them four cups of premium kibble each day, a couple of doggie biscuits, and a marrowbone to chew on once a week. Greyhounds are cheaper than kids and better behaved!"

I heard Mum sniff. "Well, you were always unnatural when it came to children. I would have liked grandchildren, but…."

I refused to take the bait. God knows, I didn't want to open that Pandora's box.

I could hear rustling in the background. "What's that crackling noise? Is it our connection? Your phone or what?"

"Rustling? Oh, no, it's the newspaper. I'm checking to see when my TV show comes on. Oh, dear. Seems that it starts in about ten minutes, so I'll have to hang up now. Call me next Sunday. Okay? Take care of yourself. Bye, bye."

"Okay, enjoy your show. Talk soon. Bye."

———

At ninety, Mum had reluctantly succumbed to the physical restrictions imposed on the elderly. She still cooked her own meals—including the infamous Victoria sponge—but she needed assistance with everyday chores. Her neighbor, Barbara, shopped for groceries, and Mum had hired a woman to clean her flat. The health insurance offered home help for the elderly, and a woman would arrive every other day to help Mum with showering and hair washing or take her to doctor and dental appointments.

Mum was an expert at multitasking before the phrase even existed. I empathized with her wistful longings for her younger years.

Once she told me that she could no longer cut her toenails. "Can't reach 'em any more. Have to rely on the chiropodist stopping by each month to trim them for me. Most irritating." At first, I found this hilarious. Visuals of Mum trying to contort her body into a position where she could trim ninety-year-old toenails teased my brain. However, she had the last laugh. A few years later, arthritis invaded my hips and knees, and I was forced to rely on a monthly pedicure to keep my feet in good shape. When I shared this news with Mum, she laughed. "Now you know what I have to go through." It was her turn to gloat. Laughter was something I rarely heard from her, so hearing her chuckle flow through the phone lines felt good.

Mum had been active and industrious throughout her life; it must have been exasperating for her to accept the inevitable. She needed physical assistance, but her mind remained inquisitive to the end, and the daily newspaper was her best friend.

———

I recalled the distress in Mum's voice after Dad died in 1988; she told me she was considering selling the house.

"I don't know what else to do. I can't manage this place on my own, but your Dad wanted you to have this house after we were gone."

I was quick to reassure her. "Mum, I have a home here in Tucson. I can't live in two places at once. Your home on East-wood Crescent is yours. You're only seventy-three, and you could live another twenty years, if not longer. I'd feel much better if you were living somewhere that had central heating and no stairs."

The mortgage on the family home was paid in full. It was time for Mum to liquidate the asset and use the proceeds to ensure that her remaining years were comfortable. We'd had this discussion several times, and each time I reminded Mum that she and Dad had toiled and scrimped to pay for the house.

"I just lived in it, so the money from the sale of the property is rightfully yours to do with as you like." I never mentioned that when I was a kid yearning for love and emotional security, this was one of her favorite "digs": they were just taking in a bastard and it was *their* house. "This is mine and your dad's house, not yours. You just live here because we let you, so remember that."

A twinge of sadness remains in my heart, writing those words on paper nearly sixty years later. *My God,* I think, *I'm writing this at the age of seventy.... Do we ever get over this stuff? Can we?*

"Are you sure? Your dad was very insistent that you inherit this house. He wanted you to have some money for your old age. When he was in hospital, shortly before he died, he told me that it was the right thing to do—make sure you were all right later in life. He made me promise."

This is a revelation, I thought. *Dad wanted me to be okay in my old age, and Mum had promised to follow his wishes to make that happen. Wow!*

I refocused my attention on Mum. "There's no way that you can keep going up and down those steep, dark stairs or live in a home with no upstairs heat in the winter. You can't manage the garden. If anything major goes wrong with the house, you don't have the money to fix it. You need to sell, get the money out, and find yourself a nice retirement home."

Confident that I supported her decision to sell, Mum went to work immediately.

Within six months the house had sold in 1989, and she moved into Chestnut Close. She told me how much she appreciated feeling warm during the winter months, thanks to the central heating, and was relieved that climbing a steep, narrow staircase was in the past.

Mum was one resilient woman and I admired her strength.

7
HERE I COME
1943

OBVIOUSLY, I have no memory of the occasion. I can only imagine that my entry into this world was routine and without drama. Had I known the path I would travel for my first eighteen years, I suspect that I would have been reluctant to push, wriggle, and ram my way out of the birth canal. Perhaps I would have tried to remain in the womb to avoid my destiny but, like most newborns, I was probably rapped smartly on the rump then wailed in protest, scooped up in a blanket mummy-style by a nurse, and carted off somewhere to be cleaned up and made presentable.

I was born in a hospital in the south of England, probably at Plymouth but perhaps at Yelverton. It was August 1943, two years after President Roosevelt finally decided that the United States would become an active ally of Britain after the Japanese surprise bombing of Pearl Harbor in 1941. It would be two more years before Germany buckled in defeat under the leadership of its charismatic but despotic leader.

The Plymouth hospital collapsed in rubble during the

bombing, so all birth records were lost. Plymouth sustained such terrible air raids that there was a general exodus to places like Yelverton to avoid the Blitz. Great Britain struggled to survive the ravages of World War II while the citizens of the small island suffered loss of life, loss of home, and loss of hope.

As a kid in the early 1950s, Vera dragged me onto the bus at least weekly, and we traveled to the city to buy groceries. I would start to feel despondent as we drew closer to the center of the city. I could see mounds of rubble from the windows of the bus, concrete and brick, block after block, where rows of homes had previously stood. The families they had sheltered were dead or homeless, forced to scatter like thistles in a high wind. It was a depressing sight.

Numerous churches, historic monuments, and commercial buildings shared the misfortune of Hitler's wrath. Walls and roofs were ripped away, leaving gaping holes and jagged walls. These war-beaten relics once defined every view of my city. They resembled battered old women, waiting still and silent, lacking the strength to fight back, their dignity shattered. The ruins were waiting to be demolished, the last chapter of their existence. For years, I watched Bristol slowly rebuild: it seemed to take forever.

Decades later in 1972, while traveling through Los Angeles on my way to San Francisco, I encountered a chubby, overly chatty, former GI working the counter in a local diner. I was familiar with his type: brash, big mouth, and confidence louder than his competence. When he detected my British accent, he began to proudly brag to me and other patrons in the diner that England and Europe would have been wiped off the map had it not been for the "Americans winning the war."

Scenes from my childhood flashed through my mind: majestic buildings lying in fragments, their former glory destroyed, while my hometown struggled for many years to rebuild after the war.

This chubby hamburger-flipper was bloody lucky. Had I been a man, I might have lunged across the counter, grabbed him by the throat, and nearly throttled the life out of him. Perhaps he would have gotten the message that the U.S.A. did not win World War II alone.

Living with the unpredictable volcano, otherwise know as Vera, for eighteen years had shown me the wisdom of controlling my temper. Still there were many times in my life when anger overpowered wisdom, but in this instance I waited for the right moment to make my point.

I ordered a cheeseburger and suggested that Chatty Chubby go to the local library and catch up on his reading about World War II. Despite repeated pleas for help from Great Britain's Prime Minister Winston Churchill, President Roosevelt continually delayed American support, although he assured Britain that America was an ally. British allies included Canada, Australia, New Zealand, South Africa, and India. Of course, the covert work accomplished by the French Resistance was also invaluable.

Several mostly political reasons influenced President Roosevelt's reluctance to supply troops and equipment to help Britain and her allies defeat Germany. America in the 1930s was undergoing an ideological clash between two groups. The isolationists did not want to enter the war since the memories of World War I were still too fresh, while the interventionists were willing to support Great Britain in its battle against Hitler. Apparently, this ideological clash became less important after the Japanese bombed Pearl Harbor. Even today, most Americans seem to forget that World War II started in 1939, not 1941.

Many years later, in 2010, watching a program about World War II on The History Channel these matters were clearly illustrated. Politics under Roosevelt's leadership appeared to trump the president's promise to Great Britain of America's friendship and alliance.

Did the United Kingdom need the United States to join us in the fight against Hitler? You bet we did. Were we thankful that the Americans *finally* became our allies? You bet we were. Did the influx of American soldiers and equipment help Great Britain defeat Germany? Absolutely. Many brave Americans fought beside courageous soldiers from Great Britain and other allies and lost their lives fighting for freedom against a lunatic dictator. However, there has always been one stark difference between America and England and Europe.

On September 11, 2001, Al Qaeda struck with such intensity that the Twin Towers in New York City's World Trade Center collapsed minutes after planes piloted by terrorists rammed into the buildings. Thousands of innocent Americans and visitors to this country perished. Prior to the attack that day, no American city had suffered the physical aftermath of political and religious brutality by an international enemy. The United States had not been invaded by any enemy force for nearly two hundred years. No historic icon or treasured commercial building had crumbled and screamed for restoration.

On September 11, 2001, America experienced the pain and damage of physical war and the universal loss and suffering it entails. The country now knew how it felt to weep, surrounded by destruction.

After recommending that Chatty Chubby the burger flipper

do a little research, I picked up my cheeseburger and headed to the exit.

"Hey," he yelled. "You haven't paid for that."

"Yes, I have." I turned back and waved. "I listened to your arrogant bullshit about America single-handedly winning World War II. It's best that I leave now with a free hamburger in hand than stay and grind it into your skull."

The burger flipper was still yelling as I pushed my way out the door and headed for the bus. I will never forget that guy and doubt he will ever forget his encounter with me.

Yes, I have an aggressive side to my nature. Controlled anger and sometimes not so controlled anger have fueled my path through life. Yes, there have been some repercussions along the way when the anger has spilled over.

However, with the passage of time, a generous amount of humor has trickled into the mix to balance any potential explosions. Most of the time it works.

8
DADDY'S GIRL
1944

M Y EARLY CHILDHOOD MEMORIES are few, but I do vividly recall times when I felt safe, secure, and loved by my dad.

I suffered severe bouts of bronchitis. Since there was no heat in the upstairs rooms to ward off the bitter cold during the winter months, Vera would place me in a large playpen at night to sleep in front of the fire in the living room.

Dad would come home around midnight, tend to me, and bank up the fire. When I heard the key turn in the front door, I'd pulled myself up in the playpen and grab the bars that faced into the living room, knowing that Dad was home. He would open the door, switch on a lamp, and walk into the kitchen to retrieve his dinner, cooked earlier but kept warm in the oven for him.

Once Dad had his plate on the dining room table, he would have time for me. He would come over to the playpen, reach in, scoop me up into his arms, and carry me to the table. I would be balanced on his knee, and he would hold me close with one arm. Between bites of dinner, Dad would talk to me. "How's my best girl? I'm sorry you don't feel well, little one. After I bank up the fire, you'll be fine and cozy. You'll sleep like an angel and feel better in the morning. Did Mum give you your medicine? I'm sure she did because your cough isn't as persistent as yesterday."

Of course, I didn't understand much of what Dad was saying, but the warmth in his voice and the comfort of his body was enough. When it was time for him to read the paper, he would kiss me and lower me gently into the playpen.

"Here you go. Dad's right here. I'll bank up the fire and then read the paper. Need to know what's going on, you know, what with the war ending and all."

I didn't protest. I rolled onto my side, perfectly content to watch Dad across the room reading his paper. I was always asleep before he turned the last page

Glenda, eight months old

I started kindergarten at age three. Vera thought it best that I be around other children. I had already created an imaginary friend with whom I would chat aloud, and therefore Vera thought that I was lonely. She was probably correct.

I was an outgoing, active youngster who had difficulty following the school requirement that all students take an hour's nap in the early afternoon. I was never tired so I would wander around the room poking other toddlers in their cots to wake them up so we could play. This did not sit well with the teachers.

"Glenda, you need to leave Susan alone and return to your cot and take a nap."

I would protest. "But I'm not tired."

"No matter. In this school, children take an hour's nap in the afternoon. Please return to your cot."

"But I want to play."

The teacher would sigh. "No more buts. Please return to your cot—now."

Looking back, I have wondered: had I been conscripted into the military at the age of three? In today's society, I might have been labeled with ADHD or Attention Deficit Hyperactivity Disorder and medicated. Back then, I was just considered an active pest.

All the children wore pinafores with different logos embroidered on the front; mine was a Cockerel. I suspect the teacher selected this image because I was very vocal as a child. Once a year, the school hired a photographer to take individual photographs of children in their pinafores, and the photographs were given to the parents. Dad carried that faded and crumpled picture of me in his wallet for years.

I was in my mid-twenties and on leave from my job in the Middle East when Dad told me a story about Bert, a bus driver buddy who had asked after me:

"Hey, Alf, how you doin'? How's that daughter of yours?"

Dad turned to his friend Bert and smiled. "Oh, she's fine."

Bert extracted a Woodbine cigarette from its pack, lit up, and took a drag. "Want one?"

"No, thanks, not right now." Dad was reaching for his wallet.

"Got a picture of your girl in there?"

"Yeah, wait a minute. Got her photo. Here… here you are." Dad handed Bert a small, faded photograph.

"This must be your granddaughter!"

"I don't have a granddaughter," Dad said.

"But this is a toddler!" Bert laughed and elbowed Dad in the ribs. "Did you and the missus get busy and produce another daughter?"

Dad told me he was embarrassed when he answered Bert. "I know, I know. It's stupid, I guess, but I like this picture. She was my baby girl… then she grew up and left me behind."

The picture Dad had whipped out of his wallet to show Bert was of me in kindergarten: three years old, wearing the Cockerel pinafore, grinning broadly with two missing front teeth.

"Oh, my God! Is that me?" I asked. "You showed him this?"

"Yes, I did," Dad said proudly. "It was your kindergarten picture. Don't you remember?"

No, I didn't remember. I grinned at him and glanced again at the picture. "I'm kinda cute, don't you think?"

A beam of parental pride lit up Dad's face. "You were a cute fireball, all right. None of your teachers could keep up with you."

"How come you don't carry a current picture of me?"

Dad averted his eyes, dropped his head, and his cheeks flushed. He scratched the back of his neck. "I dunno. Suppose I liked this picture. It reminded me of the times I would take you for walks in the fields behind our house and you had questions about everything." He put the picture back in his wallet. "I just couldn't part with it."

I felt a surge of warmth that melted some of the resentment I'd held against him for many years. When he had had to choose between his wife and his daughter, I lost out. He gradually withdrew his affection, abandoning me to cope alone with Vera's escalating emotional and physical abuse.

———

Years later, foraging through old family photographs, I came across a sepia picture of me, a chubby baby girl, eight months old, clutching a toy and looking lost. Gazing at this picture my eyes grew moist. I was an adorable baby, one who deserved to be nurtured, protected, and loved. Until age ten, I had felt loved—at least by my father—but things changed rapidly soon after. I would learn later that Vera was jealous of her husband's affection for his daughter. As the years dragged on, my sense of emotional security became a low burning candle. Once I reached my teens, the flame had flickered and died.

———

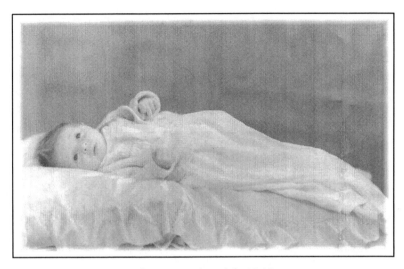

Three weeks old, 1943

Discussion was not part of Vera's vocabulary or coping skills. She was raising a child whose favorite word was "Why?" Her outlook was traditional and hierarchal: I was the child, she was the parent, and therefore, she ruled. Whatever she said was law. When she issued a command that I questioned, she became angry and confrontational. She would pace back and forth, waving her arms and shouting that I was an ungrateful child who should be thankful to be adopted and not shoved into an orphanage.

"Why can't you—just for once—do as you're told?" she would scream.

All this drama… just for asking "why?"

During my teenage years, I was well aware that Vera was prone to dramatics when she wanted to express her displeasure, which was often. Her behavior and comments were frequently degrading, and they made me feel totally worthless. No child wants to be referred to as a bastard or told: "You'll turn out just like your slut of a mother."

Time passed and I became accustomed to Vera's negative approach to life. I was an optimist; therefore, living with a pessimist was suffocating.

During one of our Sunday morning phone chats five years before she died, Vera told me that the kindergarten teachers considered me pretentious because I could read. "'Your child doesn't understand that most of the children in her class cannot read,' she recounted. 'She becomes impatient with them.' Your father spent hours reading with you. You picked it up like lightning and he was very proud."

Lack of impatience was no surprise. Patience remains one of my many challenges, especially when dealing with minutia. Reading at the age of three was a surprise. That was how I felt initially, but thinking back, I can never remember a time when I couldn't read, and for that I'm thankful. I've enjoyed many hours in the company of books. Sadly, I have no memory of the special moments spent with my dad as he was patiently teaching me to read. I can only imagine that this memory, like numerous others, faded into the background. I needed to focus all my energies to survive the constant battles with Vera.

9
HUMILIATION
1946

SORTING THROUGH FAMILY PHOTOGRAPHS, I found one of me at age three, sitting on a sofa between Dad and Vera at the home of my Aunt Rene and Uncle Len. It reminded me of how easy it was to get into trouble during my tomboy days. My cousin Stephen was celebrating his first birthday; my parents and I were attending his party.

There were many other youngsters present, mostly older than me, but we soon became bored with adult chatter. I don't recall who suggested it, but I overheard one kid say: "Let's go outside. When my dad was parking the car, I spotted a large oak tree that we could climb."

I was up for that. We sneaked out the back door, carefully unlatched the garden gate, making sure it didn't squeak, and then we were free to explore the lane outside my aunt and uncle's home. To the right was a steep grassy hill with several oak trees near the top. Tree climbing was one of my passions. The children on my street frequently played the game of Robin Hood, although I was never interested in the role of Maid

Marion. Scaling the tallest branches with the boys made me feel accepted, one of the gang. Let the other girls whimper that they were scared to climb so high—I thrived on the challenge.

Dad, Vera, and me. I'm in trouble again. 1946

On this particular day, I had been decked out in attire appropriate for attending a family gathering, not for climbing trees, in a green plaid skirt and yellow pullover. When the adults came looking for us and ordered us to return to the party, my clothing was smudged with dirt and grass and my underwear was torn from scooting down the grassy hill on my butt.

Vera was not amused. She grabbed my arm and dragged me into the living room where most of the guests were enjoying a leisurely afternoon cocktail.

"Come here, young lady! Where have you been?"

"I was outside playing."

"Why didn't you ask me if you could go outside?"

"I don't know."

"How on earth did you get dirt and grass stains on your clothes?" Vera lifted up my skirt. "Good heavens! And your underwear is torn. What have you been up to?"

"Nothing."

All the guests were looking in our direction when Vera grabbed my arms and shook me. She followed with three smacks to the back of my legs and butt. They stung like hell. I fought back the tears that threatened to trickle down my cheeks.

"You are such a handful! You drive me to distraction. Why I agreed to adopt you, I'll never know. Why can't you behave like a normal child instead of some wild animal?"

"Come on, Vera, give it a rest," Uncle Len said. "She's just a kid who wanted to play with the others."

Vera glared at her brother. "When I want your opinion, Len, I'll ask for it."

"Yeah. Well, a little brotherly advice—you're being too hard on her." He winked at me and then turned away. "Hey, Charlie! Give me another Scotch, straight up."

Flushed with humiliation, I longed to be invisible until Vera calmed down.

Dad stepped forward. "Vera, why don't—"

"Alf, let me handle this!"

Shoulders stooped, Dad slunk back to his chair.

Vera dragged me into the bathroom, slapped me several more times on the butt, and then cleaned me up, spit style, with one of her handkerchiefs. Then we joined the rest of the family in the living room.

Vera was an excellent seamstress. It must have been galling for her to have a tomboy for a daughter. I never understood why she insisted on dressing me in skirts or dresses and not pants or shorts to accommodate my athletic proclivities. Let's face it, a tomboy playing cricket and football wearing a dress is ludicrous.

I can only surmise that for Vera, having a daughter meant wearing frills and lace, and this was an opportunity for her to showcase her many dressmaking talents. I was expected to fall in line and act in ladylike fashion. Unfortunately, her expectations were incompatible with my nature.

Much to my relief, Aunt Rene gently intervened at that moment and rescued me from maternal torment. Vera continued to rant, embarrassing me in front of everyone.

"Vera, don't trouble yourself so. Let me take Glenda into my room and you enjoy yourself at the party, okay?"

"Are you sure?" Vera scowled at me. "She's such a handful. This is your son's first birthday party. Don't you want to be with my brother and meet all your guests?"

"No. Not necessary. Len loves parties. Me? Not so much. Len will cover for me. Come, Glenda. Let's go to my room. I have something to show you that I know you'll love."

Aunt Rene ushered me into her bedroom and removed a shoebox from her closet. The first time I saw a pair of Aunt Rene's high-heeled shoes, I fell in love. Aunt Rene encouraged me to slide my tiny feet into her shoes and stumble around pretending I was grown up. I always had a soft spot for Aunt Rene. Except for her hair color, she resembled Veronica Lake, a movie star of the 1940s; she was tall and willowy, with light brown hair that partially covered one side of her face. Aunt Rene was mellow and, unlike Vera, never shouted or raised her voice to anyone. She would tell me that I was pretty, something Vera never said, and promised one day I would have loads of shoes just like hers when boys would be clamoring for me to go out with them on dates.

As I grew older, I learned that Aunt Rene was an alcoholic. When she died from cirrhosis of the liver, the tears I wept were selfishly more for me than for her. I had lost a champion. I missed her gentle, sensitive soul and her touch that embraced me like a warm shawl of affection.

Uncle Len was transferred temporarily to South Africa where most of his time was consumed teaching the locals the latest printing techniques. It was rumored by relatives that he also enjoyed a little womanizing on the side. Aunt Rene consoled her loneliness and her husband's betrayal with gin and tonic, a habit she could not discard even when she and Uncle Len returned to England.

I realized that Aunt Rene's mellow persona was because she was usually drunk. She was using alcohol to ease her pain and help her cope with a rambunctious husband and life in general. In my heart, I believe that Aunt Rene and I had a special bond. I will always remember her beautiful face and gentle ways.

A couple of years after Aunt Rene died, Uncle Len remarried. This time he selected a homely, practical woman named Eleanor, a lively hairdresser from Newbury. I can still hear Vera's words of approval for her brother's choice of wife Number Two.

"Len was never good with money, so she'll keep him in line. He won't be able to browbeat this one."

Her assessment proved accurate. Eleanor's independent, outspoken personality, with her hearty laughter and fiscally conservative approach to life, was a successful coupling for my uncle, although she could match him drink for drink without any apparent ill effects.

10
A TOMBOY'S HAVEN
1943–1960

I GREW UP IN BRISLINGTON, a residential neighborhood on the outskirts of Bristol, formerly a major seaport in southwest England. The city of Bristol lies between two shires, which are now called counties, of Somerset and Gloucester. Historically, Bristol was a county in its own right, and it had traded with Europe since the eleventh century. Woolen cloth was the primary commodity for traders hailing from Somerset, Gloucester, Devon, and Dorset.

In the 1700s, trading practices expanded to include slaving voyages from Bristol, organized by local businessmen who invested in the transatlantic slave trade. After being abducted from their homes, Africans were corralled like cattle in the hulls of ships en route to Europe and the colonies of North America. Slave ships stopped in Bristol to replenish supplies and hold auctions where British gentry or successful merchants would select, bid on, and purchase an African male, female, child, or even a family to train as servants or field workers.

At the age of fifty, I watched a program on my local public

broadcasting television station and was appalled to discover that my hometown had been engaged in this shameful activity. Why didn't I know this? I did not recall instruction at school concerning Bristol's involvement in the slave trade during this appalling period in history. Was I absent those days? Was the subject covered in the curriculum? Is my memory faulty? I guess I'll never know.

Brislington is southeast of Bristol, ten miles from Bath. In 1953, there were luscious green meadows adjacent to my parents' back garden. In the spring, we were dazzled with color from an array of wild flowers. Dense woods were home to enormous oak trees, their sprawling branches cast shadows of relief from the sun, and the River Avon meandered quietly in the background, all in all a safe haven for children.

After playing in the woods with my friends during school summer vacations and on my way home, I would visit my favorite oak tree. It was my special place where I imagined that the elves and fairies of the forest had banned criticism and beatings and all corporal punishment. I could relax and daydream, stretching out in the thick, cool grass under the tree surrounded by clusters of bluebells.

My real mother would be waiting for me by the front gate, a taxi at the curb. Of course, Vera would have denied her access to the house, but my mother couldn't care less about Vera's behavior—all she cared about was finding me. We would hug and she would tell me she loved me. Leaving everything behind, we would get in the taxi and drive away. I would not look back. Sadly, the daydream would fade, replaced by reality:

it was time to go home to pick vegetables from our garden and start cleaning them for dinner.

When I was fourteen, the government purchased the fantasy playground of my childhood behind our house for a housing development. After two years, the land was studded with cookie-cutter housing estates and my favorite oak tree was felled to make room for a road. The meadows and woods that had offered me solace and shelter from chaos and pain were no more. I was lucky that an unblemished, natural playground had been available to me for nearly sixteen years, but I mourned its loss.

When I was seventeen, I discovered the coastal towns in Devon and Cornwall. The ocean with its many moods drew me like a magnate. There was something spiritual about the southern coast of England. It made my heart smile.

I vacationed for a week with my parents in Bournemouth and later in Cornwall for a seven-day getaway with my former husband. There were also several post-divorce, long weekend trips with friends to Torquay.

Mild ocean breezes swayed the Torbay palms that overlooked Torquay's sandy beaches and gave this small English seaside town a distinctive Mediterranean flavor. Agatha Christie spent many hours writing her mystery novels in this quaint southern coastal town in England.

On my trips to the southern coast, I would find a large oak tree where I could stretch out on the grass, watch birds going about their daily routine, listen to their lively chatter, and feel a sense of belonging. Other times, I would sit on enormous rocks that littered the rugged coastline, absorbing the power and scent of the ocean as waves crashed against the rocks. I always felt welcomed and hugged by the surf. Something in the back of my mind told me that I was a country gal who loved and was loved by nature. In such moments, I felt warm contentment. It was a feeling I longed to experience more often, but one that proved to be rare throughout most of my life.

When I finally traced my biological family in 1995, I was not the least surprised to learn that my roots were deeply entrenched in Devon and Cornwall.

I used to dream of having a circular, one-story home with large, tinted glass windows all around, situated atop a bluff and overlooking the ocean. A massive master bedroom with a deck would face the ocean. There would be a large guest room, two bathrooms with walk-in showers, bidets, and Jacuzzi tubs, plus an enormous living area, a well-equipped kitchen, and a lap pool at the far end of the patio. Tucked away on the other side of the house was my office-library—my private space, where visitors would not be welcome. Of course, on the grounds there were several dog runs where retired, rescued greyhounds could sprint, abandoned poodles could prance, and former Beverly Hills' accessory cuties could roll in the dirt and enjoy being real dogs.

Then I would wake up and wonder: why are there no people in this dream? I soon realized this was my haven away from the din of Vera's voice, a place of peace where I could hear birds wish me good morning and feel butterfly wings brush my shoulders.

The closest town to Bristol is Bath, a small town renowned mainly for its ancient Roman Baths and the elegant Royal Crescent of thirty Georgian homes built in the 1700s.

Construction of the Roman Baths began in 1894, but the Celts had discovered the hot springs in 836 BC. Rainwater from the Mendip Hills meanders underground to Bath, and there the water's temperature can reach up to 204.8° F. During the eighteenth century, it was widely believed by the nobility that the waters of Bath had curative powers. However, by 1979, the waters tested unsafe for public bathing, and thus the local council closed the pool.

The elegant sweep of the Royal Crescent has often appeared in historical movies, one of which was *The Duchess.* Today, this fine example of Georgian architecture includes a hotel and a museum; some of the other houses have been converted into flats and offices.

We would visit Bath five or six times a year as a family; it was one of my parents' favorite Sunday jaunts. Dad told me that babies awaiting adoption were warehoused in a wing of one of the hospitals until the adoptive families arrived to take them home.

One Sunday, walking back to the bus station, we passed an old, but well-preserved, large stone building. Dad reached for my hand, bent down, and stopped on the pavement in front of the entrance.

"Do you know what building this is?"

I shook my head.

"This is where your mother and I signed your adoption papers in October 1943."

I heard a catch in his voice before he continued. "We bundled you up in a heavy, cream-colored shawl your mother had knitted, and headed for the bus terminal, waiting for the bus that would take us home. I held you all the way, and you never cried once."

Oh, to remember being bundled up in a shawl, feeling loved, and held all the way home on the bus. Bath held fond memories for Dad.

———

Small three-bedroom homes in clusters of four, were the last row of houses in our neighborhood that curved into Eastwood Crescent, my adoptive home for eighteen years. From my bedroom I could see the meadows and dense woods with the River Avon nearby. This was exceptional terrain for any child, but for a tomboy like me it was sheer heaven.

My favorite wild flower was the bluebell. Prolific bunches nestled in groups around the bases of oak trees. I learned to resist picking handfuls of these flowers to take home because, once picked, they lost their desire for life even when immediately placed in water. I had swiftly connected with nature. I preferred to leave the bluebells with the wood nymphs under the oak tree until it was time for these glorious flowers to fold their petals one last time.

The meadow immediately adjacent to our back garden concealed an underground train tunnel. Drifting off to sleep at night, I was comforted by the rhythmic, clickety-clack rumble of train wheels on the tracks passing through the tunnel. Even today, my favorite form of travel is by train: the seductive motion is relaxing, and my eyes can absorb the ever-changing scenery.

Our family lived in one of the middle houses. Therefore,

access to our long and narrow back garden meant that the coal men had to traipse through the house lugging their sacks of coal. They were strong fellows who, with a swift twist of their bodies, successfully transferred the sacks from their backs into the coal bin by our back door.

Vera was a meticulous housekeeper. She always hated coal delivery day and would mumble under her breath. "Life would be so much easier if we'd bought a house with a side entrance. I told Alf, but no, we had to do it his way. 'Course, he's never here when the coal's delivered, so why should he care?"

She would spread large towels from the front to the back door and issue stern instructions to the coal men not to venture outside the towels. They never did. From what I recall, the coal men were large and amiable fellows, covered head to toe in coal dust, and adept at following directions from homeowners.

"Now, lads, watch where you're going! I've laid towels from front to back. Make sure you stay on the towels and don't stray onto the carpet. I don't want to be sweeping up coal dust after you're gone. Go straight through the conservatory to the back garden. No stopping, mind you. You'll see the coal bin off to the right."

"All right, missus, we'll be out of your way in a jiffy."

Although Vera and I did not share the same DNA, I certainly empathized with her distaste for dirt.

When I consider American kids who live in the inner cities, Welsh youngsters who grow up in coal-mining towns or children who live anywhere without an opportunity to run free in the meadows and woods, I feel especially blessed that I grew up in the country. Vera could keep track of me by looking out the kitchen window. If she could spot my bright auburn curls charging about in all directions, she knew I was safe.

In the 1950s, when I was between eight and fourteen, child predators in the neighborhood were unheard of, so I was free to play without my parents fretting over my safety. If I wanted to join the rest of the kids and venture further into the woods, I had to promise Vera that I would be home promptly at a set time. I relied on a neighbor boy who lived two doors up and proudly sported a watch to help keep me on track so that I returned home on time.

One day, I was playing French cricket, a game that requires the person at bat to hold a cricket bat in front of her legs and, when the ball is thrown, hit the ball either to the left or the right without raising the bat above the knees. On this particular day, I was the catcher positioned behind the batter.

Instead of following the rules, Lesley, who was the batter, swung the bat waist high and to the right and hit me square on the nose. With blood gushing from my nose, I was forced to run home, hoping that a Band-Aid would suffice and I could soon return to the game.

Vera took one look at my battered nose and the blood dripping onto my blouse, and I was grounded. That escapade caused my previously straight, but pronounced, Roman nose to develop a bump in the middle that remains to this day.

Lesley and I, both only children, lived on the same street and were school chums throughout our early school years. We'd walk home from school together, and when we reached Lesley's home, her mum would often invite me in for a cup of tea and biscuits since she knew Vera was working.

Lesley's mother Mrs. Jackson was a warm, effervescent, and chubby individual who doted on her daughter and was bountiful in her affection.

When her mother's embraces seemed smothering, Lesley sometimes became irritated. "Oh, Mum! Please don't fuss."

I would sit quietly sipping my tea and enjoying the biscuits, watching the interaction between mother and daughter, envious because I was starved for love and acceptance in a home where my adoptive mother showed me no warmth.

The Jackson household was welcoming and cozy. In the front room were a plush couch and two matching chairs covered in cream chintz printed with large red flowers. Lesley's father was a tall, slender man with slicked-back hair, a slight stoop, and slow way of speaking. Mr. Jackson was not as effusive as his wife, but when he glanced at his daughter, there was much tenderness in his eyes. It was obvious that Lesley was his pride and joy. With reluctance, I left this circle of warmth to return to the cold and critical environment that was my home.

Fast foods did not exist in England when I was growing up. Had some enterprising individual introduced processed or ready-to-eat foods to the British public in the fifties, Vera would have banned it from our home. Each year, Dad planted vegetables and fruits in our garden. We always had a plentiful supply of cabbage, kale, cauliflower, Brussels sprouts, French beans, onions, radishes, carrots, potatoes, raspberries, strawberries, gooseberries, and apples from our tree that remained generous for many years.

When I was twelve years old and Vera was working part-time, she would leave me a note instructing me to pick whatever vegetables I wanted for dinner and prepare them ready for cooking before she came home. Unlike many other children around the world, I was lucky. My adoptive parents made sure I was raised on natural homegrown foods and home cooking. Vera told me that during World War II and continuing for several years thereafter, food in Britain was rationed. My parents were allowed six eggs per week, and I consumed all of them.

Nutritionally, I received excellent care. It was in the love and affection department that I was undernourished.

11

STORY TIME

1951

WHEN VERA WAS OCCUPIED with cooking, puttering in the kitchen, or sewing at the dining room table, I enjoyed many happy times sitting on my dad's lap. He would tell me stories, one of which was how I came into his life. Dad, my knight in shining armor, had traveled to Bath accompanied by his wife, to claim a daughter. He was a great storyteller and this was one of my favorites.

"Well, it was like this." Dad sank back into his chair, smiling at his recollection of events.

I settled sideways on his lap and leaned against the arm of the chair.

"Your mum and me took the bus to Bath. It was about two hours before we got there because we first had to walk to the village and wait for the bus. The ride to Bath was a little over an hour." Dad shook his head as he recalled the trip to Bath.

"Were you excited about getting a baby?"

"Oh, yes, we certainly were." Dad smiled and patted my knees. "Your mum worried that her tummy problems would prevent her from coming with me, but thankfully her medicine worked."

"Did you talk about me on the trip to Bath?"

"Of course, we did." Dad gave me a quick hug. "I reached for your mum's hand and asked her if she was happy now that she was going to become a mother."

A few seconds of silence passed before I asked, "What did she say?"

"Your mum had tears in her eyes before she spoke. 'Every woman on our street has children except for me,' she told me. 'I've caught their sly glances, probably wondering why I had no children. I felt like an outcast. Now I will be like everyone else—a mother—and accepted.'"

I turned and looked deep into his eyes. "Do you think she loves me?"

He drew back, obviously surprised. "Of course she loves you. Why would you ask that?"

I fidgeted on his lap for a moment. "Well, she never lets me sit on her lap. She never kisses or cuddles me like you do."

A frown creased Dad's forehead, but then he smiled it away. "Your Mum is a little reserved, but I'm sure she loves you. Now, where was I? Oh yes… when we arrived in Bath, you were waiting for us in a hospital. They'd given you a bath, powdered your bottom, and dressed you up in a very pretty outfit."

Secure in my dad's arms, I always loved the part when he told me that he wanted only a baby girl, no boys for him. He selected me, a chubby girl with bright auburn curls.

"Your mum told me before we were married that she couldn't have children. I said, 'Okay. Doesn't bother me.'"

"Why couldn't she have children?"

Dad shook his head. "Don't rightly know. Something wrong in the baby-making department, I suppose. After a couple of years of us being married, your mum kept after me about adopting a baby." He laughed. "Finally, I agreed, but, as I told your mum, it had to be a girl, no boys for me."

I giggled. "No boys for my dad."

He continued. "When Matron put you in my arms that morning, you stretched out one little hand and touched my cheek." Dad wiped away a tear and hugged me tight. "You were the prettiest baby I'd ever seen and I knew you were mine. It was my job to love and care for you."

I cherished those moments with my father and hearing him relate that story always made me feel loved and wanted.

I used to think that babies awaiting adoption lived in shoeboxes and when people came calling, the babies were swiftly flicked with a feather duster and displayed to prospective parents like merchandise in a department store. I was convinced that the person who dusted the babies the day my dad came calling was especially careful and there was not a smidgeon of dust on this auburn-haired infant.

Later, I learned that shoeboxes and feather dusters were not involved in the adoption process in 1943. Prospective parents completed applications stating their preference: boy or girl. My parents had specified a girl. When a baby girl became available, the next couple on the list who wanted to adopt a girl received a letter from the hospital, and Matron set a date and time to visit the infant. If the couple were happy with the child, they would proceed with the adoption.

What role did Vera play in my adoption? She never told me that she loved me or cuddled, hugged, or comforted me when I was sad or hurt. In fact, there was no physical contact between us unless it was corporal punishment. I often wondered: why did she want me if she couldn't love me?

On Christmas Eve, for many years Dad would drape my red dressing gown over his shoulders, slap on a set of white whiskers, and enter my room play-acting as Santa Claus. I always pretended to be asleep, but Dad knew I was faking.

"Ho! Ho! Ho! And who do we have here? Let me check my list. Ah, of course! It's a little girl called Glenda, who seems to be asleep. I'll leave her a note in case she wakes up and thinks I've forgotten her. How could I forget my best girl? I'm going to put the note on the dressing table so she'll see it as soon as she opens her eyes. Yes, all right, Rudolph, I'm coming."

The note would read:

> Tomorrow you will receive your Christmas gift delivered by my favorite Reindeer, Rudolph. But now, you have to sleep and dream of opening your present on Christmas morning.

Even when I knew that Santa Claus was a fable, I played along because Dad enjoyed this role, and it was another special moment between father and daughter when I felt loved.

The sanctity of my father's arms was about to dissolve. Without warning, storm clouds foreboding family conflict were gathering speed across the universe, looming ever closer. I was about ten when the clouds burst.

Early one evening, I was sitting on my dad's lap. He was telling me another of his fabulous make-believe stories in which I was the beautiful heroine and a knight from King Arthur's court was on his way to rescue me.

"Princess Glenda has been captured by a wicked witch and imprisoned in a castle deep in the forest. The witch heard that Charles, a knight from King Arthur's court, wants to marry Glenda but the witch wants Charles to marry her daughter, Inez." He paused, increasing the drama.

"Glenda is a beautiful, slender princess with long, auburn hair, a fair complexion, and blue-green eyes. The witch's daughter is fat and ugly and eats live mice for dinner. In her dark cave, covered in cobwebs, the witch is concocting a wicked spell that will destroy Glenda's beauty and turn her into a mean snake."

I gasped and cuddled closer to my dad.

Dad curled forward, narrowed his eyes, and hissed. "I see a black pot bubbling over an open flame. The witch is tossing in dead roots and leaves and a few dead skunks to make a potion she will entice Princess Glenda to drink."

I squealed with delighted terror and grabbed Dad's arm. "How can I escape?"

"Be patient. The witch forgets that Princess Glenda loves the animals of the forest and that they love her. When Glenda roams the forest, when she sees an injured animal or bird, she always takes them home and cares for them until they're healthy enough to return to their families."

"Will they help me escape from the wicked witch?"

"All in good time," Dad said. "A butterfly is nestled in a crevice close to the cave's entrance and hears the witch mumbling to herself about how she's going to fix Princess Glenda for good so that nobody will want to marry her."

"Oh, no!" I cried.

"Upon hearing of the witch's dastardly plot, the butterfly immediately flies off and calls out to all the animals in the forest to meet at their communal watering hole. In half an hour deer, elk, bears, otters, rabbits, birds, mice, and other animals that reside in the forest, gather, very upset that their special friend is being held captive by the wicked witch. What can they do to help her before it's too late?"

I'm holding my breath. I'm really into the story. "Who's going to tell Charles that I need help? The animals can't help me. The witch would kill them."

Dad patted my hand. "Have faith. The animals and birds decide to send a pigeon to find your special knight. For centuries, pigeons have carried messages, and your knight has several pigeons that live around his castle. When a new bird arrives, he will take notice. Your knight is much like you. He is very in tune with the animals of the forest and he will follow his instincts. He will know that something is wrong."

"Are you sure?"

"Absolutely. A pigeon trained for such missions is sent off to find your knight. He flies for two days and two nights until he spots the castle where Charles lives. He flies around the castle and locates Charles's bedroom. The pigeon lands on the window ledge and starts flapping his wings. At first, Charles ignores the pigeon, but the pigeon persists. Charles strolls over to the window. 'What do you want, my friend? You're not one of my regulars.' The pigeon flaps his wings harder and Charles realizes something's wrong. 'All right. Show me the way.'"

I chortled with glee and clapped my hands, "My Knight is coming to save me."

Suddenly, sounds of spite and venom erupted from the dining room and shattered my world of make believe. "It's about time you paid some attention to your wife!" Vera, who had been sewing at the dining room table, exploded in anger. Throwing aside the jacket she was working on, she stood, raised a fist in the air, and screamed at my dad. "I'm your wife after all! When you're off working, I'm left alone to deal with her. And she's a handful, I can tell you. Constantly talks back. Never does as she's told and tries my patience to the limit most of the time."

Stunned, I cringed against Dad.

Vera broke down in tears. "And here you are, telling her these ridiculous stories, filling her head with poppycock nonsense, neglecting me and showering affection on her." Spent from her outburst, Vera turned her back on Dad and me, pulled a handkerchief from the sleeve of her sweater, and blew her nose.

I slid off Dad's lap as he stood up slowly. I hid behind him, clinging to his jacket, tears flooding my eyes.

"For God's sake, Vera, I'm just telling her a story. Where's the harm in that?"

Vera spun back around, eyes glaring, and pointed at me. "You are neglecting me in favor of her." She stepped closer to my dad, hands on her hips. "She's a bastard child from a slut of a mother who got herself pregnant when she wasn't married. We took her offspring into our home. Don't you think that I need your attention when you're home?"

I had no place to hide, just listened, hurting inside.

"I agreed to adopt a daughter rather than a son, but I never imagined that you would put her first and ignore me. I never agreed to that." Vera stamped her foot. "It's not right and I'm not going to put up with it!"

Dad thrust out his hand, as though warding off evil, and

took a deliberate step toward her. "That's enough," he snapped. "I don't want to hear any more filth coming out of your mouth. I can't believe that you're jealous of your own daughter. Try loving her instead of constantly picking fault. What the hell's wrong with you? My God, woman, you're neurotic."

"Don't be bloody ridiculous!" Vera snorted, scoffing at the idea. "I'm not jealous of her, and I resent you calling me neurotic." She kicked at the back door. "How dare you say that to me? She's not my daughter! She's someone else's mistake that I agreed to take into our home. I just want you to be a husband to me when you're home. I'm your wife and I should come first."

I stumbled into the front room and covered my ears to escape Vera's vitriolic outburst. She had finally said why she did not love me: I was someone else's mistake and I wasn't a boy. I felt as unwanted as leftover Christmas turkey in February.

To learn at such a young age that my mother was jealous of my father's affection for me was frightening. I had to protect myself. The only way I knew how was to raise my emotional drawbridge and keep it locked down, tight. I had to accept that I was not what Vera wanted in a child.

I recall several occasions after this incident when I asked Dad to tell me a story, but he always had an excuse. "Sorry, Glenda, but I promised your mum I'd fix the toilet," he would say or "Can't right now. Maybe tomorrow."

Tomorrow never came. I missed the contact with my dad and cried alone at night in the safety of my bed. I knew that Dad loved me but I also knew that I was paying the price, because Dad wanted to avoid conflict with his wife.

My paternal champion had been vanquished.

That day marked the beginning of many lonely years living with Vera without the affection and companionship of my dad. I could never have believed that my relationship with a father I adored as a child would become strained and distant as he was forced to reconcile the needs of his wife against those of his daughter.

After this devastating confrontation between my parents and dealing with Dad's distant attitude, I grew sullen and resentful toward Vera. Her jealousy had carved a deep schism between father and daughter.

Over time, my resentment smoldered into fiery hatred. There were innumerable opportunities where Dad could have stood up for me, when Vera appeared emotionally agitated and irrational, but he never did. The respect I once had for him was gradually eroding.

On one occasion, when the pattern calculations for a dress Vera was making were incorrect, she became extremely frustrated and started mumbling. "I don't understand it. It should work. I've been over this pattern a thousand times. I'm so damned mad I could scream."

I was about thirteen and had been reading in the dining room when Vera started muttering. However, whenever Vera was sewing, irritated, and mumbling to herself, it was best to retreat. I disappeared with my book into the front room.

When Dad came home from work, Vera was still at the dining room table and still in a tizzy. I overheard their conversation.

"Vera, what's the matter with you? Why are you so upset?"

"I've been working on this dress pattern for most of the day." I heard her sigh of exasperation. "You know, the one I'm making for Jean's wedding—Mrs. Miles' daughter next door. I thought I'd fathomed it out, but these final figures are wrong."

I made a big mistake: I left my safe zone and entered the dining room.

"It's all her fault." Vera tossed her head in my direction. "She's been buzzing around here like a wasp searching for its next victim. Distracted me to no end, made me make a mistake in my calculations. Now I can't find the mistake."

"That's not true," I protested. "I've been reading in the front room."

"Glenda, don't call your mother a liar," Dad said. "Can't you see she's upset? I think it best that you and your book return to the living room."

Found guilty without a trial, I was dismissed.

"Come on, Vera, put the sewing away. Let's have a nice dinner and relax. I've had one hell of a day."

Over the next few years, I would become accustomed to being the ball in my parents' Ping-Pong game of blame. I mentally filed Vera and Alf away in a compartment labeled "Bitch and Fallen Warrior." The deterioration of my relationship with my father created a gut-deep, burning mistrust of men that has lasted throughout my life.

In my late teens, during one of many screaming matches with Vera, I finally confronted her about her jealousy over my father's affection for me when I was younger. We were standing in the kitchen. Vera was making an apple pie.

"You couldn't stand it because Dad was spending time with me when I was a kid. You were so bloody jealous that I was receiving attention and affection from Dad, something you never gave me. What sort of mother is jealous of her daughter? I wish you'd never adopted me."

She tossed the dough on the counter, hands on her hips, her chin out-thrust and looking much like her mother Edith, and moved toward me, her face contorted. "Jealous of you? Why on earth would I be jealous of you?"

"Well?"

Scorn and ridicule spilled from her mouth. "Wives come first. Your father needed to be reminded of that. It was disgraceful the way he gave you so much attention and ignored me. You're a bastard child that never should have been born, except your mother got pregnant during the war, and then she dumped you. I don't believe the story about the bloke who got her pregnant being killed in the war. I'm sure he ran like hell when he found out she was having a baby."

I picked the dough up off the counter and threw it at her. "You should hear yourself. Dad was right when he said you're neurotic."

Vera deftly dodged the dough. It landed in a lump on the concrete floor of the conservatory.

The dough on the floor looked helpless, like a baby seal about to be bludgeoned by hunters—much like I felt. "You need to check into a mental hospital," I said. "You're bloody nuts."

"You'd better watch yourself, young lady."

"Oh, yeah? Or what? What are you gonna do? Bang my head against the concrete wall? Beat me with the boiler stick again? I don't think so. Those days are over."

Vera shrugged. "Well, if I wasn't on you most of the time, you'd probably turn out like your mother."

She bent down, picked up the dough, and tossed it in the trash. "I see you putting on the war paint, but let me tell you something. Boys look at faces last, and bodies and legs first. I always had good legs and a good figure. I never covered my face with makeup like you, and I had plenty of men interested in me."

I was unmoved. I had pierced her blustering armor with the sword of truth.

12
I'M A BASTARD
1955

PERIODICALLY, VERA HAD SHARED SNIPPETS of information or her opinion about my conception and first six weeks of life. She called me "a bastard," a reference with which she seemed comfortable. She tossed the phrase around whenever she was angry, totally disregarding my feelings. I looked up the word "bastard" in the dictionary: an offensive term for someone born to unmarried parents.

Factually, this was an accurate description; emotionally, it was as if I'd been stabbed in the heart. Hungry to devour every crumb of information, I chose to ignore the slur, hoping one day for a window into a world previously inaccessible.

Vera told me that my biological mother, Norah Townsend, "abandoned me." I've since wondered whether abortions were legal in those days. The National Health System, implemented in 1948, was not available to Norah in 1943. Had it been, it's probable that birth control and/or abortion would not have been included in its services. Perhaps Norah did not believe in abortion. Perhaps society did not accept abortion in the 1940s. I was troubled that Norah carried me for nine months only to leave me to others.

Many years later, I learned the facts from a member of my biological family.

———

After a few weeks in a hospital in Bath, an acceptable adoptive couple was identified. The Matron would have handed me over to Vera and Alf Taylor, a respectable, hardworking couple who were unable to conceive children of their own. How prospective adoptive parents were vetted in 1943, I have no idea. Was the ability to feel, show, and express love and affection a question for prospective mothers on the interview forms? I doubt it.

When I was about fifteen, I mentioned to my adoptive parents that I was interested in tracing my biological family. Unanswered questions were piling up, too many to be ignored. In my younger years, I'd felt a connection with Dad, but never with my adoptive mother.

Vera was sewing at the dining room table. She sprang from her chair like a cheetah chasing prey, paced back and forth, flinging her arms about and screaming. Her anger and energy filled the room.

"Why on earth would you think they'd want anything to do with you? You're a skeleton in their closet, something they don't want popping out unexpectedly! You were a mistake— one that a woman buries deep in her soul." Vera stopped pacing and faced me, her face twisted in rage.

"What does that say about us, me and your dad? We've worked our fingers to the bone to give you a good home, a decent education, clothes on your back, only to be pushed aside because you want to find out where you came from."

"But—" I began.

Nearly in tears, she continued to rant. "Sheer ingratitude, that's what I call it! If it hadn't have been for me and your dad, you would have ended up in an orphanage or been placed in service as an indentured servant."

How could I communicate with someone who believed that an adopted child should be so thankful for a home, regardless of quality, that she would suppress any longings to know her roots? It was all about Vera's needs and nothing about mine. If she'd had the ability to share love and affection, given me encouragement, comforted me when I felt insecure, my desire to find my biological family would have been mere curiosity, not a driving need to look elsewhere for love and security to fill the emptiness in my heart.

When I told Dad about the reason for my latest skirmish with Vera, he had a different perspective.

"Well, wait a minute, Glenda. Come, sit on the couch with me."

I sat next to Dad and remained quiet, waiting to hear his views.

"Let's say that your mother and her family kept your birth a secret. Nobody in the village was aware that she had given birth and surrendered you for adoption. What if your mother married and had other children but did not tell her husband or children about you? Can you imagine the shock if she received a letter from you? She would have to reveal her past to her family. Do you really want to disrupt her life?"

Dad had made some good points. He was not telling me that I shouldn't be curious, but that I should consider others' feelings. I mulled over his comments for several weeks before I realized he was right. I decided to put my search on the back burner and wait for a more opportune time.

I had not made a mistake; I was the result of someone else's. In time, I would come to realize that we all make mistakes and have to move on. Thirty-four years later, at age fifty-one, when I was living in Tucson, Arizona, I would finally decide that I'd waited long enough. The time was right to track down my biological mother.

13
DOMESTIC SERVICE
1951–1955

ONE DAY AFTER SCHOOL while Vera was folding laundry, she raised the topic of adoption. "I couldn't have children of my own, you see, so me and your dad took you in."

"But where did I come from?"

"Oh, I don't know. All I know is that the woman who gave birth to you couldn't keep you. She got herself in the family way without being married, so she had to give you up."

"Why did she have to give me up? Why couldn't she keep me?"

"Getting in the family way when you're not married is a disgrace." Folding a towel over her arm, Vera sneered, self-righteous and pleased with herself. "Young women aren't supposed to have babies if they're not married. I expect her family threatened to disown her unless she gave you up for adoption."

I stood beside her, folding towels, thinking.

She turned and looked at me. "Rightly so, in my book. Babies born out of wedlock bring disgrace to the family. So be warned, my girl. Don't make the same mistake as your mother. If we hadn't taken you in, you would have ended up in an orphanage or in service."

The laundry was finished. Vera swept the pile into her arms and headed for the stairs to the linen closet on the second floor, leaving me alone to think. Depending on the orphanage, I could have been placed into service as young as eight. I suppose I would have worked as a servant in an ancestral home, upper- or upper-middle class home. But where? Would it have been locally or in another shire?

A young girl who emerged from an impoverished home or working class background to work as a maid was frequently small in stature, undernourished, and often pegged "a shrimp of a lass." I had heard rumors and whisperings from friends' parents and neighbors that poor families sometimes sold their children to upper-crust families seeking a servant: too many children and insufficient funds to care for them was cause enough for negotiation. Money changed hands, the child left home, and the rest of the family survived, at least until the next child was conceived, which set the pattern in motion yet again.

When I misbehaved, according to Vera's guidelines, she threatened me with drudgery, long hours, low wages, and backbreaking work as a servant.

"I'll put you in service, my girl. See how you like that. You'll do chores from morning to night. That'll teach you a thing or two. "

My comeback was always the same: "I'll run away."

The only escape for a servant was through marriage, but maids had limited opportunities to meet eligible future husbands. Some maids left service to work in factories, but factory work was not considered respectable because the young women worked alongside men.

Had Vera followed through with her threat, my future would indeed have been dismal. I would have been trained as a scullery maid, classified as lower staff, the lowest ranking position, and provided lodging and clothing. I would have worked for a pittance from six in the morning until ten at night, seven days a week. My hands would have become red and sore from scrubbing pots and pans and washing clothes.

After several years, if I was lucky, I might get promoted to parlor maid and trained to polish silver candlesticks, dust lengthy wooden staircases, or tend the fireplaces in the family bedrooms. Upper staff such as butler, cook, or housekeeper would not acknowledge my presence should they catch a glimpse of me hauling a bucket of coal to the family bedrooms to bank up the fireplaces and ensure the rooms were warm during frosty nights. The master and mistress of the house would also be blissfully unaware of my existence.

I would have shared a cold, damp, dimly lit room in the attic with another maid and followed a stifling set of house rules that emphasized that my job was to serve my betters. If I was lucky, I might earn a few hours off each week. My inner voice whispered: servitude is not for me.

When Vera made these threats, I fully believe that she did not comprehend the broader ramifications of life as a servant with the constant fear of physical and/or sexual abuse. If I were to become pregnant by the master of the house or one of his sons, the family would have considered me the guilty party. After all, didn't I "lure him on"?

The local vicar would assume the starring role of intermediary and arrange a quiet adoption for the baby. As for me, the mother of the child, I could be transferred to another family in a different shire. Should the employers be morally bankrupt, I could have been driven to a different shire and tossed out into the street to fend for myself.

A biological relative, Helen Chaffe, who was born in the early 1900s, was the illegitimate child of a son of one of the local gentry. Helen's mother had worked for the family as a domestic servant and when her pregnancy became known, the son was sent away. Helen endured the humiliating experience of walking up to "the big house" to collect from the family a ten-shilling weekly subsistence.

For many in the 1940s and early 1950s, being in service was considered an honorable, respectable position. I did not share their enthusiasm. Servants were completely dependent on their masters and mistresses for their well-being. My role would have been to serve my master and mistress without question.

Were I to act above my station, protesting that some of the house rules were unfair or too stringent, or if I tried to run away, such rebellion could warrant a beating at the very least.

In Victorian England and continuing through the early 1950s, ownership of the lower classes by the upper classes, disguised in terms of employment, remained acceptable. From which class of birthing canal one emerged determined one's destiny. Slavery has never been reserved solely for those of another race.

Small wonder I threatened to run away. When Vera told me about working in service if she and my dad had not adopted me, the main words that registered in my mind were that my biological mother could not keep me. Vera frequently pointed out that I was a bad and willful child. In my mind, "could not keep me" meant I was "not worth keeping."

14
DEFENDING ADOPTION
1953

I HAD A THICK, UNRULY MANE the color of burnished copper. Vera and Dad were both brunettes without a shred of red to call their own. Whispers were circulating amongst some of the neighbors, some of which irritated Vera, who promptly set the gossipers straight: "I had tea with the milkman when Alf was at work." The gossip slid underground. After some time, all the neighbors learned that I was an "adopted child." By the time I was ten, Vera had trained me how to respond to any kid at school that teased me about being adopted. "You tell them, you were chosen by your parents. They just happened."

Once I needed to use this grenade on the playground at school. I was playing a skipping game with a group of friends when Megan Foster called, "You're out."

"No, I'm not," I said. "You're out."

"No, I'm not. I'm in and you're out. Anyway, my mum said you're adopted so I shouldn't play with you."

Without thinking, I instantly unleashed Vera's training. "Well, I was chosen by my parents, but you just happened."

Megan dissolved in tears. Later that day, I was called before the principal Mr. West, a pompous individual who sounded as though he was chewing pebbles when he spoke. I was sent home early for being mean to another student.

Vera was furious. The following day, she marched into Mr. West's office

"May I help you?"

"Yes, Mr. West, you can." Vera tightened her grip on her handbag. "I'm Vera Taylor. You and I have something to discuss concerning my daughter Glenda."

He arched an eyebrow. "We do? Very well, please sit down, Mrs. Taylor." Mr. West lowered himself into the black leather swivel chair behind his desk.

Vera sat down, leaned forward, her steady gaze never leaving Mr. West's face. "You sent Glenda home from school yesterday. I want to know why."

"Hmm...." Mr. West lowered his head and stroked his chin thoughtfully. "Let me think. Oh, yes. There was an unfortunate incident in the playground where Glenda caused another student to cry."

"Are you talking about Megan Foster?"

Mr. West raised his eyebrows. "Well, yes. As a matter of fact, I am. I thought it best to send Glenda home so that she would learn a lesson and think about her behavior toward another student before returning to school today."

Vera sat back in the chair and folded her arms across her chest. "*Her* behavior? You're talking about *my* daughter's behavior?"

"Well, yes."

"So, what was the incident?" Lips pencil thin, Vera awaited his response.

Mr. West gazed at the ceiling, arms propped on his chair as he steepled his fingertips. "Well, it appears that the girls were playing a skipping game. When Megan told Glenda that she'd fallen short in her performance and was out of the game, Glenda disagreed in a most aggressive manner."

"Really?" Vera leaned forward. "Did you speak with Megan?"

"Yes, I did."

"Did you speak with my daughter?"

"No, I did not."

"And why was that?"

"Well, it was obvious to me that something unpleasant had occurred in the playground during the break because Megan was crying."

Vera leaned back, bracing her arms on the chair and crossing her hands over her stomach "Oh, so let me see if I understand this. You spoke with Megan because she was crying, but you did not speak with my daughter. Correct?"

Mr. West frowned. "Yes, that is correct."

Vera nodded briefly. "What about the other girls they were playing with? Did you speak with them?"

"No, I did not."

Vera stood up and slammed one hand against the corner of the desk. "Well, thank goodness you're not a copper with the local police department!"

"I say there, that's—"

Vera barged on. "You spoke with only Megan because she was crying. You never spoke with the other students who saw and heard what was going on. Good heavens, are you aware that Megan told my daughter that she could not play with her? Because Megan's mother had forbidden her to play with an *adopted child?* Did you know that when you spoke with Megan?"

Mr. West stood and faced Vera across the desk. "No, I had not heard that."

"If you'd spoken to my daughter, you would have...." Vera started pacing before his desk.

"Um, well I...."

Vera faced Mr. West. "Don't you consider that an *inappropriate* thing to say to another student?"

"Yes, absolutely, but —"

"No buts!" Vera wagged her finger at him; Mr. West probably felt like he was looking down the barrel of a pistol. "You punished my daughter without hearing both sides of the situation. Should this happen again, I will take you and your pompous, pencil-pushing attitude before the School Board and seek sanctions against you. Is that clear?"

"Mrs. Taylor...." Mr. West drew himself to his full height of five foot eight inches. "I think you are getting ahead of yourself, there's no need... um... I acted...."

"I'm aware you 'acted.' You acted by doing nothing other than listen to a student who was crying. Perhaps you were worried that a crying student would turn into a complaining parent. Well, you were wrong. The student who was *not* crying has turned into a complaining parent. Good day to you."

Vera stormed out of the office and slammed the door behind her. With a few choice sentences delivered with fierce intensity, she had shredded Mr. West's pomposity. She told Dad and me later: "I left him speechless and red in the face."

I was truly proud of Vera that day. She had faced bureaucratic bullshit and felled it like an oak tree with shallow roots.

15
ACADEMICS
1954

B Y THE AGE OF TWELVE, it was time for me to move to secondary school. At the end of the school year, parents met with the school principal at the end of the school year and received an assessment of their children's intellect and future possibilities.

When it was Vera's turn, Mr. West told her: "Glenda is an average student, and I doubt she will amount to much of anything."

"I'm not surprised that you would make such a statement, I told him. You never liked my daughter, but I'm sure she will prove you wrong."

I can still see Vera's flushed face and wagging finger as she related the incident to Dad and me. "Don't you let his prediction come true. You make something of yourself, young lady."

I never admitted this to Vera, but Mr. West was correct: I was an average student.

I attended an all-girl's high school in England where the students wore grey and white uniforms and the teaching staff or mistresses, as they were called in those days, were all female. In the final year, students would complete a comprehensive examination that included mathematics. If they passed, they could attend college at no charge, and the County of Bristol would pay the tuition.

Math was incomprehensible to me. Miss Owens, the math teacher, instructed a class of over forty girls. For students like me, who couldn't keep up, it was a running joke amongst the students: "She fell off the bike and tumbled into the ditch." Once a student tumbled into the ditch, she stayed there. Math tutors or tutors in general were unavailable to working class students in the 1950s. I spent many hours "in the ditch," so I was ineligible to attend college because I could never pass the math portion of the examination.

That was fine with me because I yearned to attend nursing school. Throughout high school, I was frequently top of the class in physical science, which was taught by Miss Andrews, one of my favorite teachers. I was fascinated to learn how the body worked, and I mentally compared it to a car engine. If a car was properly cared for, it could last for years; likewise, if a person took care of his body, he could be around for years, barring unforeseen circumstances like accidents or acts of God.

I will never forget Miss. Andrews. She was a tall, gangly woman, dressed in tweeds, hair dragged back into a tight knot at the base of her neck, who barked out lesson instructions. She was probably in her early fifties; she wore no make-up and bore a slight resemblance to certain Ascot athletes. What Miss

Andrews lacked in femininity she certainly made up for in teaching skills. She was a demanding teacher, and her students had to bust their butts to earn an A in her class, but it was well worth the effort.

Thanks to her, I learned about menstruation and the reason why this monthly ritual was necessary. Vera never talked about such things but quickly snatched up my physical science book after I'd finished my homework, and she tried to educate Dad.

"Alf, listen to this. Did you know…?" Vera began to deliver specifics to Dad about the human body.

I watched Dad squirm in his chair, rustling the newspaper as he tried to cover his face. "Vera, not now," he mumbled. "I'm reading the paper."

———

Vera refused to enroll me in nursing school. "With your temperament you couldn't stand the discipline from the Matron and training staff."

What was she talking about? "How do you know that?" I demanded. "Who did you speak with?"

"I don't need to speak with anyone, young lady. I know you. I know that you would not be able handle the discipline."

Vera was correct; nursing school in England was quite rigorous. However, I was sure that Matron or staff—unlike Vera—would not subject me to corporal punishment if I failed a test while in training. What Vera seemed to ignore was that I had a passion for the subject. I excelled every year in Miss Andrews' class because I received positive feedback for my efforts, something Vera had not grasped because she never gave me positive feedback for anything. I imagined nursing school to be similar to Miss Andrews' class. If I were to work hard, praise would be my reward; if I slacked off, discipline — perhaps dismissal — would follow. What I hadn't counted on at the time was that math would probably also be a requirement in nursing school.

Sadly, my aspirations to become a nurse never materialized.

My second choice was hair styling. I dreamed of owning my own salon in the future. We were cleaning the living room when I said to Vera, "I think I'd make a great hairdresser. I'm sure I could open my own salon after a couple of years."

Vera stopped fluffing pillows, straightened up, and stared at me. "You must be mad. You want me to pay for hair dressing lessons? Absolutely out of the question, young lady."

She returned to pillow fluffing. "Just wait 'til I tell your father. What a laugh!"

"But—"

"No buts. The subject is closed."

Vera had her own agenda, one that she'd been working on for more than a year. I discovered that she and my school mistress had agreed that I would complete an additional year of school. They both knew that my admission to college would never happen because I lacked the necessary math skills. However, gaining an extra year of education would help me attain a solid secretarial position, something which Vera considered acceptable and respectable.

I had taken classes in shorthand and touch-typing in high school and excelled in both. On the manual typewriters of the late 1950s, I could whip out an error-free document at 75 words per minute and take dictation in shorthand at 100 words per minute. Once the electric typewriters appeared, my typing speed accelerated to 100 words per minute. I had excellent skills for secretarial work but no desire.

Being stuck in an office shuffling paper was not my idea of a career. In those days, women had "jobs" until they married and had children; a career was something to which only men aspired.

"If you can type, you can eat." This one of Vera's favorite sayings and it proved prophetic. When between positions throughout my working years, I could always work temporarily as a secretary or paralegal until my next permanent gig arrived. Hence, I was always able to pay my bills and have a roof over my head.

For this, I'm grateful to Vera, even though she was adamant that the role of secretary was my future until I married and moved onto the role of mother and homemaker. I believe she was looking out for my welfare based on her knowledge and experience of working women in the 1950s and early 1960s.

I had a different dream. Taking dictation and typing someone else's words were skills I would use intermittently while seeking something more challenging in a professional position.

When was I living in San Francisco, Vera wrote me that she had run into Mr. West in a local department store. When he politely inquired about me, this opened the door for her to set the record straight. She did so with gusto. Vera let the "pompous ass" (which was what she called him) know just how wrong he had been in his assessment of her daughter's abilities.

In her letter she described the encounter: "I told him that because of your adventurous spirit and excellent secretarial skills, you had worked for the Personnel Director of an oil company in the Middle East for two years and then immigrated to America, all on your own, without knowing a soul. Now you're working as a legal secretary for a prestigious law firm in San Francisco."

Vera was plucky in her defense of me against Mr. West's assault on my intellect. Of course, I thought, obviously she wouldn't have mentioned any negative reflections on her role as a parent.

In my next letter to her, I asked: "And what did he say?"

Two weeks later, her letter arrived. "Not a damned thing," she wrote. "He puffed up, got red in the face, raised his hat, and walked away."

I suspect that Mr. West and Vera had different perspectives on success. Mr. West would have recognized academic achievement alone, whereas Vera recognized my independent zeal to explore and learn outside a classroom environment.

His mistake was to predict a mundane future for me.

16
FAIRNESS
1957

O N ANOTHER OCCASION Vera showed the same relentless pursuit for fairness.

My maternal Grandmother, Edith, was also handy with the needle. She taught Vera how to sew, crochet, knit, and embroider. On November 21, 1934, at age 22, Vera applied and was accepted into the Dressmaking and Women's Light Clothing Trade Board of England and Wales. Vera met my dad when she was working as a seamstress.

One afternoon when we were sitting in the living room drinking tea, I asked her, "How did you meet Dad?"

Vera grinned. "Well, it was like this. A friend of your Uncle Len introduced us, and your dad asked me to go to the dog races. He was seven years older than me and said he'd had his eye on me for some time." She hesitated a moment, replacing her cup in its saucer. "He said that he was ready to get married."

Vera glanced in the mirror on the wall behind me and patted her hair. "I was a looker in my younger years. People used to say that I looked like Loretta Young. When your father told me that he had money in a savings account, I knew he was a good bet."

I was hoping to hear that Dad had sweet-talked Vera and that she had fallen madly in love, but that was not the case. In later years, after tracing their respective home lives, it was evident that Vera and Alf had needed to find a partner to start life anew and escape acrimonious family relationships.

Dad always objected to Vera working outside the home, which was a typical attitude for husbands in those times. This caused many an argument, one of which whipped Vera into such a tizzy she was practically frothing at the mouth.

Dad was adamant. "I make enough money to keep this house going. I work as much overtime as possible so that you can take care of the home and Glenda." It was a matter of pride for him. "I don't want people to think I can't support my family."

Dad shook out his newspaper, turned the page, adjusted his glasses, and kept reading.

Vera sighed. "Alf, be reasonable. What about holidays? We haven't had one for five years. If I worked part-time three days a week, I could make enough money for us to have a nice holiday."

Dad lowered his newspaper and fixed her with a steady gaze. "I said no and I meant no."

Dad's nephew, a builder, had recently added a conservatory to the back of the house. This now served as the kitchen. Vera flounced into the conservatory and began to do the dishes, all the while loudly spouting protestations.

Dad folded his paper, placed it on the floor beside his chair, stood, walked to the door separating the dining room from the conservatory, and locked it. He peered at Vera through the glass panes. "Now what are you gonna do? You're stuck." He laughed so hard his shoulders shook. I couldn't help it; I joined in.

I never decided which was the most distressing for Vera: being locked in the conservatory or Dad's audacity to laugh at her predicament, especially one he had created.

Vera, determined not to be outfoxed, took off one of her shoes and pummeled it against a glass pane in the door until it shattered. Tears were spilling down her cheeks. "Alf, you open this bloody door right now, you sod! Open this door or you'll be sorry!"

Dad stood there, arms folded, grinning. "I don't think you're in any position to make threats, Vera. You need to calm down."

Vera's spittle showered against the glass. "Open this door, Alf, or I'll smash every pane of glass in the conservatory."

I knew Vera's wrath. I'd seen it plenty of times when Dad was at work. "You'd better open the door," I said. "You know how she gets."

Dad glanced at me, nodded, and unlocked the door. As if nothing had happened, he walked back to his favorite chair, picked up the newspaper, sat down, and started reading again.

Once the door was unlocked, so was Vera's fury. She flew into the dining room like a hawk chasing prey and screamed at my dad. "You think this is funny? Me wanting to make some extra money so this family can go on holiday? You bloody sod! Let's see how funny you think this is!"

She stormed into the kitchen and returned immediately, egg in hand. She launched the egg toward the dining room wall closest to Dad. It hit its target. Raw egg trickled down the wall to the floor; it was the wall he had recently wallpapered during the renovation.

Delighted with her handiwork, smugly satisfied, Vera marched into the living room and switched on the television. While Victor Sylvester's band played in the background, Dad studied the wall behind him. He took a cigarette from his pack and lit up, then sauntered into the living room. "You know, you'll be living with egg on the wall for quite a while because I've signed up for overtime."

Vera did not respond. I imagine in her mind she'd won the battle.

Eventually, when I was around thirteen, she secured a part-time position as a seamstress with an upscale store downtown. I suppose that her perseverance finally overcame Dad's reluctance to having a working wife.

Vera's venture into the employment arena was rocky. If she took umbrage at something one of her coworkers said, she would grab her coat and hat and whirl out the door in a huff. Soon she would be working elsewhere. Vera's skills were impeccable. She never had a problem finding employment, but staying the course or "playing nice in the sandbox" with her coworkers was another matter. It was Vera's way or the highway.

Her proudest moment was when she was approved by the Committee for Institute Teachers, meaning that she could teach dressmaking in the evenings through the Bristol Education Institute.

I was in my early twenties when she first applied. Initially, her application was rejected due to lack of formal training. Vera had never apprenticed in dressmaking, but she had worked in the trade for many years and had letters of recommendation from various employers commending her skills. She was determined that nothing would prevent her from becoming an evening institute teacher. She appealed the committee's decision, met with the committee in person, and won the appeal. What Vera lacked in formal training, she excelled at in skill, experience, and determination. I was very proud of her.

17
ABUSE
1953–1958

VERA WOULD FREQUENTLY become agitated and rage out of control over minor issues. Prone to angry outbursts without warning, she would lash out at me verbally and physically. It was hard to pinpoint what would set her off, but it was like living with a time bomb with a short fuse. I was always tiptoeing around her emotionally, anticipating the next explosion.

Whenever she became upset with me, she would slap my face or punch me on whatever body part was closest to her. Using the boiler stick on my legs and buttocks was another of her preferred forms of punishment.

In the mid-1950s, washing machines were available to the wealthy but beyond the financial reach of the working class. We would put clothes into a tub called a boiler that heated the water, and we stirred the clothes around with a hefty stick, much like a baseball bat, to make sure they received a good wash. It was rather like the agitator on modern washing machines, but Vera also used it as an instrument of torture.

As a little kid, I was petrified of Vera when she had one of her tantrums. As I grew older, I grew braver. My fear of Vera slowly changed into strategizing the best ways to escape her abuse. When threatened with a beating, I would run away into another room or around the dining room table, with Vera chasing after me. I was faster and more nimble so Vera sometimes gave up. Instead, I would hear her say, "Come back here, young lady."

I would hesitate, momentarily unsure. "No, you're just going to hit me."

"No, I'm not."

For the first time or two, I believed her. I would cautiously return to wherever Vera was waiting. Instantly, she would grab my arm, often tugging me over to a concrete wall and then banging my head on the wall until her tirade was over. Alternatively, she would wield the boiler stick and swipe at my legs until ugly red welts rose up on my skin.

I needed another path of escape.

That path was our neighbor, Nellie Miles. She was my sanctuary. I would run out the back door, turn to the right, squeeze through the fence, and frantically bang on her back door. Obviously, she must have heard the commotion through the adjoining wall because she would open the door immediately.

We never talked about what was going on between Vera and me. We just sipped tea, and I listened to her stories about her kids, trying to gather enough strength to return home and hoping that Vera had calmed down.

In the 1950s and 1960s, society approved of corporal punishment for children, even in school. In those days, parents always backed the teachers, so it was pointless to complain that a teacher had whacked you on your behind with a wooden switch in front of the entire class. I recall vividly a male math teacher who would bend a student over a desk in the front row and use the switch. He also had a penchant for throwing wooden chalkboard erasers at students if he heard someone talking when he was writing on the board. Had an eraser struck and damaged a child, I doubt little would have been done.

There was no agency like Child Protective Services to investigate cases of abuse. The only place a child could find a little comfort was to confide in relatives and hope the relatives could be trusted to keep her secret. In my case, I found a trusted neighbor who heard the abuse and gave me shelter when I needed help. This was the era where children should be seen and not heard.

I realized early that I had a timid side to my nature. Vera's constant criticisms had eroded my confidence. This frightened me. Teachers and relatives had usually described me as an extrovert, but there were many days when I felt insecure, scared, or even totally lost.

I learned from the kids at school that timid people are picked on or bullied unless they could stand up for themselves. I was determined not to be pigeonholed as a weakling. By the time I was twelve, I had developed a sturdy outer shell and a defiant attitude that was impenetrable by people who knew me the least, and that was everyone.

When I was in my mid-twenties, my Uncle Jack and Aunt Alma took me to the airport to catch a flight to Beirut. We were sitting in the airport lounge, sipping a cocktail, when my aunt exclaimed, "Glenda, I've just noticed. Your left eye doesn't twitch any more. How's that? It used to twitch all the time when you were a kid."

"Simple." I took a sip of my drink, put the glass on the table, and met her gaze. "I no longer live with Vera."

She didn't respond, but the glance she exchanged with my uncle confirmed that I'd hit a home run.

When I was in my seventies, and Aunt Alma was in her nineties, we were chatting one morning on the phone.

"Myra and her brother rarely speak to each other," she said.

"Why?" I asked.

"Well," Aunt Alma said, "Julian is tired of his sister's angry outbursts. Myra is just like Vera—you never know when she's going to blow up!" It appeared that Myra had inherited her temperament from the Smith side of the family.

During Vera's frequent tirades and beatings, I made damned sure not to shed one tear. I would not give her the satisfaction of knowing she was hurting me. Once her anger was spent, there was always the threat that she would tell Dad that I was an insolent, willful child. Alone in my room at night, I would hear Vera regale Dad about my "bad behavior."

"Your daughter talked back to me again today. I won't have it, you hear me! You need to support me in this and help me straighten her out."

After a hard day's work, Dad did not want to listen to her complaints. He'd often say: "I wasn't here, so I don't know what went on."

Dad was aware of the friction between Vera and me. However, he never saw her physically abuse me because she did it only when we were alone, and I never told him. What was the point? He had made it clear when I was younger that he wanted no part of it.

The physical abuse continued at least twice a month until shortly before I turned sixteen.

One day, when Vera flew at me, her arm outstretched and ready to strike, I had the courage to change the rules. I grabbed her arm and yanked it down to her side. The anger I felt toward her over the years bubbled to the surface. I could see by her face that she was surprised and rightfully scared.

Holding her arm I said, "If you hit me, I will hit you back. I'm stronger than you. I will make damned sure when I hit you, I will hurt you." I was icy cold and direct; I meant every word.

I let go of her arm but continued to face her.

Vera shrank back, away from me. "I'll tell your father."

"Go ahead. And I'll tell him about all the times you've banged my head against a concrete wall or slapped my face or beaten my legs or butt with the boiler stick."

There was no response. From now on, Vera must have known that she would get back whatever she dished out. Fearful that I could not contain my anger any longer, I left the room and went upstairs to my bedroom.

When Dad returned home from work later that night, I heard the usual exchanges between them, but Vera made no mention of my threat to hit her. More importantly, she never laid a hand on me again. She knew better.

18
MILITARY SERVICE IN A DOUBLE-DECKER 1955

DAD TOLD ME THAT IN 1939, when German bombs began blasting English cities and towns, he had tried to enlist in the army. Unfortunately, the military rejected him because of a hearing defect.

Shaking his head he would say, "I really wanted to get into the fight against that mad devil Hitler, but my hearing was not up to scratch. I suppose it was not to be, but people don't forget seeing a man of draft age driving a bus around the streets of Bristol when other men were fighting overseas serving their country."

I had overheard snippets of conversations several times between my parents on Dad's inability to serve in the military. One time Vera said, "Just ignore them. What do they know? Wasn't your fault that you couldn't go to war."

"I know that, Vera, but it makes a bloke feel bad when people make snide remarks." Dad shifted his weight in the chair and stared down at the floor. "They think I didn't join up because I was a coward."

"What utter nonsense," Vera said. "We know the truth and that's all that matters."

During the blitz, without headlights to illuminate the way, Dad skillfully navigated a double-decker bus through Bristol's pitch-black streets. He always delivered his passengers safely and on time. He once told me: "You know, your dad was offered a promotion to Inspector more than once."

"Really, why didn't you take it?"

"Well, you know how it is." Dad scratched his ear. "I was reluctant to squeal on my mates."

"What do you mean?"

He sighed. "When buses were late or there was an accident or the fares collected didn't match the number of tickets sold, I'd have to report that to the chap at the depot. The bus crew would be in trouble."

Dad stood up and strolled over to the window that faced our back yard where vegetables he'd planted earlier in the year were beginning to nose their way out of the ground into the light. Even thinking about reporting his coworkers to the boss had made Dad uncomfortable. He rubbed his chin and turned to face me. "I didn't want that responsibility. Did you know that many inspectors are disliked by the drivers? I wouldn't like that." No, I didn't know, but I understood why Dad did not accept the promotion.

Vera was livid at the loss of extra income. "It's not just you, you know. What about me? I'm constantly scrimping and scraping. A little extra money would come in very handy. But no, you don't want to rat on your mates."

She grudgingly accepted the fact that her husband, lacking in ambition, balanced the score by being a steady and reliable provider.

I recall Vera telling Dad and me that during the bombing of our neighborhood, when Dad was at work and I was still a baby, she never took me to the shelter. "Filthy places, all crawling with insects. Who wants to be crammed into a shelter with the neighbors and be forced to hear their stupid cries of terror?" According to her, she preferred to stay in her own bed and leave me undisturbed in mine.

One night, German planes blitzed our neighborhood with bombs. Their targets crumbled into a mass of bricks and concrete, shooting flames and billowing black smoke. Some bombs landed so close to our home that our upstairs and downstairs front windows blew out. Vera was undeterred. "If it's my time to go, then I'll go in my own bed, thank you very much."

Dad lit another cigarette, his hand trembling. "That was a bloody stupid thing to do. You and Glenda could have been killed."

Vera waved one hand dismissively. "Yeah, yeah. We weren't, though, were we? We live on the outskirts of town, so it was a good bet that not many bombs would fall around here. And I was right."

For Vera, being right was important.

Dad continued driving double-decker buses until he retired in April 1970. After working for the bus company for thirty-one years, his retirement benefit was a simple gold watch; there was no such thing as a pension plan in those days. Thanks to Vera's excellent money management skills during their marriage, my parents had saved sufficient money that, with careful use, would ensure their survival for the remainder of their lives.

Dad was a man's man. He missed "being around the blokes" as he put it, so he found a part-time job in a factory as a sweeper. He was back with the lads and his earnings supplemented my parents' savings for several years. Finally, age and health issues convinced him to quit and retire permanently.

Throughout his life, Dad had had a sweet tooth. He would contentedly munch through a bag of candy several times a week. By the time Dad retired from the bus company, he was rather chubby, and his sweet tooth had resulted in diabetes. The doctor suggested insulin shots, but Vera was adamant: "No shots." She promptly changed Dad's diet and banned candy from the house. Within a year, Dad was svelte and free from diabetes.

Vera definitely had her good points when it came to caring for my dad.

19
CHRISTMAS MORNING
1955

ONE CHRISTMAS MORNING when I was twelve, Vera seemed excited and all aflutter.

I was sitting on the floor in the front room, watching cartoons on the television. I heard Vera say to my dad, "Alf, you go in there and tell her to close her eyes. I'll bring it in."

Dad sounded confused. "What about the...?"

Vera sounded impatient. "Yes, yes, I have it here. It will be inside. See, like this."

"Oh, okay. Um.... Glenda, where are you?"

I was still in the front room watching television. Dad came into the room grinning. "It's time for your Christmas present. Close your eyes and don't open them until I tell you. Okay?"

"What is it? Is it a bike?" I held my breath. "Is it roller skates?"

"Just hold your horses, young lady. It's coming right now."

I jumped up, sat on the sofa, closed my eyes, and crossed my fingers. *Please, please let it be a bike or roller skates.*

"Okay, you can open your eyes," Vera said.

I took another deep breath and opened my eyes. She was holding the handle of a green and cream pram. She smiled and faced me. My first thought was: *What on earth am I supposed to do with a baby carriage?*

"Look inside," she said.

Stunned, I followed her instructions. A large, bald, plastic doll, attired in a blue taffeta dress lined in pink, with blue underwear and booties to match, seemed to stare back at me, unblinking.

"What do I do with it?"

"What do you do with it?" Vera rolled her eyes. "For heaven's sakes, girl, it's a doll. Took me a long time to make those clothes, you know." Pride colored her every word. "I did it when you were at school." She held up a couple of white nightdresses. "Look, nightdresses for you to change her before you put her to bed."

She must have expected me to pick up the doll, so I did, and held it by its arms. "Why do I have to change her clothes?"

Hand on her hip, trying to contain her impatience, Vera glared at me. "Young ladies sleep in nightdresses, so you have to change her from daytime clothing to nighttime clothing. You can give her a pretend bath and then put on her nightie before she goes to sleep."

"Why?" To a twelve-year-old tomboy, this seemed nuts. "I don't sleep in a nightie."

Vera shook her head and sighed. "Yes, I know that very well. I'm the only mother on the street that doesn't wash and pin her daughter's nightdresses on the line with the weekly wash. She paused expectantly. "Well? Do you like your Christmas present?"

Fighting back tears, I nodded and shifted the doll to the

crook of my arm. I couldn't let Vera or my dad see my disappointment. I didn't understand. Did they not hear me? They had asked me what I wanted for Christmas and I told them: a bike or roller skates. What happened? Were they trapped in societal expectations for a girl? Were my wishes as a daughter not important? As always, I had questions but rarely received answers.

The day following Christmas in England is Boxing Day where trades people—coalmen, milkmen, bakers, and others—customarily receive gifts of money for services performed throughout the year. We called them Christmas Boxes. That particular Boxing Day, I banished the bald doll out of sight to the top of my wardrobe. Instead, my two faithful companions and confidantes that comforted me when I was sad—my teddy bear and the family cat—enjoyed chauffeur service in the pram, up and down our street.

After six months, the pram disappeared—probably sold—but the doll remained, planted on top of the wardrobe, always reminding me that I was not "a perfect daughter."

Vera grumbled. "There's something wrong with you. Most girls enjoy playing with dolls. I spent ages working on those doll clothes. Bought you a nice pram and all you used it for was to haul the cat around the neighborhood. I'll never understand you."

"But, Mum. I told you that I wanted a bike or roller skates. Don't you remember? You asked me what I wanted, and I told you—"

"Such foolishness! A bike or roller skates?" She grunted. "You're already a tomboy."

That caught me by surprise, and my mouth dropped open: she'd acknowledged that I was a tomboy.

"Yes, yes. I've heard the stories. Climbing those tall oak trees in the woods and jumping from high branches to the ground." Vera sighed in exasperation. "Hanging by your legs on the monkey bars, rocking high on the swings and then jumping off. You're lucky you haven't broken your neck."

I stuttered, "B-b-but I—"

"No buts." Vera kept on. "Bikes and roller skates are for boys. You're a girl. You need to learn to act like one." She picked up her purse. "I'm off to the shops. This is a good time to clean your room. I'll inspect it when I return."

This was one time that I received an answer to my question, but I didn't like it.

20
DANCING
1957

MOIRA SHEARER LEFT ME MESMERIZED in the movie *The Red Shoes*. She was a lithesome redhead, adored by millions, embracing freedom and joy through music and dance. I was entranced, my spirit twirling on air.

"Mum, can I take ballet lessons? I want to be like Moira Shearer."

Bewilderment shadowed Vera's face, and she frowned. "You? Ballet? Oh, for heaven's sakes! Absolutely not! You're like a fairy elephant."

My enthusiasm, previously inflated and then instantly deflated, was doused with icy water.

———

At the time of this brief exchange, neither Vera nor I knew of my latent talent. It was hiding, waiting for the right introduction, a fantasy—like what might have been hidden behind a Victorian bustle. I was fourteen when, metaphorically, my "bustle eventually rustled": I learned to ballroom dance at a professional level.

One Sunday afternoon, my parents and I visited Dad's brother Will and his wife Gwen. Their grown children Pat and David had married and were starting families of their own; their younger brother had died in childhood. David was a builder, a down-to-earth chap who couldn't abide his father. I fully understood why. Dad's brother Will had come from the same mold as their father, a loud, raucous, know-it-all chauvinist.

I had met Pat only a couple of times. She seemed a little aloof, but it was obvious that she was a momma's girl. I once overheard Vera tell Dad: "Pat is certainly getting hoity-toity," implying she was a working-class girl wishing to move up to a middle-class life. I wondered whether my aunt was guiding my cousin to fling her net wide when angling for a mate. If Pat "married up," she could escape the life that her mother had endured, living with the likes of her father. From what I recall, Pat was successful in her quest; she met and married a middle-class businessman.

Aunt Gwen had managed to smartly sidestep many of the crude, verbal barbs dished out by her husband and had found solace in ballroom dancing several times a week. Back in the 1950s, it was acceptable and commonplace for two women to dance together in the absence of their husbands. Gwen, always enterprising in her search for a dance partner, had found a man.

The family grapevine sizzled. I overheard conversations between Vera and my dad. "Was this man a dance partner or was there a little more to it?" Everyone was aware of Uncle Will's temperament. Nobody knew for certain the status of Aunt Gwen's relationship with her dance partner.

In those days, inquiries of a personal nature were frowned upon and considered impolite, even amongst family members. Relatives would patiently wait for someone with loose lips to gossip, revealing details, piece by piece. When I finally met him, I found Aunt Gwen's dance partner to be charming and gracious. I must admit, I tended to agree with some of the adults and wondered whether he "batted for the other team." However, it was none of my business.

Vera was a devoted fan of ballroom dancing and never missed the weekly one-hour television show *Ballroom Dancing with Victor Sylvester*. Since she was an expert with a sewing needle, she was captivated by the dancers' colorful, frothy gowns and awed by their exotic hairstyles and elaborate jewelry. Vera watched the dancers twirl through intricate steps with the speed of hummingbirds, and she was transported to another world, and her feet would try to keep pace on the carpet under her chair.

During our visit, Uncle Will was hogging the conversation as usual when the doorbell rang.

"Excuse me," my aunt said. "That's probably Jeffrey. I told him to drop by if he was passing this way."

Jeffrey? Who was Jeffrey?

Aunt Gwen observed the curious glances that passed between Vera and Dad. She paused on her way to the front door. "You'll like him, Vera. He's quiet by nature, with a gentle charm. Actually, he's rather handsome with dark wavy hair and a neatly trimmed moustache. He's about my height with a slight muscular physique—perfect dance partner material."

Aunt Gwen grinned and winked at Vera as she opened the front door. In stepped a well-dressed man who, stitch-for-stitch, matched Aunt Gwen's description.

"Let me introduce you," my aunt said. "This is my sister-in-law Vera, my brother-in-law Alf, and their daughter Glenda. Of course, you know my husband, Will. This is my dance partner, Jeffrey.

Vera was never at a loss for words, but this announcement temporarily zipped her lips into silence. Composing herself, she inched toward the edge of her chair and extended her hand. "Pleased to meet you, I'm sure."

"Likewise." Jeffrey bowed over Vera's hand. "I hear from Gwen that you love ballroom dancing, but you don't dance. What a shame. Why don't you and Alf come with us one night?"

"Yes, I do enjoy watching ballroom dancing." Vera sank back in her chair. "I don't have enough confidence to try it." She laughed nervously. "Alf doesn't like dancing. He thinks it's the devil's work—"

"Vera," Dad interrupted, "I never said that. What I said was, 'Glenda is too young to go dancing alone.' I don't want her around long-haired, riffraff Teddy Boys."

In Britain during the 1950s and 1960s, Teddy Boys were all the rage. Many belonged to gangs and "duked it out" with rivals on Saturday nights. They hung around the local pubs, drove noisy, flashy cars, and let cigarettes dangle from the corners of their mouths. They were working class lads who wore Edwardian style drape jackets, suede shoes with thick crepe soles, narrow fitted pants called drainpipe pants, and flashy ties. Their popular hairstyle was an overblown quaff in front with a "duck's arse" at the back. Teenage girls were drawn to these bad boys, and when the Teddy Boys revved their cars outside the local tavern on a Friday night, fathers wanted to lock up their daughters. Dad was no exception.

"You don't dance, Alf?" Jeffrey asked.

"No, never tried it. I prefer to watch football."

"See what I mean," Vera said, wriggling into position for a better view of Jeffrey. "Glenda asked me if she could take ballet. Of course, I told her, 'Not a chance.' Ballet is not for tomboys. But she needs to learn grace. I think ballroom dancing could help her with that, but Alf is against it."

My aunt joined in the conversation. "Alf, what if Vera brought Glenda to Mrs. Yelverton's class? She would be among adults, not Teddy Boys. Ballroom dancing is a wonderful way for a young girl to gain poise. Vera would be there, I would be there, and so would Jeffrey. Glenda would be well protected. Why don't you let her give it a try?"

Dad shifted in his seat. His cheeks reddened like Braeburn apples ripe for the picking. He grinned sheepishly. "Oh, I see. So you're all ganging up on me." He looked straight at me. "Is that right? You asked your mum for ballet lessons?"

"Yes. But she told me no. That I was a fairy elephant."

Aunt Gwen winced; Uncle Will erupted in a bellicose roar.

"Oh, dear...." Dad shook his head and looked at me again. "Well, would you like to learn ballroom dancing?"

"Yes, of course I would. But you've always been against it. I told you—"

Dad raised his hand, and I shut up. "I was only against you going dancing on your own or with a girlfriend. You're far too young for that. But...." He hesitated, rubbing his right ear, deep in thought. "As long as your mother is with you, I guess it's okay. He turned to Gwen. "Where are the classes held?"

"Just down the road. It takes me five minutes to get there. Vera and Glenda can take the Knowle bus from the village. It will take them about thirty minutes," Gwen explained. "Classes are held every Saturday. They start at ten in the morning and end around one in the afternoon."

"I see," Dad said.

"When you're not working, Alf, why not come and see for yourself. There are several teenagers taking classes right now."

"Glenda can dance her way to bronze, silver, and gold medals for the waltz, quickstep and fox trot," Jeffrey said. "Once she passes these examinations, she can start to learn the Latin dances—you know, tango, cha-cha-cha, rumba—that type of thing."

Dad looked a bit bemused, but he nodded. Recalling the event, I knew Dad had no clue about dancing in general, let alone Latin dances.

"You'd like that, wouldn't you?" my aunt asked.

"Like it? I would love it!" I said. "Dad, you'll be proud of me. I know I'll pick up ballroom dancing very quickly. I have natural rhythm."

"Well, let's not get ahead of ourselves," Vera said. "You don't want to get a big head, but I'll certainly be glad to see you learning to dance instead of climbing trees."

———

The dance studio resembled an aircraft hangar, long and narrow, the long walls broken up by an occasional window and lined with a row of chairs on either side. Overhead was a curved metal roof.

Under the watchful eye and skillful mentoring of Mrs. Yelverton, my initiation into the art of ballroom dancing was rapid and smooth. I was correct; I had natural rhythm and blossomed quickly into an excellent dancer. Finally, Vera and I shared something we both loved. She was impressed with my dance skills, and I admired her creativity in sewing my competition gowns. Like a thirsty plant absorbing moisture from an unexpected rain shower, having Vera's approval and support was a surprising gift that I cherished. For the first time, I felt a connection with my adoptive mother.

Mrs. Yelverton was an imposing figure, but she was an excellent teacher. She was tall and stout, with a powerful voice, and she usually wore her hair pulled back and twisted into a knot on top of her head.

When scheduled for dance examinations, I became nervous. *What if I didn't pass the three requisites: waltz, quickstep, and foxtrot? If I didn't, I could not move forward to the dances I was most anxious to learn.* I'd watched students of the Latin dances practicing for exhibition competitions. Their twirling bodies were pumping attitude; they were poured into skimpy, snug-fitting gowns flashing iridescence that aroused my desire. Latin music was filled with drama and passion. Its melodies and rhythm stirred within me a physical longing that, even in my early teens, I didn't fully understand, but knew somehow it was linked to boys.

Luckily, I had an experienced dance partner for the waltz, quickstep, and foxtrot, an older gentleman who provided a strong lead that allowed me to perform well. Music would fill the empty dance studio and my training took over. In my mind I could visualize the aircraft hangar filled with spring flowers, their delicate perfume tantalizing my senses. My feet glided automatically with precision into the steps of the dance. No pain, no anxiety—I was free—like a wood nymph twirling in the morning dew.

In one year, bronze and silver medals for the waltz, foxtrot, and quickstep were mine. Each Saturday thereafter was devoted to practicing the dances to earn the gold. Once these examinations were conquered, I was free to embrace Latin rhythm.

Vera was right. Ballroom dancing was definitely better than climbing trees.

Managing competition jitters was challenging, but the applause and cheers from the audience and other competitors enveloped me in such warmth and admiration that I felt validated as a person and loved.

During the break one Saturday morning, when I was socializing with the other teenage students, I saw Mrs. Yelverton huddled with Vera in one corner of the room. Both were chattering earnestly, their heads bent toward each other. There were broad hand gestures from Mrs. Yelverton and vigorous head shaking from Vera that indicated something intense was going on—but what? I watched Mrs. Yelverton pat Vera on the shoulder and turn away before calling all the students onto the dance floor.

Vera beckoned to me, and I went to her. "What's going on?" I asked.

Vera sighed. "Mrs. Yelverton tells me that you have the talent to turn professional. She says you're way beyond dancers your own age. In a couple of years, you would be ready to compete against adults."

"I told you I was a natural," I said a mite boastfully.

"You're right, you did." Vera sank into the nearest chair, the fingers of her right hand tapping against the armrest. She took a deep breath. "Unfortunately we can't afford it. It's been a struggle buying you dance shoes every couple of months. If you were competing professionally... well, I can't imagine. My fingers would be raw trying to keep up, making your dresses.

And shoes? You would need new shoes, probably every month. Your dad and I… well, we just don't have the money. I'm sorry, but that's the way it is."

As though I'd been caught in a cloudburst, I felt drenched with disappointment. I bit my lower lip, determined not to cry. The only thing for which Vera and I shared a passion and had formed a connection was ballroom dancing. We were a team. Vera would make the dresses, and I would execute the dance. When presented with medals, I would know they were for both of us because the judges awarded points for competition dresses. With limited financial resources, Vera had done an outstanding job. My competition dresses were the prettiest, and I was grateful, but I needed more.

Stellar performances and excellent examination results were insufficient. To dance competitively at a professional level, I needed something my family could not provide: money. At age fifteen, I concluded that lack of money was an obstacle to talent and therefore, I should never expect success if I needed to rely on others' resources to reach my goals.

Sadly, my dance with Vera was over.

21
DEPRESSION
1955–1958

IN A RARE VULNERABLE MOMENT, Vera once let down her guard and revealed that she had been embarrassed because she was the only woman on the street who was childless. She felt the neighbors looked down on her. She told me: "Married woman without children in the 1940s and 1950s aroused suspicion—'How come she has no kids?'"

Wives were expected to breed; that was their primary reason for existence. Vera could not meet society's expectations.

When Dad had popped the question, Vera told him that she could not have children. According to Vera, my dad had said, "Fine with me. I don't care if we don't have kids."

However, being childless was not fine with Vera. She frequently said, "I don't think marriage is marriage without children." After a couple of years of nagging, Dad finally succumbed and agreed to adopt a child.

I can still hear the wistful tone in her voice when she told me: "I wanted a boy, but your father was insistent. He would agree to adopt only a girl, so I settled for a girl."

Hugging my teddy bear, I cried myself to sleep that night: she'd "settled for me."

When Vera was in her mid- to late-eighties, her three brothers died unexpectedly in quick succession. Len was the first to go with a heart attack in 2000. He was followed by Jack, who died after a lengthy battle with Alzheimer's. Then it was Gordon, who also suffered from heart problems.

During one of our Sunday morning phone chats, Vera told me how devastated she was at the loss of her three brothers. I offered a few words of comfort. She was lonely after losing her husband in 1987. She and Dad rolled on like a tandem, bound together by culture, similar childhood experiences, and need. Vera would prattle on when sewing at the dining room table, and Dad would read the newspaper or a book, nodding or grunting occasionally to assure Vera that he was listening.

"My brothers always looked out for me, protected me," Vera confided. She recalled an incident when her brother Len had followed her and my dad on their first date.

"Your dad was seven years older than me, so I think Len was a little concerned. Anyway, your dad invited me to go to the dog races."

"Dog races? What sort of dogs?"

"Well, greyhounds, of course." From the tone of her voice, I concluded that she considered my question irrelevant. Her attendance at a greyhound racetrack seemed ironic since I had become an advocate against greyhound racing, but I kept my mouth shut. This was Vera's time to talk and the disclosure was enlightening.

"I didn't know it at the time, but your Uncle Len followed us, at a distance, of course, to make sure that your dad actually took me to the dog track."

The tempo and pitch of Vera's voice told me that she was reliving her first date with my dad and enjoying every moment. "Len stayed in the background, you know, like a detective. When we left the track he followed us to make sure your dad took me straight home too and didn't try any hanky-panky."

"Well, did he?"

"Did he what?"

"Try any hanky-panky?"

Vera scoffed at the very idea. "Course not. I had three brothers and would eavesdrop on them when they were to-gether in their bedroom next to mine and talking about their lady friends. Had quite an education, I can tell you. Your father behaved like a perfect gentleman. I wouldn't have it any other way."

"It must have been a shock," I commented, "losing all three brothers so close together."

"Yes, it was," Vera said. "And crying doesn't bring them back. They pampered me all my life, and I miss that dreadfully. Your father and I would be invited to spend vacations at their homes, and they never allowed us to pay for a thing. During the holidays, they always stayed in touch, sent a card and gift at Christmas... they never forgot."

I heard her sniff and blow her nose. "Now they're gone... all my brothers are gone. I have only my sister left, your Aunt Molly. I probably shouldn't say this, but I don't like the woman. Never did, even though she's my sister."

Vera's aunt raised Molly, not her parents, so Molly was rarely around Vera and her brothers. I could not understand

Vera's intense animosity toward Molly, but I was about to find out.

Apparently, according to Vera, Aunt Molly was lazy and selfish. "She comes over here for tea. Never asks if she can help. I have to wait on her hand and foot. She never offers to wash up the tea things."

"Well, Mum," I hesitated a moment. "Have you ever asked Aunt Molly to help you?"

"What would be the point? I know she wouldn't." Vera sighed. "Calls me to whine about her lot in life. I don't have time for that. The last time she called, I let her have it. I told her not to call me again if all she wants to do is complain."

Older and wiser now, I remained silent.

When our conversation ended, I hung up the phone, pondering Vera's comment: "They pampered me." It needled the hell out of me. If Vera had relished pampering so much by her brothers, why was she unable or unwilling, to pamper, just a little, her adopted daughter? I didn't get it. Old childhood resentments came bubbling up, and I was pissed off for a week.

I considered confronting Vera when I called her the following Sunday. I would tell her what a lousy mother she had been and how much I'd craved acceptance, love, and approval as a child and that all I'd received from her was criticism, derision, and abuse.

Was it because I was adopted and not her natural child? Was it because Dad had refused to adopt a boy, something Vera had desired, but was denied? Was it because I was a tomboy and lace and frills meant nothing to me? My mind was spinning in a circle of questions with no answers.

Perhaps I had been wrong to expect love and nurturing from her. Maybe, I was a bad kid and therefore, unlovable, but I never skipped school, passed all my examinations, never came home under the influence of alcohol or drugs, and I was a virgin until I was eighteen.

What did my adoptive mother want from me: perfection?

———

Over the years, Vera's harsh and repressive mothering style took so much energy to withstand that I was always exhausted. Intermittently, death crept into my thoughts. It was the only way to silence and banish Vera from my world, permanently. Many nights I would pray: "Please let me go to sleep and never wake up. If you can't do that, then please take away the pain."

My prayers went unanswered. I began to think about running out in front of a truck that was lumbering down the street; I would be hit and it would be over. I would be dead and at peace. Then I thought: What if the truck didn't kill me? What if it left me a cripple, and I had to live in a government-run institution for the permanently physically impaired? No, no, that was not the answer. I needed a sure thing. It never entered my mind to commit suicide overdosing on narcotics or blowing my brains out with a gun, probably because neither of these resources was available in my world of the 1950s.

Battered by Vera's tempests over the years, I felt emotionally crushed, like a brick wall continually slammed by a wrecking ball. I dreaded waking up each morning, not wanting to face another day. Most nights, to avoid interacting with Vera, I retired early with a book.

One day, our neighbor, Mrs. Miles, passed me on the street and, according to Vera, told her I looked so sad that it brought tears to her eyes.

"Is Glenda all right?" Mrs. Miles asked her.

That evening when I returned home from work Vera cornered me. "I told Mrs. Miles you were just fine." She bristled. "Don't you be out there seeking self-pity, young lady. Pull yourself together. None of us gets what we want out of life. Why should you be an exception?"

It sounded to me as if Vera was frustrated with her lot in life. I recalled her angry outburst years earlier when she felt that Dad was favoring me over her. It appeared to me that she viewed another female as competition, even her own daughter, and probably another reason why Vera wanted to adopt a son and not a daughter. It made perfect sense: he would be another male to pamper her.

All I yearned for was acceptance, affection, encouragement, and approval, but Vera could give only what she knew and I could return only what I felt.

It was not much of an exchange.

22
TOMBOY TRANSFORMED
1958

IF I'VE TOLD YOU ONCE, I've told you a hundred times, boys aren't interested in girls who climb trees, play cricket, and get their clothes covered in grass stains." Vera would stand at the kitchen sink, vigorously wielding a sturdy vegetable knife, scoring the base of homegrown Brussels sprouts as she readied them for the pot. Her frustration was blatant. "They want someone who, well… someone who's ladylike, bathes regular, takes pride in her appearance, and the like." She would swivel about on her heels and wave the knife in front of me. "I don't expect a young man to be knocking on my door any time soon looking for you."

Of course not, I thought. *Why would he? If a boy doesn't climb trees and play cricket, what good is he? We wouldn't be friends.*

Vera would sigh, shake her head, and go about her business, usually cooking or folding laundry. "When will you ever learn?"

She didn't have long to wait. My transformation seemed to happen overnight.

One night, snuggled beneath the sheets, I was a tomboy. The following morning I awoke interested in all things feminine: the latest fashions, make-up, hairstyles, and fretting whether boys would find me attractive and cast a second glance in my direction. From that moment, I knew my life would never again be the same.

Constant nagging from Vera to take a bath, wash my hair, lotion my body, file my nails, iron my school uniform, and straighten my stockings had vanished.

Going on sixteen and spending minimal time in the bathroom in front of the mirror switched to hogging the bathroom and despairing over the image in the mirror that stared back at me. What boy could possibly be interested in this freckle-faced creature with home-cropped titian hair, pale skin, bowed legs, knobby knees, and white eyelashes and eyebrows?

Vera had noticed the change. "How much longer are you going to be in the bathroom preening? Your father needs to use the toilet. Hurry it up."

I would call back to her. "I'll be out in a minute."

"Not a minute too soon, I hope." She liked to have the last word.

At other times, Vera's voice would ricochet off the staircase. "Are you running another bath up there? Didn't you just have one yesterday?"

"Yes," I would respond. "But that was *yesterday*."

"In this house, my girl, we don't take baths every day."

Frustrated, I would yell back down the stairs. "There's no pleasing you, Mum. You tell me that boys won't be interested in me if I don't bathe regularly. Now you're telling me not to bathe every day. I wish you'd make up your mind."

"That's enough lip from you, young lady. Just do as you're told."

I would finish up in the bathroom, skip down our steep staircase, run through the front room into the dining room, and meet Vera in the kitchen.

"Oh, so here you are." Her brow would wrinkle slightly while she eyed me up and down. "Well, you're certainly clean, but at this point, I doubt boys would be interested in you."

"What do you mean?" My face flushed red. "Why do you say that?" I always felt under attack but was never sure why.

"Well, look at you." She would sigh, hand on her hip, with her other hand extended toward me churning at the air as if groping for words. "You need... filling out, so to speak. I mean... well... let's face it." She rolled her eyes. "You're practically flat-chested. Your legs are a little bowed and, well... you have knobbly knees. I'm only saying that... maybe... you're not quite ready to attract the attention of boys."

Vera would pause and gaze out the kitchen window, her frown easing slowly and replaced by a small, proud smile. "When I was your age, I had a nice little figure, I did. Couldn't keep the boys away, but you... well...." Her eyes scanned my body one last time. "Let's forget about boys for a while, shall we?"

Her words stung, but I took a deep breath, kept my mouth shut, and stuffed down the pain. It was typical Vera, spouting barbs of torment. After all, I should be used to this by now. I rapidly blinked back a few tears, but anger was gnawing at my gut.

After such demoralizing encounters, I would eradicate Vera from my mind. Instead, I imagined myself as a moth, pushing itself free from the chrysalis, knowing it would emerge as a beautiful butterfly. I had begun my journey to womanhood an innocent, emerging slowly from my chrysalis, with much to learn about the world, men, and myself. Who knew whether I would ever mature into a beautiful butterfly, but I was hopeful that someday, someone, somewhere, would think so.

Vera had mentioned "boys" and that I wasn't quite ready to attract anyone's attention. In retaliation for her insensitive comments, I was goaded to pursue the topic further, approaching it from a different angle.

"The girls at school are allowed to wear makeup on the weekends and have their hair cut by a hairdresser. Boys seem to like that. Why can't I get my hair cut by a professional?"

"We don't have the money. Besides, I think I do a fine job trimming your hair."

My haircut was a constant source of embarrassment. Vera would place a bowl on my head and then trim the hair that poked out around the bowl. I had naturally wavy hair and odd strands would stick out at all angles. I would cut them off, but soon they would reappear.

I persisted. "You go to the hairdresser. Why not me?"

Vera would bristle and draw herself up to her full five feet four inches.

"You should be grateful that you have a thick head of hair." She would protectively pat the hair at the nape of her neck. "Mine is fine and thin and needs special attention. When you're earning money, my girl, you can pay to get your hair cut professionally."

Vera's attempts at being a hairdresser caused much teasing from my schoolmates.

"Guess who's had a haircut?" Roars of laughter would

follow me. "Your mum's nifty with the bowl and scissors, ain't she?"

I never told Vera about the taunts. Why bother? She always seemed disinterested in how I felt, so I didn't think she'd care. Worse, she might have found it humorous and shared it with the neighbors while chatting over the back fence. Time and experience had revealed that Vera had no respect for privacy.

I kept pushing. "Carol and Lesley's mums let them wear makeup on the weekends. How come I can't?"

I could hear from the tone of Vera's voice that she was irritated. "I couldn't care less what their mums allow. Forget the makeup, young lady. When you turn seventeen, we'll talk about makeup."

I had needled Vera enough, and I wasn't getting anywhere. It was time to shut up.

For once, Vera kept her promise. When I turned seventeen, I was allowed to use a little powder and lipstick. Mascara and eye shadow would have to wait until I turned eighteen.

Since I was a redhead, I was an easy target for teasing by my friends and the girls at school. "Coppernob" was their favorite nickname for me. I would laugh it off, but inside I would cringe at being ridiculed and made the focus of attention.

Someone would shout, "Here's Coppernob!" All eyes would turn in my direction. Like an insect on the end of a pin, I squirmed with embarrassment. Did they see what Vera saw? I always wondered what they thought of me and imagined the worse.

I was the only girl of seven paper delivery kids with Giles Groceries. When I entered puberty and became more curious about boys, my tendency to blush would reveal my vulnerability. I had a secret crush on Gerald, one of the paperboys but never told Vera of my feelings. My anticipation of Vera's sensitivity to a daughter's first crush was that it would be outside her realm of comprehension.

One local teen, Susan Jackson, who lived with her doting mother in a house on my paper route, had somehow sensed that I was interested in this young man. She frequently hung out around the store, observing the comings and goings of the paper delivery crew and chatting with several of the boys. She was cute, flirtatious, and popular.

When I was at the store one day, checking the newspapers in my bag and getting ready to walk my route, Susan approached me. "I thought you'd like to know that Gerald wants to ask you out. You like him, don't you?"

I stopped sorting my papers and gaped at her. *Was she kidding?* Gerald was popular with all the girls—he was medium height and blonde and had a good build. He usually dated girls like Susan, not girls like me. I blushed, which gave Susan the confirmation she sought.

"How do you know that he wants to ask me out?"

"He told me."

"When?"

Susan shrugged. "Last week, I think. He's going to ask you for a date sometime soon when you're picking up your papers. See ya." With a pert, saccharine smile, Susan left the store.

I was suspicious but also a little hopeful. Susan and I were acquaintances, never friends. Why was she giving me this information? I decided that a wait and see attitude was the best strategy.

Later in the week, after I'd delivered the papers, I stopped at the local candy store next door to Giles Groceries and bought my favorite, sherbet lemons. I'd popped one into my mouth when Gerald walked into the store. We stared at each other. I recalled Susan's words and blushed.

Gerald, sweat beading on his forehead, appeared agitated and uncomfortable. "What Susan told you... well, it's not true." He shuffled uneasily. "She shouldn't have done that. It wasn't right." He spun around, heels scraping against the floor, and started to leave the store, but then turned back. He glanced toward me, avoiding my eyes. "I'm sorry," he mumbled and raced out the door.

I slunk out of the store and hurried home. I escaped to my bedroom, telling Vera that I wanted to read. Emotionally scorched, I cuddled the family cat, crying and praying that this latest humiliation would go away. I never again spoke to Susan Jackson. Why would I?

I continued to deliver papers for another six months. For a while, I dreaded running into Gerald, but I had no need to fear further embarrassment. When our paths occasionally crossed, we exchanged a brief greeting and went our separate ways. I suspected that Gerald had integrity. Since none of the other paperboys teased me, I believed that he never repeated the incident. For this, I was grateful.

When I would have wanted to be skipping through a rose garden, after Gerald's rejection and Susan's deception, I felt like I had slipped and fallen into a garbage dump. Throughout my teenage years, self-esteem remained a stranger. I had no one to turn to for help. No one who would listen to my fears and insecurities, give me advice, encourage me to keep going and, most importantly, tell me that I was loved and loveable.

Although I had an extended adoptive family, they could not help. They were strangers to me. I did not feel close to any of them except Uncle Jack and Aunt Alma, but they lived in Exeter, not Bristol, and in those days, we didn't have a phone.

Vera's bullying and abusive behavior toward me had killed any chance of affection or trust I may have developed for her as a mother. I was just biding my time until I could branch out on my own and leave her behind.

23
PEDESTALS
1958

B Y MY EARLY TEENS, I believed that I had conquered my need for Vera's love and approval. With the pain stuffed deep inside, I had convinced myself that only weaklings whined for love.

Despite frequent bouts of depression, I had survived without love for fifteen years. After all, she wasn't my real mother. She had adopted me to meet the societal expectations of her time in order to be seen and accepted as a mother. Vera told me that she wanted a boy, but settled for a girl. I assumed I was window dressing for the neighbors.

Academically, I did fine. Athletically, I excelled. Vera remained unimpressed with any of my sporting achievements. Her usual comment was: "Yes, very nice, I'm sure, but that won't get you a job."

Mrs. Welsh, the gym teacher, and the student body had elected me captain of the netball and field hockey teams. My diving skills earned me a place on the swim team. During my last three years in high school, I had triumphed over high jump competitors from all the other schools and remained the champion.

I was preparing to compete in my final year when Mrs. Welsh approached me one morning after gym class. "Are you going to enter the high jump competition this year?"

"Yes, of course."

"Well, you should know that your major opponent has recently been taught the Western Roll, so there's a good chance she'll beat you."

Stunned, I stared at her. "What?"

Mrs. Welsh shrugged. "You have to understand, this method will increase her jumping ability by several inches. Western Roll will beat the Scissor every time."

I froze. Did I want to relinquish my title of champion in my last year of school? Of course not. I stepped nearer. "Mrs. Welsh, how does the Western Roll work?"

Mrs. Welsh crossed her arms, cocked her head to one side, probably visualizing a jump. "The athlete runs toward the bar from the side. She jumps up and then twists her body and rolls forward over the bar."

That didn't sound too difficult. "Can you teach me the Western Roll in time for the competition?"

Mrs. Welsh laughed. "Oh, Glenda, of course not. The competition is in a couple of weeks. You would need at least a month of intensive practice to master the Western Roll and significantly increase your jump."

"Then I won't compete."

Her laughter ceased abruptly and she frowned. "But you must compete, you always represent the school."

I faced her, my mind made up. "If the school wanted me to represent it, then it should have taught me the Western Roll."

Tears threatened to flow. "I have no intention of entering a competition knowing ahead of time that I will lose."

I was angry and disappointed. I had placed Mrs. Welsh on a pedestal because she had always encouraged and championed my athletic accomplishments. Now she too had abandoned me.

Mrs. Welsh must have realized I was intractable. She turned on her heel, cheeks flushed, and left. I watched her white shorts jiggle their way down the corridor, hoping that guilt was licking at her heels as she made her way toward her classroom.

She had fallen from her pedestal, and I had watched her butt bite the dust. The experience taught me a valuable lesson: no more pedestals, for anyone. The English actress Samantha Bond once commented: "If you put people on pedestals, there's only one way to go and that is down."

Dad always attended my sporting events when his schedule allowed, but Vera never did. Sometimes, he chided her. "Why don't you go and cheer Glenda on? She's a very good athlete, but you never bother to go."

"Does any of this teach her to earn a living? No, it doesn't." Her exaggerated sigh would follow. "I have better things to do with my time."

During my last two years of high school, the headmistress appointed me prefect.

Vera's only comment was: "Do your best."

"Do my best"—at what? She had no idea about the responsibilities of a prefect, never showed any interest in learning, or realized that the headmistress selected few students for this important position. As prefect, I was to set a good example with the younger students, arrive on time to school, ensure appropriate conduct in the playground, teach sportsmanship, and encourage study and homework obligations.

I had learned semaphore as a Girl Guide, an organization similar to the Boy Scouts but for girls. I was so fast flashing letters with those flags that few of my peers could keep up with me. It was the same with shorthand and typing. I took to it like a greyhound chasing a rabbit. I learned later that I had probably inherited my abilities in shorthand and typing from my biological mother.

I suspect that from Vera's viewpoint nothing else mattered other than the shorthand and typing. She'd already made it clear that she saw no value in athletics or music, let alone my ability to communicate using semaphore. After all, World War II was over. Who needed semaphore in the late 1950s?

24
MONKEY SEE
1959

ON WEEKENDS, when Dad was not working, Vera and I would drag him off to the Saturday night dance at Knowle. We'd meet up with Aunt Gwen and her dance partner Jeffrey. These evenings were reserved for adults, but exceptions were made for teenagers like me who met Mrs. Yelverton's high performance standards.

On and off, until I was close to seventeen, I continued to accompany my parents to the weekend dances. Vera's focus was no longer on me and what type of dress she would design for my next competition. She was now concentrating on learning to dance and enjoying spending time with her husband. The respite from mother and daughter arguments was a blessing, although I suspected that the hiatus would be temporary.

Over time, it became obvious that Dad didn't need to be dragged to Knowle, not any more. His passion for football had waned as his intrigue with dancing flourished.

One afternoon, Dad walked into the kitchen where Vera was making a steak and kidney pie. "What do you think about me not signing up for overtime on Saturday nights? It'll give us a chance to go dancing every weekend."

Vera finished rolling out the pastry for the pie and turned to my dad. "That would be nice, but that's four days a month. I don't think we can manage without overtime pay four days out of a month."

"What if I sign up for two Saturdays a month? Would that work?" With arms raised as if holding a lady partner, Dad began a dance routine in the living room. "We could dance two, I could work two... although I'd rather dance four. Know what I mean?" Dad nudged Vera with his elbow and laughed. Her normally grim mouth curved into a smile, and she glanced at my Dad through lowered lashes.

"You cheeky devil." She flicked some flour in Dad's direction. "Well, let's try dancing two Saturdays a month and see how it works without the money and all."

As I watched this unexpected private exchange between my parents, I felt like a peeping Tom. Obviously, that special spark had not fizzled despite their frequent arguments.

I teased my Dad. "Do you still think that dancing is the devil's work?"

He grinned, gazing off into the distance. "Course not. I think now I understand why you and your Mum love it so much."

"Good, I'm glad."

Dad nodded. "I enjoy watching bodies bend and sway to the music, the precision of the steps, the routines, and all. It's similar to football, you know, precise steps, strategic moves, and then shoot for the goal, but dancing has an elegance that football lacks. I like that."

"Are you saying that dancing is better than watching football?"

He winked. "Darned close."

Mrs. Yelverton and other experienced dancers would invite Dad onto the floor so that he could practice the steps of the dances he was familiar with or gradually learn new routines. I watched his face light up when Aunt Gwen offered her expertise to Dad as his dancing partner. She always chose a dance Dad had not previously tried. She would patiently teach him the steps, guide him through the movements, and commend him on his progress.

From the sidelines, Vera watched her husband glide and twirl, looking amazed that he was doing so well. "Blow me down with a feather! Never thought I'd see the day when your father would be out on the floor ballroom dancing."

When the dance was over, Dad returned to sit next to Vera, his face beaming with the pride of accomplishment. After six months, he had a solid repertoire of dances tucked away in the cummerbund of his memory.

I could tell that Dad was excited with his progress. He told me he wanted to teach Vera these dances, but this proved difficult.

On the dance floor, she was rigid as an iron gate, solid and inflexible. Her grip on Dad's right arm was as firm as a wrench on a pipe. There were times when my partner and I danced close to my parents, and I could observe them and overhear their conversation. I watched Dad guide Vera around the floor and saw her frequently stumble, her features crimped in tortured embarrassment. He was counting out the steps, expecting Vera to follow his lead. She tried, but she couldn't keep up.

Raw impatience flared across Dad's face. "No, no! Turn to the right. I'm leading you. Follow my lead and turn to the right."

Vera was flustered. "All right! All right!"

Dad would suddenly stop. "Why are you trying to turn left?"

"I'm not," Vera would protest, "you're confusing me, making me lose my confidence."

Dad would count—one, two, three—and they would start dancing again. "For God's sake, Vera, just relax! I know the steps. You should know the steps by now too. Obviously you don't, so just follow my lead and you'll learn the damned steps."

"If you don't stop bossing me around, I'll walk off this bloody dance floor right now."

I actually felt sorry for her.

A twinge of compassion shot through me every time she stumbled or when Dad became impatient with her. She was right: she lacked confidence. From my observations, she also lacked rhythm and was petrified for fear she might make a mistake. Aware that other dancers had watched her struggle to keep up with Dad, I could see the apprehension on Vera's face. She was probably wondering whether the women were sniggering about her behind her back.

Sometimes, at home, I would try to help her with segments of a dance that she had failed to grasp. As we danced around the living room, I was careful to keep my voice calm and be supportive and encouraging as I guided her through the steps. She was receptive, but there were times when she gripped my right arm so tight that I could feel her fear shooting up through my right shoulder.

Despite Vera's insecurities and Dad's lack of patience, Saturday remained their night for dancing, and they danced together for many years.

25
No Soup
1960

A SEVERE WINTER STORM was blasting our neighborhood; freezing rain slashed at windows and formed rushing rivers in the street gutters. It was a Saturday and Dad was working overtime. I was curled up on the sofa in the front room reading a book. My peaceful haven was disrupted the moment Vera entered the room.

"Once the rain stops, I need you go to the grocery store."

I looked up from my book. "What for?"

"I want you to return the Brussels sprouts I bought this morning. I don't think they're fresh."

"Mum, you know I hate doing returns." I groaned inwardly.

Vera grinned. "Yes, I know you do, but you have more cheek than me. Old man Giles will give you a refund. You're just a kid. He may grumble a bit, but he'll do it."

"Why can't you go?"

"Well, for instance, we might get into an argument." She sounded exasperated. "Or worse, he might refuse to give me my money back—in front of some of my neighbors. I want to avoid that at all cost."

I got the point. How would it look if she and Mr. Giles had a public confrontation? Oh my, that would never do. I was living with a tyrant in the home and a mouse in the world.

I put down my book, got up from the couch, and wandered over to the window to check the weather. "It's raining very hard. It doesn't look like it'll stop any time soon."

Vera joined me at the window. "Oh, it'll stop in an hour or so. Then you can go to the shops." She went upstairs for a nap.

My stifled need for maternal love unexpectedly resurfaced. *If I come home with the refund,* I thought, *perhaps she will be appreciative.* Here was a wonderful opportunity to gain my mother's approval and perhaps a show of affection. Once that thought whipped through my mind, a second swiftly followed: *How pathetic you are, still pining for your mother's love and approval. You know it's never gonna happen. She's not capable.*

I shrugged off such pessimistic thoughts, returned to the sofa, squished myself into a comfortable position, picked up my book, and continued to read.

Two hours passed. The rain did not let up. Dusk was dusting off the day and preparing to enfold the streets in shadow. My chance at "saving the day" and showing Vera that I deserved to be loved was fading rapidly.

I made a quick decision. I pulled on my Wellington boots, donned my mackintosh, grabbed the umbrella, picked up the Brussels sprouts from the kitchen, and set off for the store. With head bent, I battled the strong winds and stinging rain; I was relieved and exhausted when I arrived at the grocery store.

"Can I help you?"

"Yes, please, Mr. Giles." I handed him the bag of Brussels

sprouts. "Mum bought these this morning, but when she got them home and looked at them, she doesn't think they're fresh."

Mr. Giles glowered at me. "Not fresh? Of course, they're fresh! I got them in only a couple of days ago. You tell your mum there's nothing wrong with them."

Two women in line behind me were getting restless. "What's holding up the works?" said one.

"Nothing, ladies," Mr. Giles said and turned to me. "I think your mum needs her eyes examined. She does this a lot. She returns things that other customers find perfectly acceptable. I'm getting tired of it."

Red-faced, I dropped my head. "Mr. Giles, I'm just telling you what Mum told me." I raised my head and looked Mr. Giles square in the eyes. "If she's mistaken and the sprouts are fresh, I'm sure you can sell them to someone else. You know Mum's a regular customer here. Please give her a refund."

Mr. Giles sniffed. "Hmm... it's a shame your Mum sends her daughter to do her dirty work."

"Can we hurry things along here?" the woman directly behind me said. "I want to get home before it gets dark. This weather is treacherous."

Mr. Giles went to the cash register, punched a key, and opened the drawer. Counting out coins, he handed me the refund. "Be careful walking home in the storm."

I pocketed the money. "I will, and thank you." I turned and left the store.

The storm was unrelenting, and there was limited visibility. I opened my umbrella and stepped out onto the pavement. A gust of wind propelled me forward and my imagination took flight.

How would Vera react if I were to return home soaking wet? Would she be grateful to me for taking care of something that was rightfully hers to resolve? Would she help me get out of my wet clothes, bring me my dressing gown, hand me a bowl of warm soup, and lead me to the chair closest to the fire? Would she show me that she loved me?

The words "You're pathetic!" screamed in my ear but I ignored them.

I meandered down the road, dragging my feet, my umbrella threatening to fold with every swipe of the wind. I shuffled through muddy puddles and played a few games of hopscotch. By the time I arrived home, I was soaking wet and freezing cold.

I rang the doorbell. Vera opened the door and gasped. "Just look at you. I told you not to go to the store if it was raining. Why can't you do as you're told?"

She hauled me into the house by one arm and pushed me against the wall of the entryway. "Get out of those wet clothes and go to bed. No dinner for you tonight, young lady."

Technically, Vera was correct. I had disobeyed her instructions, but she apparently forgot that I had met the objective: getting the refund from Mr. Giles.

I learned a valuable lesson that day. My gut had warned me that Vera would not show appreciation in the way I needed and wanted. Never again would I ignore my intuition and try to manipulate *any* situation, hoping for love.

My trying to gain Vera's approval and affection was akin to firing up a truck that had an empty gas tank: I was going nowhere.

26
BIOLOGICAL MOTHER
1960

A S THE YEARS PASSED, I had learned to stop asking questions about my birth mother. It was unnerving for Vera. It would provoke another episode of her frustration and anger—at least, that was my perception of her behavior. Vera viewed my desire to know about my roots as disloyalty. Many years later, after reading several books about adoption, I would learn that this was often a typical reaction of some adoptive parents when their adopted child voiced curiosity about birth parents.

"We took you in, your father and me," she would say. "We fed you and clothed you and made sure you received a good education—and you reward us with questions about that woman!"

I would frequently respond defensively. "I never asked to be adopted. That was your decision." Did I hit a nerve? Oh, yes, I must have, because Vera would get worked up into a tizzy.

"If it hadn't been for us, you would have ended up in an orphanage, my girl." Such comments were a constant reminder that she had done me a favor.

One weekend, when Dad was home, I was surprised when they revealed what they knew of my birth mother. I was seventeen then and had a burning desire for more information. So many unanswered questions lingered in my heart, like cold ashes in a fireplace.

I never felt that I belonged with Vera and Alf. I was a stranger in their home, lonely and confused. When I was eight years old, I was sitting down to dinner and silently scrutinizing my parents. I had already concluded that we were mismatched. Yes, I loved my Dad, but I was not bonded to the rest of the family. I felt no connection to any of them, especially Vera. *Why was I here?* I thought. *I didn't belong in this family.* Later I wondered that such insight and thoughts could have come from an eight-year-old.

Decades later, I read a book written by a psychologist who for years had worked with adopted children and was familiar with their many issues. She believed that babies bonded with their mothers while in the womb. For nine months, they are one with their mother's natural rhythm: they know when she's hungry, when she's tired, learn her moods, hear her voice, feel her hands on their internal bassinet, learn what foods she prefers, sleep habits, moments of happiness, joy, pain, despair, even addictions like alcohol, cigarettes, and drugs.

The author's supposition was that once the child is born and held in its mother's arms, it knows the difference between the arms of its biological mother and the arms of a stranger. Some adopted children adjust, depending on the personalities and parenting skills of their adopted family. Some, like me, would always feel like an outcast, a black sheep, definitely unloved, and an unwanted bastard.

———

"Your father and I have been talking," Vera said. "You've asked us questions over the years about your birth mother. For the life of me I can't think why. I've tried—"

"Vera!" Dad's tone of voice cut her off abruptly. He turned to me. "I think I understand your need to know. We think now is the time to tell you, but it isn't much."

"Tell me! Please tell me." I felt as anxious as at Christmas. Would I receive the gift I really wanted or something like the pram that they thought I should like?

"Well, it was like this," Dad said. "Sometime in the autumn in 1943—it was late September or early October, I think. Is that right Vera?"

"Yes, I think so."

"Okay. So we received a letter from the adoption agency in Bath telling us that a six-week-old baby girl was available for adoption. And would we like to travel to Bath to see the child and perhaps adopt her?"

"Do you still have the letter?" I asked, hope in my voice.

Dad shook his head. "No, I'm sorry, we don't. Anyway, I sat down immediately and wrote back. I told them that we would be there the following week on my day off, on Wednesday."

I scanned Dad's face for his reaction. "Were you excited?"

He beamed. "We were thrilled."

They were thrilled. A burst of pleasure filled my heart. Such an unfamiliar feeling brought tears to my eyes. For an instant, I felt loved.

Vera picked up the story. "Me and your Dad were sitting in the hospital waiting room along with the other adopters when—blow me down!—the door swung open and in marched this tall, buxom blonde. She was probably in her late-twenties and wearing a fur coat. Bold as brass, wasn't she, Alf?"

"Well, she didn't waste any time. She got right to the point," Dad said. "Her eyes scrutinized every occupant in the room before she asked, 'Which of you is Mr. and Mrs. Alfred Taylor?'"

"I stood up," Dad said. "Doffed my hat and said, 'I'm Alfred Taylor and this is my wife, Vera.'"

"Not a shy bone to her body," Vera said. "She made herself comfortable in an empty chair and announced, 'I'm Norah Townsend, the baby's mother. I wanted to meet you... before I sign the papers... in case you had questions.'"

I took a deep breath and nearly forgot to exhale, fearing I would miss something.

Dad smiled. "Sort of reminds me of you." He nodded in my direction.

Vera sniffed. "I was flabbergasted. The audacity of that woman! I told her, 'This is against the rules. Birth mothers and adopters are not supposed to meet.'"

"Norah just ignored your Mum." Dad chuckled. "Made her mad. You know your mother, she hates to be ignored."

"Oh, very funny," Vera snapped at him.

"Okay, okay," Dad said. "Carry on with the story."

"So," Vera said, "I pressed Norah further. How did you find us, me and Alf? Why are you here? You gave up the baby for adoption."

Dad started to laugh and again interrupted her. "Glenda, you are definitely your mother's daughter. Norah waved impatiently, dismissing your mum's protests. 'Yes, yes. I know all about the silly rules. So absurd. The bottom line is this: until I sign the release papers, I'm still the baby's mother. I'm here because I wanted to meet the people who will take care of my child. I want her to have a good home with decent people who will bring her up right. So, what do you need to know?'"

I knew Dad was right. I had inherited my biological mother's personality. A longed-for piece of my jigsaw fell neatly into place: I knew that Norah had loved me.

Vera and Dad's main concern were any possible health issues. They asked Norah about the family's medical history.

"Our family suffers with bronchitis," Norah had said, "but apart from that, nothing major."

That part turned out to be true. As a small child I had to go to hospital twice a week for electrical heat treatments to my cheeks to ward off sinus problems, a therapy that continued for several years.

During the meeting with Norah, Vera and my Dad also learned that my biological mother was twenty-four, not married, and my father was a twenty-two-year-old, red-headed fighter pilot, who had recently been killed in the war.

Vera pursed her lips and crossed her arms, assuming a self-righteous pose as she continued. "I asked her point blank: how on earth did you get pregnant at your age? You're getting on for thirty."

"Norah wasn't the least intimidated by your mum." Dad chuckled. "She simply said, 'Thirty is six years away. These things happen. Next question?'"

"Yes, she quickly skipped over that fact." Vera's retort was smug. "Probably too embarrassed to give an honest answer."

Decades later, after tracking down my biological family, details would surface concerning my mother's relationship with a red-headed fighter pilot that trampled Vera's caustic assumptions about Norah.

Based on my research, input from the military, and World War II veterans who had known a red-headed fighter pilot in their unit, it's highly probably that my biological father *might* have been Richard Brian Dunsmuir. Research showed Richard was of Scottish descent and was a fighter and test pilot. A new plane that he was flying developed mechanical problems. Sadly, carbon monoxide seeped into the cabin, the plane went out of control, flew into a mountain, and Richard was killed.

Vera and my Dad knew none of this at the time they told me of their meeting with Norah Townsend. Satisfied that they were decent people who could provide for her child, Norah signed the necessary papers, left Bath and me, and returned to Plymouth.

Little time passed before Vera's tongue was shredding Norah's reputation, labeling her a "loose woman."

I can still see Vera's face, pinched and superior, as she shared her perception surrounding the circumstances of my conception. "She should have known better at her age. She was probably just a loose woman. Whoever it was obviously dumped her when he knew she was pregnant. Don't believe a word of it. 'Killed in the war'—humph!—a likely story! Who does she think she is, wearing a fur coat? Be careful, my girl, that you don't turn out to be like your mother."

For once, Dad spoke up. "Vera, you know darn well that Glenda's mother was an attractive woman who, like so many others, got caught up in the war. Wasn't it you who told me that when your brothers were overseas in the war, your mother and sisters-in-law received nylon stockings from the G.I.s? Didn't you tell me that you suspected there was some hanky-panky going on to get the nylons? It's not our place to judge Norah or anyone else. War changes people."

Vera's pressed her lips shut; she stood and headed for the kitchen. "Right, then. I'll start dinner."

Vera's scathing comments about Norah stung and, for a brief moment, I felt ashamed of my biological mother. Was she really the tramp that Vera was making her out to be? Stifling tears, I asked my Dad, "Do I really look like my mother?"

Dad glanced over at me. "Yes, you have her eyes, and she was about your height. Your red hair comes from your father because Norah was a natural blonde."

"Yes, well...." Vera called from the kitchen, "That's what she told us, but—"

"Vera, she looked a natural blonde to me, and a good looking one at that." Dad winked at me. "Rest easy, Glenda, you look a lot like your mum."

Those words lit a fire in my heart. I had something to hold onto: I looked like my mother and I had her eyes.

Ever since I was a kid, people had commented on my blue-green eyes fringed by thick, long white eyelashes that touched my eyebrows and made wearing sunglasses uncomfortable. When I started wearing mascara, people compared my lashes to Elizabeth Taylor's. I was always rather embarrassed by the attention. If Vera overheard such comments, I was promptly reminded: "Don't let that go to your head, my girl. You're no Liz Taylor."

I would mentally remind myself that her demeaning comments about Norah and me could only be uttered by an uncaring bitch.

It was a comfort knowing that my biological mother had traveled many miles to meet my adoptive parents, violating the stringent rules that existed in 1943 forbidding contact between birth parents and adoptive parents. Norah had taken the time to meet and evaluate Vera and Alf. On the surface, they were a respectable and responsible couple. Norah had no way of knowing that Vera's nature included a generous dose of the devil.

Norah's trip to Bath told me that she had guts, ignored policies that made no sense, and most of all, she loved me. I suspected that due to the societal and familial expectations in the 1940s, my biological mother was forced to part with me. Much later in life, in my fifties, after I had located my biological family, I learned this to be true. It felt good to know that I had been loved by the woman who had carried me for nine months before she had to let me go.

27
CIGARETTES
1960

FOR THE MAJORITY of his working years, my father was a bus driver. Dad's personality was mostly low-key, but occasionally he displayed bursts of impatience especially when Vera's "tummy troubles" flared or she nattered on about things he considered inconsequential. To support the family, Dad worked shifts and all available overtime so he was frequently absent from the home.

When not smoothly navigating a double-decker bus, Dad's off-duty pleasures were simple. He devoured the newspaper from front to back, and he would regularly comment on topics that piqued his interest. The stronger Dad's interest in an article, the more scathing his comments, especially when it came to politics. Sometimes his only companion was Keela, our family cat. Whether she agreed with Dad's assessment of world, national, or local affairs remained a secret between human and feline.

Dad thoroughly enjoyed tobacco although his budget could accommodate only inexpensive unfiltered Woodbines. In the

1950s nobody worried about lung cancer. His other passion was candy, particularly sherbet lemons. For Dad, these indulgences were close to a fantasy: sitting in a deck chair on the beach, waves lapping at his feet, toes flirting with the ocean....

I started smoking at age sixteen, using the money I earned from my paper route to buy cigarettes. Five unfiltered Senior Service cigarettes cost one shilling. The quality of the tobacco was a major upgrade over Woodbines.

Sometimes Vera found my stash.

"And what did I find in your coat pocket again? Cigarettes! I've told you, no smoking while you live in this house. How many times do I have to repeat myself?"

Something resembling a self-righteous smirk would cross her face. "Well, now they're confiscated. I'm going to give them to your father. He enjoys a good Senior Service." She would hand them over to my dad.

"Caught again, I see." Dad would lower his newspaper and look at me, eyes twinkling. "Smoking isn't ladylike you know."

Selecting a cigarette from the pack, Dad would fumble in his trouser pocket for matches, then light up one of *my* Senior Service cigarettes, inhaling smoke deep into his lungs. Exhaling, a wicked grin of satisfaction would light up his face. "Nice that my daughter can afford the good smokes. I could get used to these."

I rolled my eyes in frustration.

He noticed and would continue. "You'd best find a better hiding place. You know your mother. If she thinks you have cigarettes, she's like Sherlock Holmes. She'll make it her mission to find them."

The newspaper would rustle, and Dad's attention would be diverted to something else.

At least twice a month, when Dad's work schedule allowed, he walked with me to the public library to return our books and select new ones. "Adventures for the mind," Dad would say. He expected me to do my best in all things and to read anything and everything within reach. I marveled at how easy he was to please.

By contrast, most of Vera's expectations were insurmountable. A daughter should always obey her mother without question. Rather than climb trees and play sports, a daughter should act like a girl—enjoy playing with dolls and wearing dresses trimmed with lace and frills. A daughter should want to babysit for the neighbors, and an adopted daughter should be grateful that someone plucked her from the mire of rejection and gave her a good home.

She was always far more complicated than Dad and, depending on her mood, her demands shifted like sunlight on crystal.

Vera Smith Taylor was an industrious and strong-willed woman. The eldest of five children, she had three younger brothers, Gordon, Jack, and Len, and one sister, Molly. The three brothers were ambitious and had driving personalities much like Vera, but Molly did not share these characteristics.

Vera shared little with me about her life before she married. She revealed that her physical constitution had been frail and her attendance at school was irregular. My maternal grandmother Edith had taken Vera from school early and given her the responsibility of helping rear her siblings; Edith herself worked full-time as a seamstress and took in ironing in the evenings to sustain the family.

The youngest child Molly did not grow up with her

brothers and sister. Her father, my maternal grandfather Archibald, was financially unreliable. Therefore, Edith relinquished her rights and role as mother, allowing her sister Elsie and brother-in-law Albert to raise Molly as their only child.

Elsie had been incapable of bearing children and had longed to become a mother. Since Edith's finances were precarious, this was a win-win situation for the adults. For Molly, it was not so perfect.

Aunt Elsie was always demanding of Molly's time. Like a grouchy parrot that needed a nail trimming, her frequent shrieking demands of Molly would usually give me a headache. I never liked the woman, and it distressed me that my Aunt Molly grew up as an only child instead of with her four siblings. Maybe I felt compassion for Molly because I, too, was an only child in an alien environment.

Molly and I had worked as secretaries for the same company for more than five years. This gave me ample opportunity to chat with her on tea breaks, and thus I avoided visiting her at home, where I would be forced to interact with the "Grouchy Parrot." It was selfish of me, but true.

Aunt Elsie would vigorously interrogate any young man who dared to show interest in dating Molly; no one was good enough. Reluctantly, Molly succumbed to spinsterhood. In her later years and after the death of her aunt and uncle, Molly continued to reside alone in the small, dingy house she had inherited from her surrogate parents.

Toward the end of Vera's life, she confided in me that she had never liked her sister. "Can't help it. It's probably wicked of me to say so, but I could never abide my sister, your Aunt Molly. She's lazy and weak-willed." *Was this another case of a female competing with Vera for male attention—in this case, that of her brothers?*

———

I later learned from a family member that Archibald, whom I never recalled meeting, was a highly skilled and well-paid printer. I was told that he was also a philanderer, gambler, and boozer who squandered his paycheck on his passions and neglected to provide for his wife and children. Indirectly, I heard from Vera's brother Gordon: "Archibald was a wicked old man who eventually ended up in an asylum." Gordon later told his son, Robert, that the Smith household was so volatile he left home early and took a job as a traveling salesman.

This was news to me. Vera had never talked about her childhood or mentioned any volatility in the household where she grew up. However, this would certainly explain why she appeared tightly wound, always ready to pounce on Dad or me when she felt we were teasing her. Much like a party balloon set free long ago to drift about, Vera's sense of humor—if she had ever had one—had been released, never to return.

———

Grandmother Edith was tall and relatively slim with fine bone structure, brown wavy hair, narrow eyes, a strong jaw, and pencil-thin lips. I saw very little of my grandmother while growing up and recall her visiting us only a couple of times at Christmas during my preteen years. When she laughed, it was more like a cackle; when she hugged me goodbye it would make me squirm.

Alfred and Vera, their wedding day, 1941

Something about Edith made me uncomfortable. I felt that she was shifty and untrustworthy, another reminder that I didn't connect with this family. When Edith reached for her purse and announced it was time for her to catch the bus home, I would breathe a sigh of relief. My instincts about Edith were later confirmed. At Vera's insistence, I had taken the long ride on two buses to visit Grandma. During tea, Edith lulled me into confiding in her about my feelings for a young man whom I was dating casually. A few days later, Vera parroted back some of my conversation with Grandmother Edith. Obviously, she and her mother had set me up.

"Since James is twenty-five and you are seventeen, he's far too old for you," Vera said. "He's only interested in one thing. I don't want you to see him again." Convinced that her word was law, Vera strode past me into the living room and prepared to switch on the television and watch one of her shows.

"I've been dating him for two months." I yelled in the direction of her departing hemline. "And I'm still a virgin. I'll make the decision who I sleep with and when—not you!"

Vera paused, spinning around to face me, sneering in contempt. "So I gather from your diary."

I gasped and stared at her in disbelief. "You've read my diary?"

"Yes I did," she replied. "But if you do get pregnant, don't come crying to me and your father. We'll wash our hands of you. You'll be on your own."

Stunned, I groped for an armchair and sank into the seat, my mind reeling. Vera had actually read my diary, my private thoughts and feelings. There was nowhere to hide in this house.

"You read my diary," I repeated disbelievingly "How despicable! You have no sense of personal privacy." I stood up, a little wobbly, and stumbled past her, bound for my bedroom.

Vera followed closely behind, her harsh and grating voice chasing after me. "While you're living under my roof, young lady, you will obey my rules. I don't want you socializing with that young man any more, do you understand me?"

Halfway up the stairs, I turned and faced her. "You and Grandma set me up, and I won't forget it. Understand me—I will never visit her again. You explain that to your mother."

"You will do as you're told."

"No, I won't. I will not visit any family member who spies on me."

Edith died a few years later; I did not attend her funeral.

In her younger years, Vera was an attractive woman. Tall and slim like her mother, with light brown hair and a good figure, Vera had softer features and larger eyes, but she could not escape inheriting Edith's thin lips and strong jaw.

Vera Smith Taylor, Engagement photograph, 1939

As she stormed through life, the less attractive features Vera inherited from her mother became more pronounced, especially when she was encountering real or perceived obstacles in life, which included me.

In contrast, Dad was gentle and peace loving and more in tune with my evolving sensibilities. Always an avid reader, he would take me to the library every week and help me select books, usually the classics: *Jane Eyre, Sons and Lovers, Pride and Prejudice, Sense and Sensibility, Oliver Twist, Little Women,* and the stories of Sherlock Holmes. I shared Dad's passion for reading and, while Vera was in the back room sewing, Dad and I would sit in the front room, quietly reading. When I encountered an unfamiliar word, I would ask my Dad, "What does this mean?" His response was always the same: "Let's look it up in the dictionary."

Enjoying these quiet moments with my Dad and the freedom to immerse myself in adventures laid out in the pages before me is a fond memory of those times when we were close.

Vera regarded reading as a non-productive pastime, and she would make snide remarks when Dad and I retreated into the front room to read, seeking peace and quiet. "The toilet handle in the bathroom needs attention," she would remark. Receiving no response, she would try again. "The apple tree could use some pruning. Glenda, you could help your father, but I suppose both of you prefer wasting your time reading those silly stories."

She never got it when it came to the pleasures of reading or, for that matter, when it came to me.

Vera's claws-like hands and prying eyes had invaded my privacy: I was savagely angry and needed to avoid her. I didn't know what I might be capable of when dealing with this crazy woman. Once I turned eighteen and could legally leave home, I would.

I burned my diary, bought a new one, and started logging my entries in shorthand. A month later, one night after work, I was ironing a blouse that I intended to wear to work the following day when Dad told me that Vera had found my new diary.

Holding the iron in midair, I asked, "Are you kidding?"

"No, not kidding."

Another battle of wills was about to begin.

I never left my diary lying around the room so obviously she had been snooping through my bedroom and found it under my pillow. There was no such thing as privacy, a space I could call my own, like my bedroom should have been. Vera had a rule that I could not be in my bedroom alone with the door closed. It took me years to figure out the reason why: she was worried about masturbation. *God forbid!* I thought.

"I'm sorry, but you know your Mum," said Dad. "She's relentless. She took your diary to work to see whether any of her coworkers could read your shorthand."

"What?" I screamed. "When?"

"Some time last week, I think."

I banged the iron down onto the ironing board, switched it off, removed my blouse, slipped it onto a hanger, and draped it over a chair. Trembling, I faced my Dad, fighting to control my anger.

"And that was okay with you?"

Dad looked away, avoiding my eyes. "Of course not. I told

her, 'Vera, that's Glenda's private property. If you want to know something, well, you know, just ask her.'"

"And what did she say?"

"She told me that you never talk to her or confide in her. If she wants to know what's going on, she goes behind your back."

"Good God, that is so disgusting!" I brushed away the tears that were welling up in my eyes. "I don't talk to her because she doesn't respect confidentiality. She blabs everything to the neighbors—like I'm some form of entertainment or something. Well, I'm not gonna let that happen. Which of her coworkers could read my shorthand?"

"Well, none of them, of course." Dad grinned. "I told Vera she was wasting her time."

My shoulders relaxed, and I took a deep breath. Now it was my turn to be smug: I'd outsmarted the intrusive bitch. I couldn't wait for Vera to return home from work. When I heard the key in the lock and her voice echoing through the living room, I greeted her when she entered the dining area.

"I hear that you took my diary to work to see whether your coworkers could read shorthand. Any luck?"

Vera was pulling off her gloves, then stopped and stared at me. "Who told you that?"

"Dad."

She pivoted to Dad, who was seated in his favorite chair, the newspaper on his lap.

"Alf, why did you tell her that?"

"Well I...."

"You know I did it only because she never talks to me. She shuts me out." Vera turned back to me. "Other daughters share their thoughts and feelings with their mothers, but not you. You're unnatural."

"And why do you think that is, Mum?" I took a step toward her. "Over the years, I've told you stuff. Then two weeks later, in retaliation, you've used it against me. Or you've shared my personal life with the neighbors. I learned early on that you couldn't be trusted to keep anything confidential, so I stopped sharing."

Dad interjected. "Vera, you forget. Glenda is nearly eighteen—you need to back off."

Vera yanked off her gloves and tossed them onto the dining room table. "Back off? Back off? She's still living under our roof, and I have a right to know what she's up to, whether she's nearly eighteen or close to fifty."

"As soon as I turn eighteen," I shouted at her, "I'm outta here. I can't wait to get away from you."

Dad started to fold the newspaper. "Now, Glenda, don't say that to your mother. You know you're welcome to stay here as long as you like."

Tears trickling down my cheeks, I faced my Dad. "You know that's not true. I'm not welcome here by her and haven't been for years. She's been an absolute bitch to me since I was a little kid—and you allowed it."

"That's enough." Dad's voice became stern. "Don't talk such nonsense. You have a hard side to your nature, Glenda, and it's not becoming."

"You're right, I do. And it's all thanks to your wife."

Dad was up and out of his chair like a sprinter breaking free from the blocks. With his right hand, he slapped me hard across the face. I turned on my heel and walked out of the room, determined not to let either one of them see my tears.

28
LOCKED OUT
1961

SNIDE REMARKS AND CRITICISM from Vera grew relentlessly as I grew older and my body developed curves. From Vera's perspective, everything about me was wrong: my appearance, my clothing, my make-up, and my choice of friends. Comments referring to my biological mother as a whore, followed by a warning that, if not careful, I could turn out just like her, would hiss from Vera's lips, usually when I was applying make-up and getting ready to go out with friends or on a date.

When I recall one particular Friday evening, I still cringe. I had had a date with Sean, a sales representative and coworker. Sean was Irish and proud of it; he was tall and slim and had wavy black hair, alabaster skin, and green eyes—he was a looker.

I had transferred from working with George Moore in Advertising to working with the Sales Director and had regular contact with most of the sales force. A sales conference, held at the Bristol offices, started on a Monday and concluded early Friday afternoon. That night, a group of us were going out for drinks and dinner and then on to a club. It was September, one month after my eighteenth birthday. Although the law now considered me emancipated, I was living in Vera's home and still had to follow Vera's rules, one of which was to return home no later than midnight.

That evening, snow thick as a polar bear's coat covered the city, and flakes continued to fall throughout the night. Buses had ceased to run. The long taxi queue in the city center was a certain indication I would not meet the midnight deadline. Shivering, unable to feel our feet, Sean and I eventually bundled into a taxi and headed for home. We arrived forty minutes after midnight.

The house was dark. I put my key into the lock and tried to turn it. It didn't work. I tried it a few more times. Still, it didn't work. Sean had a go with the same result. We looked at each other, completely baffled, until Vera's strident voice, emanating from the upstairs front bedroom, reached us.

"I suggest you sleep where you came from. You were supposed to be home by midnight. Now you're locked out."

"We couldn't get a taxi," I shouted up at the window. "Ask the taxi driver. His cab is at the curb waiting to take Sean home."

"What's wrong with the bus?"

"The buses aren't running, Mum. It's been snowing for hours."

"All the more reason for you to come home earlier, my girl."

"I say, Mrs. Taylor." Sean was trying his best to reason with her. "We waited for an hour to get a taxi, so we did—"

"You keep out of this, whoever you are. You should have had my daughter home by midnight. Now she's your problem."

Dumbfounded, my date shook his head. "Is your mother always like this?"

"Oi! 'Ow much longer you gonna be?" yelled the taxi driver.

"Just a minute!" Sean shouted back at him. "I'll be there in a minute."

Teeth chattering, I looked at Sean. "Sorry, so sorry about my mother. Obviously she's out of her mind." Stepping back, I yelled up at her bedroom window. "Mum!"

I banged hard on the door-knocker. "Mum, come down at once and open this door! When Dad gets home from work, I'm gonna tell him that you locked me out. I don't deserve this treatment. It's bloody ridiculous."

A minute or so ticked by before I heard the inside bolt slide back. I tried my key again. This time it worked, and the door opened.

I turned to Sean, head down. I was too embarrassed to face him. "I'm so sorry about this. She's a bloody raving maniac!" I choked back tears that were threatening to spill onto my cheeks. A sudden honk from the taxi interrupted this possibility.

"I ain't waitin' much longer. Are you comin' or what?"

Sean waved to the taxi driver. "Hold your horses! I'll be there, hang on. Just give me a minute." Shivering, he turned back to me. "Hey, it's all right. Honest, it's all right. No need for tears. Damn, I'm just glad she let you in. Okay, I'm off. See you Monday."

Sean scrambled into the back of the taxi and slammed the door shut. Its tires carved deep tracks in the snow as the taxi crunched its way back to the center of the city. Sean waved to me from the back seat.

Cold, humiliated, and exhausted, I climbed the stairs to my

bedroom and began shedding my clothes. Since the house had no heat upstairs, the faster I undressed, the faster I could leap into bed, snuggle below flannel sheets and thick wool blankets, and get warm. I always slept with my head under the covers because during the winter, my nose would get cold and I could see my breath in the air like a Scottish mist. Vera's voice penetrated the sanctuary of my bed covers.

"I hope this will teach you a lesson, my girl. Rules is rules."

I ignored her.

I made sure to stay busy and out of the house that weekend to avoid Vera's harping about me coming home late.

On Monday, I took my usual morning tea break. I walked into the dining hall and saw Sean and the other sales representatives huddled together at a nearby table. I picked up a cup of tea and a biscuit from the ladies who were serving, overhearing comments and muffled laughter from Sean's table.

"You're kidding! She locked her out. Why?" Obviously, they were talking about the incident with Vera. The only way for me to overcome my embarrassment was to join them and face them down.

"Good morning." Silence greeted me at Sean's table.

I placed my cup of tea on the table and slipped into a chair. "I heard some of your comments, you know, when I was picking up my tea. You should keep your voices down." I took a sip of tea and observed the faces of the salesmen at the table. None, including Sean, would meet my eyes, preferring to sip tea and dunk biscuits. It was obvious they were all uncomfortable.

"Yes, my mother is a bloody nut case. But...." I faced Sean directly. "I'm disappointed that you told everyone here about the incident last Friday night. Sean, I thought you would have kept that private, between us."

Sean blushed and ran one hand through his thick, black hair. "Look, I'm sorry, but... well... I've never experienced such a crazy situation. My God, you have to admit, it has its humorous side, right?" He laughed nervously; the rest of the group followed his lead. I stood up, no longer interested in tea or Sean. "Please, enjoy my humiliation with your morning tea. I hope you all choke on it."

I left the room and returned to my workstation. Was Sean correct? It was a crazy situation, but my humiliation was so fresh that I failed to see any humor. Perhaps I was being overly sensitive.

That weekend, Dad was not working and heard both versions of the event while we were sitting in the living room before the fireplace. My story was brief and to the point. "Do you know how humiliating it was? Locked out in front of my date, someone I work with?"

"Well, calm yourself and tell me what happened," Dad said.

I grabbed a tissue and blew my nose. "Yes, I was late, but I had a legitimate reason. There was a snow storm, the buses stopped running, and it took a long time to get a taxi." I pointed toward the dining room where I suspected Vera was listening at the door. "She needs to get off my back and knock it off. She's suffocating me. I've about had it with her."

"I see." Dad nodded. "Okay, I'll talk to your Mum." He hesitated. "But, be respectful. After all, she is your Mum."

Dad loved Vera. I never figured out why. I fumed silently. How could my Dad ask me to respect her? His expectation was as difficult to accept as was his pattern of continual denial of her behavior. From my perspective, respect was earned through words and actions; it was not a right based on status or position—and that included parents. Another pebble of dissatisfaction was added to my path already littered with rocks.

In light of Vera's behavior over the years, I've found it difficult to embrace the teaching: "Honor thy father and mother." Did that mean, regardless of their treatment of their children? There were many times that I've longed for a face-to-face, sit-down with Jesus.

I returned to reading my book until I heard the raised voices of my parents coming from the dining room. Vera was defending her decision. "She knows she had to be home by midnight on a Friday night. She was late, more than half an hour."

"But Vera, there was a snow storm that night," Dad said. "Transportation was hard to come by. I know, I was out in the middle of it myself."

"That's not my problem. She could see it was snowing. She should have made tracks for home sooner. But she didn't—did she?"

She snorted angrily and then Dad spoke. "If you keep this up, Vera, we'll lose our daughter. And I don't want that to happen. You hear me? I don't want to lose my daughter."

There was a moment of silence. I held my breath, heart pounding against my chest, wondering what would come next.

The door between the living room and front room burst open. Dad, grim-faced, stalked through, turning to yell back once more at Vera. "Glenda's just turned eighteen! It's time you loosened the reins."

Without glancing at me, he went upstairs.

I felt a surge of unexpected relief knowing that my Dad had finally stood up to her on my behalf. Protected and not abandoned to Vera's wrath was a gift.

Of course, Vera ignored Dad's warning. Although the beatings ceased when I reached age sixteen—after I told her I would hit her back—the verbal attacks continued.

Each confrontation left me drained and frazzled. I compared fighting with Vera to killing a vampire, only the vampire never died. Apparently, I was using the wrong weapon.

I would try to avoid her as much as possible. If we argued, she would pout for days, muttering to herself and refusing to speak to me. This upset Dad. I tried tuning her out, like turning down the volume on a radio. Sometimes this worked, but not often enough. It was like being scratched over and over with a dull needle: I was bleeding inside.

What did it take to survive an abusive mother who's a bully?

29

THE GRANDFATHER BULLY
1961

D AD WAS A WHIZ AT MATH, which was my weakest subject, so while in school, I relied on his expertise to help me with my math homework. I would make a list of numbers and spout them out with instructions to add, subtract, or multiply, and Dad would arrive at the correct answer by calculating them in his head. This was amazing. Of course, I had no way of checking to make sure that he was right and hand-held calculators did not exist at that time, but I believed him. He was my dad and dads never lie.

Dad had told me that, prior to his marriage, when he was living at home with his parents and brother William, he had qualified to attend Bristol University to read accounting and obtain a degree. In the early 1930s, if a student passed the rigorous university entrance examination, tuition was free. However, Dad would have been responsible for purchasing course books and other educational materials.

My paternal grandfather Wilfred, an unpleasant individual whom I never liked, had other ideas. He was miserly by nature and small in stature, but Will dominated the household and demanded that my father put such thoughts out of his mind.

According to Dad, his father told him: "You need to get a job and bring money into this house. Forget all that nonsense about college."

Dad was crushed by his father's lack of support, but he was a dutiful son and buried his dream of becoming an accountant. After working several years earning a paltry salary as a bookkeeper, he felt fortunate when, in the late 1930's, he found a more lucrative job driving double-decker buses.

Dad, Alfred Taylor, 1939

Grandfather Will was a Cockney, as was my dad. The word "cockney" originated during the seventeenth century and referred to anyone born within the sound of Bow-bells, the twelve bells located in the tower of St. Mary-le-Bow, a church designed by Sir Christopher Wren.

Cockneys were working class Londoners known for certain traditions, trades, and activities. There were the familiar Pearly Kings and Queens; the "pearlies" were easily recognized by the mother-of-pearl buttons decorating their clothing. Another identifying characteristic was their rhyming slang. For example, "apples and pears" would be slang for "stairs". Cockneys had a great sense of community and neighborliness and were always quick with humorous repartee. Many were active in market trading; some were taxi drivers, but occupations ranged from street criminals to traders on the stock exchange.

People born in the East End of London usually considered themselves Cockney. They were bouncy, humorous characters who would stand up for themselves and others they cared about, especially their family and friends. They had the gift of the gab and an opinion on everything.

Grandfather Will certainly met the standard for Cockney when it came to gift of the gab and an opinion on everything. As I grew older, I formed an assessment of my grandfather: he was a lying, blustering, lazy, know-it-all, loud-mouth bully who actually knew very little.

Some people have considered me judgmental; Frankly, I've always preferred the word "discerning."

Dad told me that my grandfather used to make and sell ice cream and pedal it around the streets in a cart, similar to vendors who sold ice. I surmised this was before my arrival into the family because I never tasted homemade ice cream at my grandparents' home and never saw my grandfather make or sell French Vanilla around the streets. When I asked my Dad about that, he said, "Well, that was before you were born. Your grandfather's since retired."

I don't know how lucrative my grandfather's ice cream business was or whether he was able to save for later in life, but I do know that Dad gave my grandmother money every week, which would make Vera furious and caused bitter arguments between them.

Vera detested my grandfather. On this subject, we agreed. Vera considered him a bully and told me that Grandfather Will was not beyond cuffing his wife Florence in the back of the head or slapping her around when he was angry.

Grandmother Florence was a timid, apprehensive individual. She rarely joined in any conversations, having learned from experience to expect biting sarcasm from her husband in return. When visitors arrived, Florence usually stayed in the kitchen, while Will held court in the living room. Florence was short and stout and could have flattened my scrawny grandfather at any time when he lashed out at her. She had enough girth to defend herself but not the courage.

My grandparents' neighborhood was gradually transitioning utilities from gas to electricity. For many years, my grandfather stubbornly refused to spend the money necessary to make the switch. On one of our family visits to my dad's parents, my grandmother's face lit up with excitement for a brief moment when the subject arose. "Oh Will, it would be so wonderful to have electricity, don't you think?"

There was a short pause, after which followed a tongue-lashing from my grandfather. "You don't know what you're talking about, woman. Shut the hell up! Get in the kitchen and make us some tea. If gaslight is good enough for me, it's bloody good enough for you. I don't know why I put up with you, you stupid cow!"

I watched helplessly as my grandmother, head bowed, wilting like a daisy, her tears brimming, struggled to regain her composure; she hurried into the kitchen. I wanted to mash my grandfather into the ground, but I was a kid and in no position to intervene.

Dad tried to stick up for his mother. "I say, Dad, there's no reason…. Why did you speak to Mum that way? You embarrassed her and hurt her feelings. What's—?"

"Mind your own damned business," Grandfather snapped at him. "This is my house, she's my wife, and I'll say and do whatever I bloody want. I'm the husband and I'm in charge. I guess that's not the way it is in your house, eh? You have to deal with her." He pointed toward Vera.

Dad shrank back into the gloomy shadows cast by the dim gaslight, but Vera did not. When Dad moved toward the kitchen, probably to comfort his mother, Vera spoke up. "Right you are then. Alf, let's go. I don't want to spend another minute under this roof. " She turned to my grandfather. "As for you, you old sod, your son may overlook your bullying ways, but not me. Don't you ever come knocking on my door asking for any favors because it won't open, not for the likes of you."

Vera grabbed my arm. "Glenda, we're leaving. Come, Alf." We marched out, my Dad trailing behind. I admired Vera's spunk but again questioned why and how I had become a member of a family constantly at war with each other: it was exhausting.

Grandma Florence's death was not unexpected. She was worn down and worn out, battered and exhausted by life. I cried over her passing, but part of me was glad she had finally escaped the abusive servitude she'd suffered living with my grandfather. I would miss those moments in Grandma's kitchen, quietly enjoying a cup of tea, brewed so strong we would joke: "You can stand a spoon up in it."

Vera's resentment lingered over Dad giving his mother money throughout their marriage, while she was struggling to make ends meet. "You've always put your mother before me. Gave her money when I didn't know where the next penny was coming from! I am not going to her funeral and that's that."

Could it be that yet another woman had threatened to usurp Vera's position as the number one female with my Dad? I would always wonder.

Dad was overwrought and pleaded with Vera to change her mind but she was pigheaded. I was accustomed to her moments of spiteful vindictiveness, but to abandon my Dad when he needed her support seemed heartless.

I accompanied my Dad to his mother's funeral. We stood at the cemetery and Dad's eyes filled with tears. "I loved my mother, but I detested my father. Always have."

I handed Dad a couple of tissues. He blew his nose and continued. "I hated the way he treated her, knocked her around, bullied her. I know that he withheld money from her—that's been going on a long time. Mum was struggling. I had to help her out. That's why I gave her a little money from my paycheck each week. I thought Vera would understand but…."

I passed over more tissues and patted Dad's arm.

At a low point in her husband's life, Vera had turned her back on my dad out of spite.

One of Vera's favorite sayings was: "Charity begins at home." For me, that philosophy never made sense. Surely, charity began when someone saw a need for help and rendered assistance, regardless of familial association. Toward the end of Vera's life, when we were in regular communication and I was again calling her Mum, she eventually understood the meaning of *giving.* She would proudly tell me about things she had given away or money she had donated, and I always validated her efforts: "Good for you, Mum. I'm proud of you."

According to Grandmother Florence's wishes, her earthly body would embrace the flames of cremation.

While waiting for the service to commence at the ashes burial site and meandering through the cemetery grounds, Dad inadvertently took a wrong turn and found himself in the area where bodies in their temporary coffins were stacked and awaiting cremation..

Before he realized that he was in the wrong place and turned to leave, he overheard one of the fellows: "Next up, the Taylor body." He knew they were referring to his mother.

When he returned to the burial garden, he said, "I broke out in a cold sweat. Thought I was gonna be sick. I imagined Mum lying in the coffin. The flames leaping higher, she was feeling hotter, the coffin engulfed in flames, I thought I heard Mum call out, 'Son help me!' Isn't that stupid?"

Dad was shivering. I hugged him and pulled him close to me for warmth and comfort.

When I later learned that my grandfather was devastated at the passing of his wife, I felt a secret thrill of vengeance.

"After all I did for her. Gave her a good life, I did," he would say. "Put a roof over her head, food on the table, gave her two sons. And she ups and leaves me."

I thought with grim satisfaction: The temerity of the woman. She left him to fend for himself!

Florence had been servile to her husband throughout their married life. That was what society expected in the early 1900s. The career for most women was marriage and motherhood. For years, Florence had been a wife and mother, bossed and slapped around by her husband. According to my dad, Grandfather Will cried and whined: "Who's gonna take care of me now that your mother's gone?"

Dad repeated his words to Vera. I saw her mouth narrow and stretch into a long, thin line, "Not me, so forget it," she snapped.

Dad wisely dropped the subject. His loyalty was to his mother, not his father. His mother had passed. There was no reason to expect anyone else to mollycoddle his father, especially not me.

Grandfather Will lived more than fifteen years after Florence died. Alone in the house, he finally understood the wisdom of having electricity installed, something he had mulishly denied his wife while she was alive.

I had no respect or love for the man, but as time progressed, I found myself feeling sorry for him and would stop by and visit once or twice a month. When his work schedule allowed, Dad also made weekly visits to his father, but Vera never did. I recall her saying on several occasions, "I'm through with that old bastard."

During one of my visits, Grandpa started ordering me around like he did his wife. I quickly set him straight. "I'm not your wife, so I won't put up with your nonsense. If you want me to continue visiting and helping you, you'll be civil to me and thankful that someone in the family is still willing to check in on you." Will's bullying days were over.

When he died, Vera danced a jig around the room. She finally had Dad to herself—well, that is, except for me.

30
THE FAMILY CAT
1962

IT SEEMED THAT A SOUL MATE for me was not in the cards, no matter how often I shuffled the deck. Fur companions have been plentiful throughout my life, and for this I'm grateful. I have always been able to communicate with cats and dogs, and they with me.

When Vera behaved callously toward Keela, the family cat, my empathetic nature asserted itself. Keela was a sleek, black feline stray; she wrapped her silky paws around my heart the moment we met. She gave me the love I needed, and I recall well the day I brought her home.

"I don't want another cat," Vera said. "They're messy. The other two died on me, and I don't want to go through that again."

I appealed to Dad. "If we take her to the shelter, she'll be killed. I'm working now. I can pay for her food and kitty litter and take care of her. Mum won't have to do a thing. Please let me keep her."

Dad lowered his newspaper. "Well, Vera, I don't see the harm in—"

Vera rolled her eyes. "That's right, side with her. You always do. I don't want another cat dying in my arms."

Dad sighed. "Well, you two work it out. Doesn't bother me whether we get another cat." He returned to his newspaper.

"Mum, I'm working. I can get Keela her shots to protect against the flu. We never had the money for medical care for the other cats—that's why they died." I sighed in relief. Dad was not opposed to another family cat. I was certainly earning sufficient money to pay for her keep.

Vera was shrewd and recognized this as one argument she could not win. "Fine. Make sure that you hand over £10 every payday for your room and board and keep the cat out of my way."

"Yeah, I can do that," I said. What intelligent creature would gravitate to Miss Sour Puss anyway?

"Okay, Vera. I think it's settled," Dad said. "Glenda will be responsible for the cat. Now, can we get some dinner around here?"

Dad was listening and his heart was open; he'd found in my favor. This time, I was the victor.

I was eighteen and working as a secretary for a stockbroker. My earlier fears of boredom and paper shuffling were now a reality. At least I was making money and could take Keela to the vet should the need arise. Veterinary care had been a luxury not available to our two previous cats that had died from feline influenza.

Unfortunately, Keela became ill before I could get her to the vet for her shots. I didn't have a car; my parents didn't have a car. I had to rely on public transportation. I wrapped her in a blanket and held her in my arms as we traveled by bus to the vet's office. Keela never struggled or tried to get away from me. She must have known I was trying to help her. When we reached our destination, I carried Keela from the bus, walked half a block to the vet's office, and a blonde, older receptionist warmly greeted us and added my name to the client waiting list.

"Come along in," she said. "You're lucky. It's not been busy today. The doctor can see you right away." She escorted me to the consulting room where the vet was waiting. He examined Keela and diagnosed her with feline influenza.

Tears welled up in my eyes. "Oh, no! We've already lost two cats to the flu."

The vet patted my shoulder. "Don't be too concerned. The illness is in the beginning stages. Keela has an excellent chance for recovery as long as you follow my instructions: keep her warm and hydrated and administer the medicine three times a day with food. Bring her back to see me in two weeks."

I thanked him, rewrapped Keela in the blanket, and headed for the bus stop. When I got home, I said to Vera, "Please make sure that she stays warm and give her the medicine at noon, with a little food. I'll feed her and medicate her in the morning and when I return home from work in the evening. The vet said she has a good chance of pulling through."

Vera sighed. "Well, that's all well and good, but the other cats died from the flu…. Why should this one be any different?"

Two days later, when I returned home from work and called Keela, she didn't come. This was unlike her. She would always come to me or meow to let me know where she was when I called her.

"That daft cat jumps up on the window sill in the front

room about four thirty in the afternoon waiting for you to come home," Vera had often told me.

When I would open the door to the front room, Keela would wind her warm, velvet body through my legs, and her purr was like an aria to my heart. But not today. I searched the house, but no Keela. When I couldn't find her, I became frantic.

I walked into the kitchen and asked Vera, "Where's Keela?"

Vera was making an apple tart, her forearms covered in flour. "I don't know."

"What d'you mean? 'You don't know?' She's not upstairs, she's not downstairs. When did you see her last? She has to be somewhere—where is she?"

Vera turned to face me, hands on her hips. "Oh, all right. She's outside."

I felt my face flush; I was livid. "Outside? What the hell is she doing outside?"

"You keep a civil tongue in your head, young lady." Vera wagged a finger at me. "Keela started coughing and then she threw up. I can't have that in my house. I don't want to keep cleaning up after a cat." She sniffed. "I put Keela out in the garden. If she makes it, fine. If she doesn't, so be it."

I went to the window. Keela was curled up in a ball on a pile of snow. It was the middle of winter and the temperature was about thirty degrees. I threw open the back door, scooped Keela up in my arms, and brought her into the kitchen. I could see hope in her eyes as she snuggled against my shoulder. My throat filled with loathing at Vera's cruel disregard for a sick animal.

Vera glowered at me and took a few steps toward me. "What are you doing? I don't want her in this house. Get that damned cat out of here!"

I glared back. "No. She stays. She's not going to freeze to death in the snow." I looked Vera up and down. "You know, I think there's something wrong with you. What type of person is cruel to sick animals? I'm gonna tell Dad about this."

Vera returned to making her pie. The bottom layer of pastry was covered with sliced apples and sprinkled with cinnamon. She rolled out the top layer of pastry, laid it across the pie dish and pinched the pastry around the edge of the dish with her thumb and forefinger. She looked up at me. "Your father will agree with me." She was gloating, her smile victorious. "Wait and see."

"No, he won't." I started to leave the room to take Keela upstairs to the small bedroom and make her comfortable. "He likes Keela."

Vera raised her voice. "Now listen here—"

"I don't wanna listen here. I'm not interested in what you have to say."

"I'm telling your father—"

"Go ahead, tell him whatever you bloody like. While you're at it, tell him what a cold-hearted bitch you really are."

"You watch your language you little—" Vera started toward me as I moved through the living room toward the front room, headed for upstairs and the third bedroom.

I stopped and faced her. "I wasn't kidding when I said I would hit you back if you ever touched me again, so be warned."

Vera stepped back, turned around, and dropped into a chair.

I carried Keela upstairs to the spare bedroom, my tears falling on her fur. How Vera could have tossed her out into the snow knowing she had feline influenza made me so damned angry that I wanted to choke her. How could she be that callous?

I took a blanket from the cupboard and fashioned a bed for Keela, placing it in the corner of the small room far away from the draught of the door. There was no heat in the upstairs rooms, but I filled a hot water bottle, wrapped it with a thick towel, and inserted it into the folds of the blanket to keep Keela warm during the night when the temperature dropped. I loved this cat and she loved me. I wanted her to live.

I returned to the living room. "I'm going to the butcher's to get some liver, kidneys, and perhaps a heart for Keela. Stay away from her while I'm gone."

Vera was sitting in front of the fire, arms wrapped around her body, slowly rocking, her face pinched in anger. "I want you and that bloody cat out of this house. You don't belong here, you never did."

Finally, we agreed on something. "You're right. I don't belong here, but I'm here for now. I'm caring for Keela. If anything happens to her when I'm at work, I'll hold you responsible, and I will tell Dad. He's very fond of this cat, so you'd better watch your step."

Vera's lower lip was thrust into a pout. "I'll tell your father that you threatened me."

"Go ahead and then explain to Dad how you threw a sick, helpless animal into the garden in frigid temperatures. Just remember, I'm no longer afraid of you—those days are over."

I hand-fed Keela cooked organ meat, sliced into little pieces and blended into white rice for two weeks, twice a day with her medication. I kept her bed clean, changed her kitty litter daily, and made sure that her water bottle was warm when she snuggled down in her blanket at night. When she refused to drink, I hydrated her with water through a syringe. I cried and prayed every night that she would get well.

After two weeks, Keela was showing signs of recovery. I cuddled her into a blanket and we returned to the vet for a checkup.

"She's perking up," the vet said. "The medicine must be working. What are you feeding her?"

"Cooked liver, heart, and kidney mixed with rice twice a day. She's now voluntarily drinking. Before I had to hydrate her with a syringe."

"Well, you did a good job, young lady. I think she's going to make it. I'll give you some more medicine for the next two weeks. If Keela's back to normal after that, then you don't need to bring her back. If she's still under the weather, well, you know where I am. Okay?"

Tears spilled down my cheeks, my heart was filled with hope.

The vet patted me on the shoulder. "Okay?"

I nodded and spluttered, "Okay."

Keela recovered from her bout of feline influenza. Once again, she was allowed to curl up happily in her usual spot in front of the fireplace.

Vera appeared glad that Keela had recovered. Therefore, I was left wondering: did she toss the cat out into the garden because she couldn't face another cat dying in her arms, or did she toss the cat out because she didn't want to be bothered caring for a sick cat? I concluded it was a little of both.

31
FINAL CONFRONTATION
1961

I CAN'T RECALL what started the argument, but I think it was something about makeup. In 1961, after the release of the movie *Cleopatra* starring Elisabeth Taylor and Richard Burton, every teenager I knew mimicked Liz Taylor's eye make-up in the role of Cleopatra. It was all the rage. At eighteen, I was no exception to the lure of this elaborate, eye-catching fad. Dark liner close to the lashes on the upper eyelids, extended out and up at the corner, with green shadow on the lids, and softer liner on the lower eyelid. The final step was loads of mascara. Looking back fifty years later, I imagine that I probably resembled a raccoon, but I loved the look.

Dad did not approve, but his method of showing displeasure was very different from Vera's. After thirty minutes of trying to create the perfect Cleopatra look, I turned away from the mirror and looked at my Dad. "What do you think?"

He set aside his latest Sherlock Holmes mystery and peered at me. "What am I looking at?"

"My eye make-up, silly. Don't you think I look like Cleopatra?" I struck the pose that I'd seen in the movie. I placed my palms together, raised my arms waist high and, keeping my torso steady, shifted my neck slightly from side to side, eyes following with each movement.

Dad stood up and came over to the mirror next to me. "Yes, very good, but...." He removed his spectacles, stared at my reflection in the mirror, and shook his head. "Hmm.... Colorful but looks to me like... well, traffic lights. I mean... all that green stuff. Are you going out tonight looking like that?"

I grinned. "Course I am. I'm going to the jazz club with Irene. This is the look right now. It's groovy. I like it."

"Well, suit yourself, but don't expect to catch a husband looking like that."

"Oh, Dad!" I laughed. "I'm not interested in catching a husband, I'm only interested in looking good."

"Okay, then. But... well... that's not my idea of looking good. Just my opinion." He replaced his spectacles on his nose and shuffled over to his chair. Sitting down, he lit a cigarette, picked up his book and returned to *The Speckled Band*, one of Arthur Conan Doyle's more intriguing mysteries. For Dad, our difference of opinion was over.

All the while, I believed that Vera had been absorbed with her sewing at the dining room table, mumbling under her breath when she ran into difficulties and grunting with satisfaction when she had conquered the problem.

I was wrong. She had been listening to my conversation with Dad. I was surprised when she struck out at me like a cobra. "You look like a tart—a floozy out on the town. Where's your pride and self respect? Only the wrong sort of bloke will be interested in you, looking the way you do. I keep telling you, you'll turn out just like your mother, you will. But of course,

I'm always wrong." Vera stared defiantly at my Dad, and then she glared at me.

This woman was a downpour on sunshine.

For a few seconds, I felt as though a shard of glass had nicked my throat. I felt dizzy and was having trouble breathing. I had not seen this attack coming. Swallowing my anger yet again, I slowly turned away from the mirror and looked at her.

"All the magazines—I mean, just look in all the magazines, Mum. For instance, *Vogue*. All the models have this look, the Cleopatra-look. All the kids my age want to look like Cleopatra. What's so wrong with that?"

"Considering your background, my girl, I would think that you would reconsider going out on the town looking like a whore. Just remember, if you get pregnant, you will keep the baby, and you will raise it. I'm not going to raise it—that will be your job."

I took a deep breath and turned to face her. "First of all, I'm not planning on getting pregnant. Secondly, if I did, I would make all the decisions about the baby. Your opinion would be unimportant and unwelcome."

"That's enough—both of you. Vera, give it a rest." Dad placed his book on his lap and glared at his wife. "Glenda doesn't look like a whore. She's just trying out some new fandangled make-up craze that all the kids are using. I don't particularly like it, but she doesn't look like a whore."

"I disagree." Vera turned in her chair to face Dad and me. "Look at her! My God, she came from a whore and now she's looking like a whore. All that makeup! Only loose women go around looking like that." She sighed, rolled her eyes, picked up her needle, intent on sewing.

In seconds, Dad was up, out of his chair, and marching

toward her. "You don't get it, do you? I don't want to hear any more of that bloody nonsense spilling out of your mouth about our daughter, do you hear me?" Spittle burst from his mouth like spray from a popped soda can. He spun around and walked back to his chair. His hands shook as he lit a cigarette.

With the sewing needle poised in her right hand, Vera sat transfixed, as if struck by God. I stayed silent. I had never heard Dad so angry.

Dad turned around, pointing at Vera. "Your daughter does not come from a whore. She came from a woman who could not keep her." He took a deep drag on his cigarette and looked at me. "Remember, Glenda? We told you about her."

I nodded but dared not speak.

"We met her, Vera, in Bath. Norah Townsend. Glenda's biological mum, don't you remember?" Dad glared at her. "You know the story. Norah told us... her father said to her: 'Take care of the problem, and then you can return home.' The problem was the baby, meaning, get rid of the baby."

Dad pointed toward me. "Norah had no choice but to give up Glenda for adoption. For God's sake, it was 1943, the war was raging. Norah had to live in a home for unmarried mothers, give up the baby, and then return to her parents' home. Her family would have disowned her had she tried to keep her child. Have you forgotten our meeting with Glenda's mother?"

"Well, no. Of course not." Vera said, nose in the air. "But clean-living young women did not get pregnant by fighter pilots, even in 1942."

Dad slammed his hand against a wall. "Have you no empathy? Have you no understanding of wartime? Are you that bloody dense?"

Vera sniffed. "I don't know what you mean."

Dad stepped so close to Vera they might have exchanged breath. "You have no idea of what went on in war-time, or you refuse to accept reality. I'm not sure which. Many children were born out of wedlock during the war and were given up for adoption."

Dad started pacing. "Norah's pregnancy was no exception. How the hell do you think we got Glenda? From Santa Claus?"

For a few seconds, all three of us stood in silence; Dad and I were staring at Vera. Her tears were falling freely, down her cheeks and spilling onto her blouse. "You've always sided with Glenda against me," she sobbed.

I thought her tears stemmed from self-pity.

Dad threw up his hands. "Oh, for God's sake, woman. Look at the facts. Glenda is our daughter. I told you when you asked for a child: only a girl. I would adopt only a daughter! You knew that from the outset. The last eighteen years, well, I haven't been around much... I've always been working.... I don't know why, but things have always been rocky between you two. Seems to me you're jealous of your own daughter."

"What utter nonsense." Instantly, Vera's tears ceased flowing. She clenched her fists and confronted my Dad. "If you had supported me when...."

Dad raised his hand. "Quiet. Somewhere during those eighteen years, we lost our daughter, and I'm sickened by it. That's all I have to say. I'm going to the shops for cigarettes."

Dad left the dining room and headed toward the front door. I heard the door open and slam shut. Dad had left, and I was alone with Vera.

She turned to me. "Well, I suppose you think you have your father wrapped around your little finger." She dabbed at her eyes with a handkerchief. "But you don't. Let me warn you, my girl, I'm his wife. I come first. I'll make bloody sure he remembers that."

This threat was one of Vera's favorites. I had heard it frequently while growing up. I didn't want to hear it any more.

I left the room and headed upstairs toward my bedroom, hoping to find a little peace with a book and our cat that always followed me to wherever I landed.

Halfway up the steep, narrow staircase, where the last three steps curved slightly to the left, I could hear Vera still coming behind me. Her mouth was in constant motion, spouting insults about my birth, what an ungrateful child I was, how convinced she was that, like my biological mother, I would turn up pregnant and not married, and on and on and on.

When I reached the top stair, I swiveled around and looked down at her. All the fear, hurt, shame, humiliation, and sadness that my heart had absorbed year after year, at Vera's words seemed knitted together into a tightly anguished pattern of pain with the thought: *She will destroy you unless you destroy her.*

My body became strangely calm. I felt chilled. My heartbeat slowed. My mind disconnected from my churning emotions, and I focused solely on surviving. Vera and I were at war: we were enemies. I was determined to claim the rest of my life without her.

In a low, controlled voice, I said, "You need to stop talking."

Vera's shrill tones bounced up the stairs. "Since when have you told me what to do? You're just—"

"You're not listening. It's in your best interest to stop talking."

"Oh, really? And what are you going to do if I don't? Who are you to tell?"

I raised my voice. "This is what I'm going to do if you don't shut up. If you take one more step up, and I mean one more step toward me, I'm going to push you down the stairs. I hope it bloody kills you."

Vera shrank back. "I'll... I'll call your father."

I could hear the fear in her voice but I kept on. "Go ahead, but it's too late. He's not home. He won't be able to save you. You will either die or end up a cripple. I prefer that you die."

Vera stepped back two more stairs. One hand to her mouth, her eyes wide, she knew I meant what I said, and I knew that I had the upper hand.

I raised my voice. "Getting rid of you will stop the bloody bullying and the pain. You will no longer be able to make my life a living hell. Do I make myself clear?"

Vera stared into my eyes. I stared back and never blinked. Tears were trickling down her face and she nodded slowly. She finally got it: I was deadly serious.

She started slowly backing down the stairs, "Just wait 'til your father gets home. You'll be sorry."

As long as she continued to back down the stairs, whatever came out of her mouth was irrelevant.

I heard a key turn in the front door. Dad was home.

I went to my bedroom, hauled my suitcase down from the top of the wardrobe, and started filling it with clothes.

"Alf! Alf! Glenda's gone mad." Vera was sobbing. "She threatened to kill me. She needs to be locked up."

I heard Dad, confused and bewildered. "What the hell happened while I was gone?"

Vera repeated the threats I had made. In the middle of stuffing a sweater into my suitcase, I paused, listening. For several seconds, all was quiet. Then Vera broke the silence. "Alf, what are you going to do? You need to protect me from her."

Dad's voice, measured and strong, bounced up the staircase to my bedroom. "Vera, if Glenda doesn't leave this house after what you've just said to her, and all the criticisms you've dumped on her while she was growing up, I will have lost all respect for her. You wanted a child, and you got one, but the way you treated her ... well.... I'm going to work."

The front door slammed shut again. I heard Vera stumble down the rest of the stairs; I suppose she was headed for the dining room.

I picked up a scarf and mopped beads of sweat from my upper lip. It was now or never. I'd made my break for freedom and I'd won. Packed and ready to go, I hauled my suitcase down that steep staircase one last time, flung open the front door, and slammed it shut.

The she-devil was behind me.

Women who cannot love and nurture a child should stick to housework, flower arrangements, and volunteer work, and forget about having kids.

32
STEPPING OUT ALONE
1961

LUGGING MY SUITCASE, my adrenalin pumping, I strode up Eastwood Crescent toward Broomhill Road to catch the bus for work. I was not scared or worried about the future, just relieved that I had slammed the door closed on an eighteen-year nightmare. Five minutes ago, I had threatened to kill my adoptive mother. Had she not backed off, I would have followed through with my threat. As I drew closer to the bus stop, I must still have been in shock: my mind was on automatic pilot, able to perform normal daily functions, on a day that was far from normal.

The regular riders were standing around waiting for the eight o'clock bus, smoking cigarettes, and nattering. Several bid me good morning.

One woman asked, "Are you going on holiday?"

I nodded. "Yes." I looked down the road and saw the bus approaching. "A long holiday."

"Oh, how exciting." The woman moved closer. "Where are you going?"

The bus pulled up at the stop and, one by one, we started boarding.

"Not sure," I said. I grabbed the vertical bar in the middle of the platform and stepped up, glanced at her over my shoulder, and winked. "But when I get there, I'll send you a postcard."

I climbed to the upper deck, hauling my suitcase behind me to avoid more questions. I found a window seat and placed the suitcase between my knees. My heartbeat slowed as my emotions calmed and my brain slid into survival mode.

Where would I sleep tonight? On a secretary's salary, my funds were limited. I could sleep on a park bench, but how could I clean up the next morning and be sufficiently presentable to report for work? In the 1960s, inexpensive motels and restaurants that catered to the breakfast crowd or gas stations with restrooms did not exist in Bristol.

There was also the chance that some crazy drunk would stumble my way and steal my suitcase. Worse, a gang of Teddy Boys could rape or kill me. Dad had warned me more than once about what he called "those louts." Sleeping in the open was not an option.

I looked out the window. Looming ahead was Bedminster Bridge, which was my stop. I stood, grabbed my suitcase, pushed the bell, and clambered down the circular flight of steps until I stood on the platform. People lined up behind me and, when the bus stopped, we streamed out in all directions, like shoppers seeking a bargain during the English January sales.

My hand tightened on the suitcase; I would explore options on my lunch hour.

Peggy, the supervisor, did not approve of her staff being late, so I hurried to the entrance, waved to the security guard, punched in, hustled to the elevator, stepped in and hit the button for the third floor. The elevator started to move slowly upward. I made sure not to make eye contact with anyone. Questions I did not want; answers I did not have.

The elevator stopped at the third floor. I got out, walked to the engineering department, nudged open the office door with my suitcase, and came face to face with Anne, one of my coworkers. Her looks reminded me a little of Marilyn Monroe: generous curves, wavy blonde hair, easy going, and a wink in her smile. Of the other four girls in the typing pool, all of whom I liked, Anne was my favorite. She was unmarried, in her mid-twenties, not wound too tight, more open-minded than most, and nonjudgmental. Imagine a 1960s equivalent of a young woman with purple hair, tattoos, and piercings working in a modern, buttoned-up, work environment.

She eyed me up and down. "What's with the suitcase?" She knew a little about what was now my former home life.

I shrugged. "Little problem I need to resolve."

Anne cocked her head to one side. "Hmm.... Don't think you're going on vacation." She stared me straight in the eyes and then glanced again at the suitcase. "My bet is that you're leaving home, right?"

I nodded and tears threatened to flow; I wiped my eyes on my sleeve.

"Watch out," said Anne. "Here comes the sergeant major," which was our code for referring to the supervisor. "Shove your suitcase under your desk and act as if nothing's going on."

Anne went to her desk, and I went to mine. I followed her advice and shoved the suitcase far under my desk as Peggy walked through the office. As usual, she was in a flurry, a sheaf of papers in her hand. "Ladies," she said, "I have two engineers who require immediate stenographic assistance." She announced the names, selected Megan and Doreen, the two most experienced stenographers, and instructed them to whom they were to report. My coworkers left the office after collecting their pens and steno pads.

Peggy settled into her supervisor's chair, slipped on her glasses, and started sorting the department's mail. "Anne, you and Glenda can deliver the mail once I have it in order. In the meantime," she pointed toward a large basket of filing atop a cabinet, "you two can make a dent in filing last week's correspondence and memoranda. If you have any questions what should be filed where, please ask me. Don't guess!" She peered over her glasses. "Is that clear?"

Anne and I answered in unison: "Yes, Peggy." I nudged my suitcase further back under the desk, fearful that Peggy might spot the intruder in the office. That would have opened a dialogue as broad as the English Channel.

After lunch, Peggy directed Anne to another engineer who needed stenographic services and left me to complete the rest of the filing. She gathered together files and papers and plucked her sweater from the back of her chair. "Remember, if you're not sure where to file something, don't file it. Discuss it with me when I get back." She opened the office door, paused, and looked back at me. "I'm off to my weekly meeting with the Chief Engineer. If you need me, you know how to reach me."

I managed to get through the day without mishap or a discovery of my suitcase. Later that afternoon, I checked my watch. It was four thirty. In another thirty minutes, I would be out on the streets, alone, with nowhere to go.

A breeze swept through the office as the door swung wide and Anne strode in, fanning herself with her steno pad. "Phew, his office is like a furnace. I hate taking dictation from that pig. He stinks! I don't think he's ever heard of deodorant." She looked at me. "Where's Peggy?"

"You know. Weekly meeting with the Chief Engineer."

"Good." Anne sat at her desk and lowered her voice so that Megan and Doreen, busy transcribing their notes, couldn't hear. "She'll be gone for quite a while. Let's meet in the ladies' room in five minutes. I have a plan, but I need a few puffs on a ciggie first, okay?

"Okay, but what are you up to? Why are we—?

"Trust me. It'll be okay." She rummaged in her bag, found cigarettes and matches, rested her heels on top of the desk, took a cigarette from the pack, lit up, and inhaled deeply.

Megan pulled a document from her typewriter and glanced over at Anne. "You'd better keep an eye on the door. If Peggy catches you with your feet on the desk, well... you know Peggy!"

Eyes closed, Anne blew a plume of smoke into the air and groaned. "I needed this."

She looked back at Megan. "S'okay. I have excellent hearing. We all know that Peggy will be all a-twitter, fluttering her eyelashes like Lucille Ball at the Chief Engineer—pompous ass." We all laughed, recalling Peggy's various attempts at flirtation with some of the engineers. After a few more drags, Anne stubbed out her cigarette in the ashtray and reluctantly removed her feet from the desk. "I doubt Peggy will be in a hurry to return to the steno room at this late hour."

I left the office and walked to the ladies' room. The door slammed closed behind me and seconds later swung back open as Anne marched in. We stood face to face. She grinned, looking pleased with herself, like a hawk that has snagged a mouse before it tried to disappear under a hedgerow. "I have a plan."

"What plan?"

Anne leaned against the sink. "I called Mum. Told her about you and... well, you know. She said to bring you home after work. We have a spare room and you can stay with us as long as you like, until you find a place of your own. Okay?"

Tears mingled with mascara spilled over my cheeks and dripped off my chin, and I covered my face with my hands, my shoulders heaving as I sobbed. I had held my emotions in check to get through the workday, but this unexpected gift of kindness shattered my pretense of invulnerability.

Anne put her arm around my shoulders. "Hey, steady on there, you're melting into a puddle. Like a snowman in summer."

I relaxed, sniffed, and we both giggled.

"I don't know how to thank you and your mum," I said. "I had no clue where I was going after I left work today."

"Well, now you do. So, blow your nose, wipe your eyes, and let's get outta here." Anne glanced at her watch. "Yep, it's two minutes to five, time enough to grab our bags and your suitcase and hit the road for home."

We returned to the office where the other girls were packing up, getting ready to leave for the day. Peggy was nowhere in sight, presumably still fluttering her eyelashes at the Chief Engineer. *What a godsend for me!*

I bent down and yanked my suitcase from underneath my desk. I stood up and was eye to eye with Megan and Doreen. I held my breath until Doreen said, "Don't worry, Glenda, we suspected something was going on." She stepped forward and gave me a quick hug. "Your secret's safe with us. Best of luck to you." Megan blew me a kiss and they left the office.

Again, I felt like crying and started sniffling.

"No, no! Not that again," Anne said. "I can't handle any more waterworks." She slipped into her coat, flung a scarf around her neck, and pulled her purse over her shoulder. "Let's get outta here, go home, have a stiff drink or two, and enjoy a nice home-cooked dinner."

All I could do was nod.

Anne's voice softened. "Don't worry. It's gonna be all right. It'll work out. You're safe. Mum will take good care of you until we find you somewhere to live so.... Please, don't worry, okay?"

Hearing Anne's words of comfort thawed some of my fears. We caught the bus to Anne's home where her mum welcomed me and showed me to the spare room. "Dump your stuff and come downstairs, dear. Dinner's nearly ready."

After a meal of steak and kidney pie, fresh vegetables, and a glass of wine, I was ready for bed. It had been an emotionally exhausting day. Snuggled between fresh cotton sheets and several woolen blankets, it felt good to know that I had a friend who cared, a friend who would help me move forward and away from my past. I slept easy that night.

The following Friday night, Anne and I stretched out on the living room floor sipping wine and scanning the classifieds in local newspapers for flats and bedsitters. Those in acceptable areas cost more than I'd anticipated.

I was beginning to feel despondent.

Anne exclaimed, "Here's one! A bedsitter in a Victorian house on Landsdown Place in Clifton."

Bristol University was close by, so Clifton was a well-known area for student living accommodations and recreational hangouts.

"Hmm... a good area," I said, "but I'm not sure I can afford it."

I don't remember the price quoted in the newspaper, but I do recall telling Anne that my moving in could happen only if I went on a permanent fast.

"What about this?" Anne said. "How would you feel about working a part-time job?"

"Doing what?"

"Bartending on Friday and Saturday nights at The Albion Pub."

I laughed. "I don't like beer. And I have no idea how to pour a pint, so why would they hire me?"

"The ad says, 'will train' and it pays £3.00 an hour plus tips." With the newspaper in hand, Anne rolled over and sat up, her voice raised in excitement. "Oh! And what about this! The bar's across the park from that bedsitter we were just talking about." She cocked an eyebrow and winked. "So! Shall we check them out tomorrow morning?"

"I think we should and the earlier the better." I thought for a moment. "I may not be an intellectual, but I'm sure I can learn to pour a pint."

"I agree." Anne raised her glass. "Let's drink to a new beginning and freedom."

We laughed, finished our drinks, and retired for the night.

As I brushed my teeth, I was thinking. Freedom is never really free. I would be exchanging one set of circumstances for another. If I rented the bedsitter, I would need to work a part-time job on the weekends to help pay the rent, buy food, clothing, and have money for bus fare to work. Time for a social life would not be in my immediate future.

Just as quickly, I realized that freedom could also mean snuggling in bed with a good book, hanging out with friends at a local coffee house, no curfews, and most important of all, peace: freedom from Vera's constant critical, scathing, and hurtful remarks. That form of freedom I could embrace.

The following morning, Anne and I were up early and heading out the door when Anne's mum called, "Girls, don't you want some breakfast before you leave?"

Tempted, we hesitated a moment.

"No, we want to get to Clifton as early as possible," Anne said. "You know what they say about the bird and the worm!"

"All right. Well, I'll have lunch ready for you when you return." As Anne's mum started to close the door, she reached to hug me. "Good luck, dear. I hope this works out for you."

Tears of gratitude started to well up again; Anne saw me brush them away. "Oh, my God, don't tell me you're at it again!" she said.

I sniffed and smiled. "You don't understand," I said. "I'm not used to being hugged. My mother is not a warm, affectionate person. For me, hugs are a little overwhelming."

Anne lowered her head for a second. I sensed her embarrassment.

"Sorry." She looked up. "I didn't realize. Mum's a hugger. I can't imagine what it would be like to live in a home without hugs." She continued to tease me. "I promise I won't nag you any more if you start blubbering."

"Blubbering?"

"Well, you know what I mean." Anne grinned and her warmth soothed me. We linked arms and set off for the bus stop.

After changing buses twice, Anne and I arrived in Clifton. The house on Landsdown Place was one of many well-maintained, four-story Victorian homes that encircled a small park. Large trees on either side of the park, their boughs bending toward each other like Elizabethans bowing to their dance partners, provided shade for visitors who rested a short while on one of the park's many benches. The house was close to the bus stop and soon we arrived at the front door.

"Well, here we are," said Anne. "Come on. Knock on the door and see what they have to offer."

I grasped the knocker and banged it against the brass plate.

"Coming." We heard a woman's voice call from inside. A few seconds later, the door was opened. "Can I help you?" A slightly stooped, elderly woman, her hair streaked with white, peered up at us through glasses perched on the tip of her nose.

"I… um… I came to look at the bedsitter," I managed to say. "If it's still available, that is."

The lady nodded. "Well, it's not actually a bedsitter, dear. More a room in an attic but—"

"The attic?"

Mrs. Foster glanced my way. "Yes, the attic. But it's clean and cozy, and you're welcome to look at it. It's still available."

I felt a strong jab in my back from Anne's elbow. "Yes. Yes, of course. I would like to see it," I said.

"All right, dear. Follow me. We have four flights of stairs to climb. I hope your young knees are in good shape." She laughed. "Mine are worn out, so I hope you'll forgive me if I just walk the first two flights. The room for rent is the only room on the fourth floor."

"That's okay," I said. "We can find it, I'm sure."

"Yes," Anne added. "Please don't hurt yourself climbing all these stairs. By the way, I'm Anne." Then she gestured toward me. "This is Glenda. She's the one interested in renting the room."

The woman smiled and nodded. "I'm Mrs. Foster. If you don't mind looking around on your own, that would be a blessing for these old knees. When you're done, come down to the first floor and knock on the door to the right. I'll meet you there. Would you like some tea?"

"Yes, that would be lovely," I said. "Thank you."

"We'll look at the room and be back in a jiffy," Anne said. She dragged on my arm and we started the hike to the fourth floor.

Finally, we reached the attic. I opened the door and stepped into my future.

It was a medium-sized room with a single bed piled high with bedding and draped with a silk, forest-green bedspread. Hanging above the bed was a round glass lamp; its switch was on the wall to the right as we entered the room. I sat and bounced on the bed. It was comfortable and firm without being too hard.

Against the foot of the bed was a five-drawer oak chest that could accommodate my sweaters, underwear, and nylons; a few feet to the right was a sturdy, medium-sized oak wardrobe for coats, skirts, and dresses. On the other wall was a large mirror; under the mirror was a low, squat bookcase with two deep shelves, and on the bookcase was a large, decorative Victorian basin and tall matching water jug.

Heavens! I thought at the time. *What was I supposed to do with that?*

Two large windows on each side of the room would allow me to watch the stars waltzing across the night sky as I drifted off to sleep. The promise of peace and tranquility was tempting.

"What do you think?" Anne asked.

I surveyed the room once more. "Well, it's extremely clean but, I would need a part-time job to make sure all my expenses were covered and I had a little financial breathing space."

"Okay," Anne said. "Let's go back downstairs and meet with Mrs. Foster. It's time to negotiate."

"Wait a minute," I said. "What's with the pitcher and the basin?"

"That, my dear, is how the Victorians bathed."

I gasped. "You're kidding! She expects me to—"

"Nope, don't worry. I've figured this into my pitch for cheaper rent."

We traipsed back down four flights of stairs and knocked on the first door to the right. It opened instantly, as if Mrs. Foster had been waiting behind the door, listening for us as we descended the stairs.

"Come in, come in. Make yourselves comfortable over there on the couch. Tea will be ready in a minute."

We did as she suggested.

"What did you think of the room? It's pretty sparse, but I keep it clean and well aired."

"Does that mean that you clean the room and change the sheets?" I asked.

"Yes, of course," Mrs. Foster replied. "Every week."

"How much is the rent per month?"

She quoted a figure that I no longer remember, but I recall Anne interrupting her. "Hmm…. Let's see. That's a tad high considering the room is four flights up, and there's no bath or toilet."

"Well, there's the pitcher and basin—"

"Yes, very nice and decorative," Anne said, settling down to negotiations. "But I'm wondering whether you really expect a lady tenant who works outside the home to use them for washing... actual bathing. You see my point?"

"Well." Mrs. Foster slowly adjusted her glasses. "There's also a chamber pot under the bed for night emergencies."

Anne completely ignored the reference to the chamber pot as she continued her critique. "Oh! And one other thing—there's no way for a tenant to cook or heat up food. So I'm sure you would agree that the room, though quite charming, has drawbacks."

"Hmm...." Mrs. Foster peered at me over her glasses for a few moments. "You seem a nice young lady. Are you permanently employed?"

"Yes," I replied. "I've been working as a secretary at the same company for over a year. I can provide you with a letter of reference, if you like."

Mrs. Foster nodded quietly, contemplating.

"I'm also looking for a part-time job to increase my income," I added. "But I have to be able to make my rent and pay my expenses on my salary from my full-time position."

A tall, slender young woman entered the room and placed a tray containing china cups and saucers, a milk jug, a sugar bowl, a plate of lemon slices, and a pot of tea on a small table close to the couch.

Mrs. Foster smiled. "Thank you, Susan." She then turned to us. "How do you ladies like your tea?"

I later learned that Susan was Mrs. Foster's daughter and she lived on the second floor. "I like mine black with lemon and a little sugar, please," I said.

"I'll take mine with a little milk and sugar, no lemon. Thank you," Anne said.

In silence, Mrs. Foster poured three cups of tea, added our individual preferences, and passed us each a cup and saucer. She took several sips of her tea and carefully replaced the cup in its saucer.

"I'd be willing to rent the room to the right person for...." Whatever amount she stated was less than I expected, and I certainly don't recall how much it was now. "There's a bathroom and toilet on the second floor that you can use."

Anne glanced over at me. "What do you think?"

I'd already done the math in my head. I could have breakfast—tea and biscuits—and eat a cooked lunch in the cafeteria at work, and buy cold cuts and bread for sandwiches for evenings. "Yes, that works for me."

"Okay," Anne said to Mrs. Foster. "What else would you like to know?"

My future landlady had prepared some personal questions about the type of hours I kept, whether I was dating anyone in particular, and previous rental agreements, of which there were none.

"I'm not dating anyone but that could change," I told her. "I'm usually in bed with a book around nine thirty. I'm very particular about my personal hygiene and that of my surroundings. I'm looking for an environment that's clean and peaceful."

"Well, if your dating life should change," Mrs. Foster said, "be aware that I don't allow men to stay in the house after ten at night. Is that agreeable to you?"

"Absolutely, no problem," I assured her. Like most in her generation, I suspected that Mrs. Foster believed sex occurred only after ten o'clock at night.

It seemed that my right shoe had suddenly acquired its own personal polishing machine. A chubby tabby cat was rubbing against my shoe, purring contentedly.

"Shoo! Go away!" Mrs. Foster said, yet she didn't seem to really mean it because she was smiling.

"No, don't worry about me," I said. "I love animals. Could she keep me company occasionally in my room?"

Mrs. Foster smiled and nodded. "I'm not a big cat lover, but she's a gentle creature that could use a friend." She looked me up and down. "All right, the attic is yours starting the first of next month. I'll throw the cat in for free." Her shoulders hunched up and shook slightly, laughing at her little joke.

I paid a month's rent in advance, and received a receipt and a front door key. Anne and I skipped out of there like a couple of happy children.

I had taken my second step toward freedom.

———

"Let's go for lunch and celebrate," Anne said. "And I know just the place."

"Really? Where?"

"The Albion Public House, of course." Ann stopped and turned to me. "The place where you're going to interview for a part-time job in about two hours. This is a perfect opportunity for you to check out the place where you might be working— the clientele, the staff, the owners, how the owners treat the staff—you get the gist?" She rolled her eyes and we both laughed.

I vowed to never believe anyone who told me that big boobs are an indication of small brains.

We walked through the park and down the cobbled street to The Albion; we settled in a corner spot in the lounge. In those days, public houses were divided into two sections: the bar where the working class played darts, celebrated, or drowned their sorrows with beer and the lounge where the purported gentry or upper crust celebrated or drowned their sorrows sipping on European Lager, Worthington beer, or gin and tonics, commonly referred to as G&Ts.

"Ladies, what can I get for you?" Laurie, one of the owners, a tall, affable, hefty man with slicked-back, dark hair and a black moustache, took our order. He was chewing on a cigar while he talked to us.

Anne and I ordered a slice of veal, ham, and egg pie, a pickled onion, and a gin and tonic. Working class we were, but our palates were definitely more in tune with the locals that lunched in the lounge.

Soon we were nibbling, sipping on our drinks, and assessing the place. Laurie's wife Pat came into the bar; she was a slim woman, barely five feet tall. I had a chance to also observe her before the interview. Both owners seemed warm and friendly to the staff and customers, which settled my nerves.

Later that day, I arrived for my three o'clock interview. Pat and Laurie recognized me from the lunch crowd earlier in the day. Laurie was busy moving barrels of beer, so my interview was primarily with Pat. We chatted and I told her that I was about to become a neighbor and that I had rented a bedsitter on Landsdown Place, across the park from the pub. This seemed to please her since she also knew Mrs. Foster. She thought it ideal having an employee who lived close to the pub. Pat showed me around, taught me how to pour a pint from a bottle and from the tap, and then observed me as I followed her instructions.

I was right. I didn't need to be an intellectual to pour a pint. I just needed the confidence to know that I could. Pat made a quick decision. If I wanted the job, it was mine, she said. I accepted her offer.

Life was looking up.

33
TOBACCO ANGELS
1963

SHORTHAND WAS A VALUABLE SKILL in the 1960s, when secretarial work was confined solely to women. In 1962, I was delighted when I was offered a position by a reputable tobacco company and assigned as a stenographer to the typing pool in the Engineering Department. Even with excellent skills, securing a position with a large company that also offered job security, advancement within the secretarial field, benefits, and a pension plan was quite a feat.

The work environment of the 1960s was rigidly structured. Secretaries were like serfs to the engineers, and we wore uniform, light green nylon coveralls that resembled prison garb. There were six of us, all young women who reported to Peggy, the head secretary. Conservative by nature, unmarried, and never without a string of pearls, Peggy fawned over the male engineers but snapped out instructions to the female stenographers.

As our supervisor, Peggy would oversee work assignments and dispatch stenographers to various engineers to take dictation, after which they would return to the typing pool to transcribe their notes. Unfortunately for me, this particular position was mind-numbing. I was making numerous mistakes in my transcription and Miss Clarke, Director of Personnel, had summoned me to meet with her in her office.

"Come in Glenda, please take a seat."

I sat facing her desk, fingers laced, hands in lap, and waited.

Miss Clarke was a tall, willowy woman with short silvery hair; she frequently dressed in soft grey. Quietly spoken, civil, professional, and always gracious, she was no push over. On several occasions, I'd heard from others that a touch of steel would creep into her voice when she had to deal with unpleasant situations or difficult people.

Miss Clark slipped on her glasses and rustled through the documents she was holding. "Glenda, I've reviewed your shorthand and it's correct, but you're making errors in your transcription. Can you explain this?"

I wanted to scream out: *Yes, that stupid bitch Vera forced me into taking shorthand and typing. She pushed me toward becoming a secretary, but that's not who I am or who I want to be!* Fidgeting in my seat, I met Miss Clark's gaze. "Because I'm bored," I said, relieved to say it at last.

Her eyebrows rose slightly, perhaps surprised at a forthright admission from an employee who was "on the carpet" for her poor performance. She peered over her glasses "Bored?"

"Yes, bored." I leaned forward in my seat. "Sorry, but engineering is boring to me. There are so many engineering terms, many of which I've never heard before, and there's no engineering dictionary available for us. Peggy usually assigns me to an engineer for dictation who rarely gives me any corresponding documentation. You know, a letter or something that would include names of people and machinery parts."

Miss Clark replaced the papers on her desk and leaned back in her chair. "Peggy tells me that she is working with you on your mistakes but you don't seem to be improving. Why is that?"

I stiffened in the chair, instantly defensive. "Peggy is not working with me on mistakes, Miss Clarke. She just points out that I've made yet another mistake. I've told her about the lack of documentation but nothing has changed. She continues to send me to the same engineer whereas my coworkers are sent to engineers who are more considerate. They provide documentation to help the stenographer. It's obvious to me that Peggy doesn't like me."

Miss Clarke removed her glasses and leaned toward me, forearms resting on the desk. "Glenda, to remain employed with us, you need to improve your job performance."

Tears stung my eyes. "I know. I'm sorry," I said. "I have good shorthand and typing skills, but I can't get enthusiastic about engineering, and Peggy is no help." I briefly looked at the floor. "Actually, she reminds me of my mother and, well, we don't get along, so....."

"Hmm…. Oh, I see." Silence hung heavy in the air. "Well, we're through here for today." Miss Clarke stood up. "Let me look into this further, and I'll get back to you. You can go now."

A week later, Peggy was practically drooling with delight when she informed me that Miss Clarke had transferred me to a vacant secretarial position in the Advertising Department. She was that glad to get rid of me. A secretarial position was a significant boost over a stenographic position. Peggy was elated; I was knocked-out thrilled. The boring typing pool and grumpy engineer was behind me. I was to report to George Moore, my new boss, on Monday morning.

George was an energetic, garrulous individual with an earthy sense of humor and kind heart. Later he told me that he had taken me on as "a project." Miss Clarke had told him about my situation, and George apparently had said: "If anyone can whip her into shape, I can."

He was right. Working for George kept me busy and engaged. Taking dictation from him was easy. He maintained a steady pace, usually knew exactly what he wanted to say, and always gave me corresponding documentation. Letters and internal memoranda regarding cigarette advertising, the content or appearance of point-of-sale items in stores, new brands coming onto the market, or disagreements with the London advertising agencies responsible for producing advertising materials were all far more interesting and definitely more entertaining than engineering.

Now error-free, I operated very efficiently. My dictation speed accelerated to 120 wpm, and my typing speed on a manual typewriter whizzed along at 75 wpm. I recall only one occasion where the accidental misspelling of a name became a cause for mirth in the department. There was no initial contact information, and George had forgotten to spell out the name. He had dictated what should have been spelled Mr. Fuques. I had typed "Mr. Fucks."

At age twenty-one, how was I to know? I'd heard that word only once when Dad was wallpapering one of the bedrooms. The wallpaper detached from the top of the wall down— probably a result of insufficient glue—and covered him from head to foot.

George also taught me an effective and easy system to monitor workflow and follow up on outstanding situations so that nothing would fall through the cracks or be overlooked. An accordion file numbered 1–31 soon became my best friend. For any written contact that required a response, I made an additional copy, anticipated a response date, and placed the copy under that date in the accordion file.

Every morning I checked and reviewed with George matters filed in the "follow up" accordion. The system was flawless. I used it during my fifty years of continuous employment, whether in an administrative support capacity or in a professional position. It has never failed me. Later in my working life, when computers became available, I swapped my "A 1–31" for the Microsoft calendar: same system, different tool, same results.

I left the tobacco company when I was twenty-four to work abroad. George and I have remained friends ever since. Even though he is in his eighties, when he calls me on the phone, he has the same robust voice and projects enthusiasm for life.

I truly believe that angels come in various forms and at certain times in our lives when we need help. Miss Clarke and George Moore were two more angels: she gave me a second chance, and his mentoring skills and encouragement upgraded my skills. Their combined efforts saved my job.

34
DAMAGE
1965

EMOTIONAL AND PSYCHOLOGICAL damage from my childhood began to re-emerge in various forms when I was twenty-two and still working for George Moore in Advertising. An unexpected challenge was eroding what little self-confidence I possessed: the simple matter of taking a break in the cafeteria, alone.

Continual disparagement by Vera about my personal appearance had rendered me insecure and emotionally fragile. Only when buffered by the company of my coworkers could I enjoy a morning or afternoon tea break.

I always tried to take my breaks with one or both of my coworkers, Christine and Rita. Sometimes, due to workload, this was not possible. I was forced to choose between not taking a break or taking my break alone. The thought of taking a break alone made my pulse race, and I would break out in a cold sweat.

Spiteful comments from my mother about my appearance had saturated my brain thoroughly, seeping through every bit of my self-esteem and destroying it. The cafeteria easily held a hundred people. Sheer torture was entering the cafeteria alone, picking up a cup of tea and digestive biscuit from the serving table, and then turning to face those hundreds of inquisitive eyes staring *at me*. What were they thinking or saying about me? My nose was too big. My teeth weren't white enough. I had bowlegs. I was too skinny. My red hair was too thick, too bright, too wild, too out of control. I was convinced that I was an unattractive insignificant person. Alone, I felt self-conscious, believing Vera was right. My many deficiencies were attracting derision, ridicule, and unwelcome attention.

I would mentally brace myself when I drew near the entrance to the cafeteria, and keep repeating: *These people look at everyone who enters the cafeteria, not just you.* The fear of ridicule by groups of sniggering employees was so overwhelming that many times I retreated and ran outside the building. My hands would shake as I lit a cigarette and inhaled deeply, hating myself for being such a coward.

On those occasions when I mustered enough courage to enter the cafeteria alone and find an empty place to sit, another problem confronted me. If I had to sit alone at a table that accommodated eight, I felt very conspicuous. When I tried to raise the cup to my lips, my hand would shake so violently that tea would splash onto the white tablecloth and my cheeks would flush with humiliation. I couldn't look to the left or right. I could only stare straight ahead and try again to raise the cup to my lips. Some days, when I could not conquer my fears and paranoia, I fled the cafeteria, leaving the teacup in its saucer and a tea stain on the tablecloth.

If I was at a table with other employees, even if we were not acquainted, my fear of judgment and criticism from people sitting at other tables would greatly diminish. I wrestled for two years with this particular demon, and gradually, I became relatively comfortable taking a break alone.

For more than twenty years, my tempestuous journey through life was plagued with obstacles that stemmed from lack of confidence. By 1985, I was struggling with depression, shyness, and a fear of attending large social gatherings, which I would mask with humor and feigned lightheartedness. I distrusted most men and suffered with jealousy occasionally when I met people whom I perceived were genuinely confident. It never entered my mind, of course, that perhaps they were playing the same survival game as me. By 1986, I was working for the office of the Arizona State Attorney General.

In the 1980s, when I was in my mid-forties, I forced myself to join Toastmasters in Phoenix, Arizona. Too nervous to sleep, I would toss and turn the night before it was my turn to speak the following morning. Unlike the others, who would stroll back and forth during their speeches, I always had to rely on notes and white-knuckle the podium.

The day arrived when, even with my notes, my brain froze. I felt like a dead tree; my mouth might have been stuffed with twigs: I couldn't speak. Several members shouted words of encouragement, but it didn't help. Mortified, I grabbed my jacket and purse and fled from the room. I rushed to the parking lot, clambered into my car, fired up the engine, and floored the accelerator. I longed to put as much distance as possible between the adult who failed at the podium and the child shaking in fear behind the wheel of the car.

None of this made sense. I could speak to a group of five hundred or more people on the benefits of mediation but could not make a short speech to a small group of forty? Perplexed, I pondered on my inadequacy for a few days until the penny finally slipped into place. Intimacy scared me. In front of small groups, the audience was too close. I could see their facial expressions and they could see mine, and I could see whether the audience appeared to be entertained or bored by my speech. Small groups were much too close for my personal level of comfort.

Public speaking was an integral part of my position with the State Attorney General's Office. It was imperative that I overcome this fear, but how? I faced more sleepless nights and came up with no solution.

The following month, pretending that I didn't belong, I slunk into the Toastmaster's meeting late and sat at a table farthest away from the podium. Some of the members saw me come in. They came up to me and assured me that my experience the previous month was not unusual; they had lived through the same embarrassment. Such admissions from people whom I suspected were far more confident than me helped calm me down, and I began to feel normal, not a pathetic misfit. I looked around and noticed four or five new faces looking slightly lost as the rest of the group mingled before the meeting began.

When one of the scheduled speakers failed to show up, a call went out from the President for someone to make an impromptu speech. My hand shot up before my fears could shoot me down. There were new members present. Perhaps they would receive some comfort knowing that sometimes people can't fulfill their public speaking mission, but there's always another day, another opportunity.

When the leader called on me as the next speaker, I calmly approached the podium, but I did not stand behind it. Instead, I strolled back and forth before the group and spoke openly about why I joined the group, my need to improve my public speaking skills, my failure at the last meeting, and my distress and embarrassment at my failure. With no notes, I spoke directly from the heart.

At the end of the meeting, the members of my Toastmaster group voted me Best Speaker of that morning. That experience taught me much about public speaking. Know your material, love what you do, speak from the heart, make eye contact, interact with your audience, and most of all, don't try to whitewash them with bullshit.

Finally, after having lived for two decades in the United States, self-confidence had finally become part of my identity. Apart from Toastmasters, I attributed this to various bosses, mostly lawyers, both male and female, who entered my life in the 1980s and 1990s and offered me opportunities for growth.

One in particular nudged me forward. The public speaking and training assignments he directed my way, and his confidence in my abilities to succeed, played a huge role in helping me move from a support into a professional position, even though, initially, I was petrified.

To the other professional angels who assisted me during the 1980s and 1990s, I am truly grateful. It made me realize that—unlike Vera—not everyone was always judging and criticizing me. I realized that many people actually liked and respected me.

That discovery melted away twenty pounds of unwarranted

and unwanted excess baggage that I'd carried around for over twenty years, heaped on me by a woman who desperately needed to be a mother but was temperamentally unfit for the role.

✑ 35
MARRIAGE AND MOTHERHOOD
1965

VERA HAD HAD A HYSTERECTOMY in her late twenties which left her unable to bear children; this was prior to her marriage and World War II. The surgery was followed by a series of radium treatments. I learned from my aunts that, as a consequence, she viewed herself as an incomplete woman.

Motherhood was something Vera desperately wanted. She longed for the societal recognition and acceptance that she was a respectable married woman with a family, and in the 1930s, having children was society's expectation for married women. I recall Vera mentioning that married women without children were often targets for vicious gossip: "Something's wrong with 'er. She doesn't 'ave any kids," women would whisper.

Longing for motherhood was yet another characteristic that I later discovered Vera and I did not share.

Wedding day, 1965, with cousin Myra

When the first man I dated told me he loved me it made me feel as though monsoon rain had drenched an arid desert. Vera's inability to show love or affection had left me emotionally parched, thirsty, longing to simply hear the words. When my future husband proposed, when I was nineteen and quite naïve, I was convinced that marriage would fix my problems. I was wrong.

On my wedding day, I walked down the aisle, my hand on my father's arm, tears trickling from my eyes. I kept blinking, trying to make them stop; the last thing I needed were trails of wet mascara sliding down my cheeks.

My father noticed, patted my hand and said, "Don't worry, love. It's just nerves."

If only that had been true.

My tears stemmed from sheer panic. Instinct told me that I was not ready to be a wife and live with the same person for two or three decades, and I was ambivalent toward motherhood. In 1965, no "good daughter" would flee the church and dump the groom. I mumbled the vows, looked forward to a couple of strong drinks at the reception, and hoped I could live with my decision.

Years later, I noticed that the only person not smiling in all but one of the wedding photographs was the bride.

Vera had asked me several times when I intended to start a family.

"Pretty soon," I would say.

I lied. She was my only role model, and the experience had taught me that her parenting skills were sadly lacking. There was a chance that I would repeat her methods of parenting and impose psychological, emotional, and physical abuse on my child. I was scared and reluctant to take the risk.

My husband, a former merchant seaman who was now working for an engineering company, was anxious to become a father. He was seven years older than me and began to pressure me to start a family. One night, as I was getting ready for bed, he asked, "Are you still on the Pill?"

"Of course. Why?"

"I've been thinking." He was sitting on the edge of the bed, watching me lotion my legs. "I'm close to thirty and I'd like to have some kids. Two, maybe three. My mum wants to be a grandmother. Your mum probably wants the same thing. I want you to stop taking the Pill."

Speechless, I froze. Scared, I nodded. I promised him that I would stop using birth control.

I never did.

Marriage for me was a monotonous routine. I worked full time as a secretary. It was a position I enjoyed, but it consumed my day from eight thirty in the morning until five in the afternoon. On my lunch hours, I shopped for fresh meats and vegetables and scrambled to consume a sandwich before I had to return to work. Upon arriving home at the end of each workday, a couple of hours were devoted to chores and pre-paring a home-cooked meal. My husband usually worked overtime several nights a week. He would rev his motorbike engine in the garage around seven in the evening, announcing that he was home and hungry. After dinner, I washed and dried the dishes, by hand. Dishwashers were available, but a luxury we could not afford. By then, it was close to nine o'clock, and I was exhausted. It was time for bed and sleep; romance was not on my calendar.

My weekends were arduous and humdrum, filled with housework, cooking, and the weekly washing of clothes in the bathtub. I scrubbed and rinsed sheets, pillowcases, towels, and clothing, and plopped the finished wash into a basket, which I hauled down the stairs, and out into the back yard. Each item was securely pegged onto a clothesline that stretched the entire length of our garden. It took two years of pinching pennies before we could buy a washer and dryer.

Our neighbors, all young couples, were similarly struggling financially, but the wives, apparently woven from different cloth, had shared with me that marriage and babies was their ultimate goal. Grappling with limited finances was all part of the program.

Drudgery was dragging me into a tedious future.

Our marital social life was similarly unremarkable. Meeting up with my husband's friends and their wives for drinks and clubbing on a Saturday night was the highlight of the week.

Jean and Reg were very much the traditional couple. Reg acted as though he was the boss, but his wife was actually in control. She was perceptive and knew which buttons to push and at precisely the right moment to coerce her husband to accomplish what she wanted.

Mike and Linda were recently married, a vivacious young couple. Mike was Irish, obvious by his soft, elfish face and natural charm. Linda was an attractive young woman with gentle features and sparkling eyes.

Maureen, Mike's sister, a bodacious blonde with a slight gap between her front teeth, was married to a quiet, steady man. Her laughter was always just seconds away. The last time I saw her, she was pregnant with her first child. Eight of us were in a bar when Maureen ordered her second and last half pint of Worthington beer for the night. When her baby arrived, I recall hearing that Saturday was the only night that child slept without waking the parents. Maureen was convinced it was the Worthington.

Bouffant hairstyles, mini-skirts, and high heels were all the rage in the 1960s. For the first year of our marriage, we did not own a car. My husband's mode of transportation and his prized possession was an Enfield motorcycle. He fussed over that bike like a mother hen hovering over her chicks.

The Enfield held no charms for me. As a passenger, I would sit behind my husband, arms clasped around his waist, frequently pelted with rain or snow in the colder months. I yearned for something with four wheels, a roof, and an efficient heater.

I would spend an hour arranging my hair, applying make-up, and generally titivating, only to shove my bouffant into a motorcycle helmet and hoist one leg over the back seat of the bike, my white thighs exposed to the world. When we arrived at our destination, a quick dive into the ladies' room was always required to rectify the damage to hair and makeup.

Come the end of the evening, after hubby had a few too many pints, the toes of my prized, suede high heels would be tar-scuffed. We would cut too close a turn on a corner, the Enfield would wobble and skid, and off the bike we'd tumble. I was never injured and didn't even snag a stocking because I always fell onto my husband who bore the brunt of the spills: mostly scratches, bruises, and torn pants. Many times, during that first year, I mourned the loss of my suede elegance but not quietly.

May the joys of two-wheel transportation remain in my past—forever.

———

The words of Peggy Lee's song "Is That All There Is?" made me wonder. Our friends lived similar lives: were they satisfied with their routines? Was I the only discontented wife?

At age twenty-three, I knew marriage was not an institution in which I thrived. I found it boring and restrictive. I also realized that I had been born without any ticking, biological clock. I did not feel the need to become a mother. In fact, motherhood would only suffocate me further. What I needed was a divorce and the perfect set of circumstances was about to unfold.

By 1967 we had been married a little over two years when my husband's employer assigned him to a project in Liverpool, Monday through Friday, and he would return home on the weekends. As time passed, the weekend visits became less frequent.

My mother-in-law expressed concern. "You need to go to Liverpool, find out what's going on," she said. "I have my suspicions. Aren't you worried?"

I didn't reveal that my sexual desire for her son had dwindled to a faint trickle, much like the amount of wine left in a glass at the end of a party. If he was carrying on with some woman, it was probably because he wasn't getting enough sex at home. How do you tell your husband or your mother-in-law that you no longer want to "jump your husband's bones?"

It was obvious that my mother-in-law expected me to drop everything, take time off work, and visit Liverpool. That was not going to happen.

I tried to reassure her. "I'm not worried, so don't you worry. As long as he doesn't bring her home and expect me to feed her, why should I care?"

She returned my attempt at humor with a frosty glare; the subject was dropped.

A few weeks later, my husband came home for the weekend. After dinner on Sunday night, I asked him, "How come you're not coming home as often?"

He mopped specks of gravy from his beard with his napkin. "This is a big project, love. It's developed problems we didn't anticipate. My job is to solve those problems and that takes time." He leaned over and patted my hand. "Be patient. It'll all work out." He winked at me. "And we can sure use the overtime, right?"

─────────

Shortly after my husband returned to Liverpool, I had a need to visit the doctor. At the conclusion of the examination, the doctor avoided my eyes as he peeled off his gloves. "I'm afraid you have *Pediculosis pubis*, commonly known as crabs."

"What?" I sat up and swung my legs over the side of the table. "I don't even know what that is!"

"Well," the doctor explained patiently, "It's a type of lice. You get them from having sex with someone who's already infected."

The word "infected" made me cringe. I felt dirty. "But that's impossible! I'm a married woman. I haven't had sex with anyone except my husband!"

In silence, the doctor looked at me and then hastily looked away. I imagined he was probably embarrassed too. He glanced back. "I'll write you a prescription. My nurse will tell you what you need to do. Don't worry, it's curable." He shook my hand and left the room.

My mother-in-law's instincts were right. Hubby was having quite the time of it with the floozies in Liverpool. When I returned home from the doctor's office, I called hubby on the phone and left a message with the receptionist for him to call me as soon as possible.

Later that evening, he called back.

I took a few deep breaths to calm myself before I picked up the phone. "I went to the doctor today."

"Oh, yeah. Are you sick?"

"I guess you could say that. I have crabs."

There was a long pause. All I could hear at the other end of the line were swift exhalations of what I presumed was ciga-rette smoke.

"Some whore gave you crabs!" I yelled. "And you passed them on to me, you son-of-a-bitch!"

"Oh, Jesus!" Another pause on the line. "Sorry."

"Is that all you have to say?"

"Well, what do you want me to say?"

"I want you to say that you're going to stop fucking around in Liverpool, return home, and work locally."

"No can do. The boss told me this morning that the project requires two or three more months."

"Well, in the meantime, can you keep it in your pants?"

"If you wanted more sex and kids," my husband shouted into the phone, "I wouldn't have to look elsewhere."

"And if you can't keep it in your pants," I shouted back,

"don't bother coming home." I was starting to tear up. "You can't believe how fucking embarrassed I was when the doctor told me what was wrong with me."

"Well, I don't have them." His tone was defiant. "Perhaps you caught them from some other bloke."

"You prick!" I screamed. "You thought your shenanigans in Liverpool would remain a secret, you fucking asshole. And no, you insulting bugger, I didn't get them from anyone but you. Do us both a favor, stay in Liverpool. I don't want to see your lying face around here." I slammed down the receiver.

Shaken, I walked into the kitchen, leaned against the sink, and let loose with tears of anger, embarrassment, and guilt. Just thinking about crabs crawling on my body made me feel like a dirty slut, even though I had acquired these unwanted guests from my husband's dirty slut. I felt guilty because I should have taken steps earlier to end the charade of our marriage.

I needed a boost. I grabbed our one and only crystal goblet and filled it half way with brandy; I downed it in seconds, but it didn't help. Then I called my mother-in-law.

"Well, you were correct. Your son gave me crabs, meaning he has been screwing around on me."

"Good gracious!" She gasped. "Well, I told you to go to Liverpool, but you refused. You didn't seem to care if your husband was cheating on you."

She was right. I had refused. I'd refused because I didn't care. I wanted out of the marriage. During the 1960s, married couples in England needed grounds for divorce: adultery, domestic battery, desertion, or other illegal acts. A dose of crabs might be helpful in a claim of adultery but, without direct evidence from the "slut," or an admission from my husband, how could I convince a judge that it was someone, other than my husband, who gave me crabs?

If I had been mature, I would have been honest about my lack of sexual desire for my husband and my lack of desire for motherhood. I tried to broach the subject once with hubby, but he disappeared into the garage, saying that he had to fix the brakes on the bike. I was a coward. I didn't prevent his departure. How do you tell your spouse without hurting his feelings that your passion for him and marriage in general had died?

What the hell did I know? I was an emotionally damaged, psychologically screwed up, twenty-three year old trying to make sense of life and longing to be free from the shackles of marriage.

Instinct told me to wait. It was only a matter of time before hubby would again betray his marriage vows.

A few months passed and I had become quite comfortable living alone with two tabby cats, puttering around the house and garden on the weekends, or visiting with girlfriends. One Saturday morning, the mail carrier delivered a letter; it was from my husband. I opened it and saw that there was no customary *Dear Glenda* greeting. It was straight to the point: "Glenda, my girlfriend is pregnant. I need you to give me a divorce."

A shiver of elation passed through me. *Yes! He needed my permission to start divorce proceedings.* Now I had what I needed: grounds for divorce, in writing.

I picked up the phone, dialed my husband's number, and insisted the receptionist find him to take the call. A minute or so passed until I heard, "Hello?"

"I received your letter this morning."

There was silence.

"If you want a divorce, you need to come home. We need to work out a settlement acceptable to a judge. Check your schedule and let me know when to expect you." I hung up, heaved a sigh of relief, wandered into the kitchen, reached for the crystal glass, and poured a generous glassful of Cabernet. This time the promise of freedom boosted my mood.

I phoned my mother and my mother-in-law to tell them the marriage was over. They sounded far more emotional at the news than I felt.

The next weekend, my husband arrived home. There was no yelling, no slamming doors, no throwing of sharp objects. We both had what we wanted: the chance for a new life moving in different directions.

It took little time to divide our limited assets and liabilities. Hubby would return to Liverpool. I would contact a divorce attorney to set things in motion, handle selling the house (a two-bedroom, one bathroom starter home), sell some of the furniture, and move the bedroom suite to my parents' home, where I would stay until I found a suitable place to live. My husband would take the stereo system as it was his sole and separate property.

The only heartbreak for me was finding homes for our two adorable tabby cats, adopted together as kittens, that were now two years old. Thankfully, I found wonderful homes for each, with children who adored animals and parents who had taught them how to respect their furry friends. I bawled my eyes out more over parting from those cats than I did parting from a husband.

The separation was cordial. I asked no questions about the other woman and the only item that caused tension between us was the refrigerator. Both of us wanted it for our mothers. I believed that my mother-in-law, widow of a Master Mariner, probably received a generous pension, and she had boarders in her three-story Victorian home. She was in a better position than my mum to buy a new refrigerator.

It turned out that she who wore the wedding ring had power over he who had knocked up another woman and provided legal grounds for divorce. The negotiation over the refrigerator was resolved. My mum became its new owner.

Two months later, my husband traveled back to Bristol to collect his stereo system and sign the divorce documents. We had equitably divided the assets and liabilities; our tabbies had moved to their new homes and were adjusting well. Our house was in escrow, and I was moving back temporarily with my parents.

Both of us were ready to start a new life. We agreed to go out for farewell drinks, dinner, and a surprisingly interesting conversation. After my husband had downed several beers followed by a couple of rum and Cokes, I learned the real story.

———

According to hubby, he had been dating his boss's daughter; a boss who thought my husband was single. Hubby would enjoy Sunday dinners at his boss's home and had ingratiated himself with the family, especially his girlfriend's young brother with whom he had developed a close relationship.

Then—*oops!*—the girlfriend's menstruation stopped, and she began to gain weight. I can only speculate that the boss demanded that my husband do the right thing. He must get a quick divorce from his wife and arrange an even quicker marriage to his daughter.

My husband bemoaned his inability to buy the girlfriend an engagement ring, due to lack of money. He rested his head in his hands. "She keeps complaining how embarrassing it is for her to be pregnant and not have an engagement ring. I told her, I just don't have the money now."

This remark rang a familiar bell in my head. When my soon-to-be former husband and I had shopped for an engagement ring in 1963, I instantly fell in love with a diamond solitaire in the setting of a partially opened rose.

I was over the moon in love with this ring. "This is it! This is the one I want."

My husband looked at the ring and then at the sales clerk. "How much is it?"

The clerk checked the tag. "£25, sir."

In the 1960s, that would have been an average price for people in our socioeconomic world.

"No, that's too much," said my fiancé. "I can't afford that. We need something closer to twenty pounds."

I felt my heart drop to my shoes; it was bleeding on my toes. He was unwilling to spend £25 for me.

The clerk showed us several rings in the £20 range, one of which I eventually selected. It cost £21 and was 18-carat gold, the setting shaped like a butterfly, with a sapphire set in platinum and two rows of tiny diamonds like wings on either side. It was attractive, but not the ring of my choice.

Perhaps I should be called a saint. I took off my engagement ring and dropped it on the table before him. "I don't need it. I won't wear it. It's not a cocktail ring—it's an engagement ring. You don't have to tell her it was mine. If it doesn't fit her, then you would need to resize it, but at least she'd have an engagement ring."

I sat back, waiting for my husband's decision. He picked up the ring and stared at it. Time ticked on. I remained silent.

He must have studied that ring for close to two minutes before returning it to me. "No, I can't do that."

I didn't ask why. I didn't care. Years later, Mum and I exchanged rings: she slid my engagement ring onto her finger, and I rejoiced in receiving a beautiful aquamarine stone set in 18-carat gold that fit me perfectly.

I struggled, silently resentful over that ring for a long time. My future husband had shown me that he was cheap. Frugal I understood, but not cheap. For me, an engagement ring was something sacred; he knew that but ignored my feelings.

A few months after we were married, one evening around seven o'clock hubby rolled his motorcycle into our driveway, revved the engine a couple of times, and then switched it off.

Carrying a beer for him, I had gone outside to greet him when I noticed two new bike accessories. "Is that a new mirror on the handle-bars?"

My husband beamed. "Yeah, isn't it great?

"Why do you need it?"

"Well, it helps me check traffic behind me. Don't wanna get into an accident, right?"

"What was wrong with the one you had?"

"Oh, it was okay, but this is bigger. I've had my eye on it for several months."

"How much did it cost?"

My husband removed his helmet, looked at me, and frowned. "What does that have to do with anything? It's a safety feature."

I nodded. "You've had this bike for over four years. I don't remember you getting into an accident without...." I pointed at the new mirror. "Without that safety feature. How much did it cost?"

He sighed. "If you must know, a couple of quid."

"What about that little gizmo by the muffler? What does that do?"

Hubby launched into a lengthy, technical explanation, which I didn't understand and, frankly, didn't care about.

"How much did that cost?"

"Jesus, what is it with you. How much does it cost? I feel like I'm being quizzed by a solicitor."

I persisted. "How much did it cost?"

"If you must know, probably about the same as the mirror. A couple of quid. Satisfied?" He pushed past me into the house. "I hope dinner's nearly ready. I'm starving."

A couple of quid times two equaled four pounds! It appeared that trinkets for the Enfield were more important than an engagement ring for the fiancée.

In December of that year, my husband asked me what I wanted for Christmas. I told him about a plain, 18-carat gold ring I'd seen in the shape of a buckle. Come Christmas morning, when I opened his gift, I found a signet ring.

I couldn't believe it. "What happened to the buckle ring?"

"Oh, you don't want that," my husband said. "Buckle rings are for blokes, not married women. The signet ring is more appropriate."

The signet ring went missing several months later. Probably

I lost it while fumbling through thick advertising files at work. My husband was furious; he thought I'd lost it on purpose. Not so, but I do admit that the ring meant nothing to me. It's possible that karma played a role in its disappearance.

———

My husband's betrayal had other interesting facets. The young brother of my husband's girlfriend turned out to be her son, yet another liaison without marriage that bore fruit. I knew from experience that condoms were definitely available in the 1960s. My husband was going to adopt her child and welcome his child into the world in a couple of months. He said he wanted children, and soon he would have two.

No, I was not a saint when I offered him my engagement ring for his girlfriend. I was offering him something that meant nothing to me.

⨋ 36
DAD'S OBSESSION
1969

A DECADE HAD PASSED since my parents took up dancing as a hobby. I had graduated from high school, joined the work force, left home, became engaged at nineteen, was married at twenty-one, and returned home at twenty-four, separated from my husband and awaiting final divorce documents.

Any day, I expected the mail carrier to slide an envelope containing these long-awaited legal papers through the letterbox. I planned to retrieve the envelope from the front door mat, wave it above my head, and shout: "I'm free!" They would be my passport to a new life and a new job in a new country, and I was excited at the prospect.

When Dad was not working, my parents continued to dance twice a week, throughout the ongoing changes in my personal life. Despite my distractions, I had noticed that Dad's conversations mostly revolved around ballroom dancing.

It seemed to me that his passion for dancing had gradually transformed into an obsession. Dad's earlier dream of attending college on a scholarship to earn a degree in accounting, which had been thwarted by his miserly father, had been replaced with a new dream: an opportunity to learn, excel, and perform as a dancer. The wheel of life had turned, this time in Dad's favor; now the arrow-like needle was pointing to entertainment. Dad was delighted that he picked up dance steps as fast as pigeons snatched up breadcrumbs in Trafalgar Square. And this from a man, who, according to Vera, had once thought "dancing was the devil's work."

As I observed them, it seemed that when it came to dancing, Dad was unstoppable while Vera was still neurotic.

One evening Dad and I were chatting in the living room. Vera was in the kitchen when he told me, "A dance class is starting next week in the hall up the street, you know, for old time and modern. Tuesday and Thursday nights. What do you think of that?"

"I think that's great." I was pleased to learn there was another option for my middle-aged parents to get their dance fix without the need for the hour long trip to and from Knowle by bus.

I could hear the mounting enthusiasm in Dad's voice. "Only five minutes away from our house. Do you know what that means? It means if I'm not working, me and your Mum can dance two or three times a week without traveling to Knowle!"

"Oh! That sounds great. What does Mum think about it?"

Dad frowned. "You know your mother. She likes dancing but seems to prefer to sit on the sidelines and watch others. Me, I like to get in there and learn. Here, let me show you what we learned last week."

Dad pulled me from my chair, rested his left hand on my waist, clasped my right hand in his, and we were off.

"Now, see. This is how it goes. Coming out of the turn, step back left, right, left, and then turn to right, step once and twirl."

I had never seen Dad so animated. His eyes sparkled, reflecting a man half his age.

"Dinner's nearly ready," Vera called from the kitchen.

"We're coming," I said. "Dad's showing me some new dance steps."

"Alf, you're always so ready to show off. Not everyone is interested, you know."

Dad grinned and winked at me. "Glenda's interested, aren't you?"

"Of course I am. I love to dance, and I'm happy that you two have found an interest that you can share."

"Sit down both of you," said Vera. "I'm ready to serve."

I think we had shepherd's pie that night, one of my favorites.

Vera scoffed and chided Dad for showing off, but I could sense there was pride behind her words. For a while, Dad's passion for dancing matched Vera's passion for designing and sewing the prettiest dresses, which made for a compatible twosome. Unfortunately, Vera could not match Dad's ferocious need to learn and, even more importantly, to perform.

According to Dad, she refused to try. This infuriated him. He said, "What would happen if Stanley Matthews was ready to score a goal at a football match, but nobody passed him the bloody ball? I can't dance by myself!"

———

It was at this point that Mrs. H. entered the picture. My parents' twirls on the dance floor would never again be the same.

In her early fifties, Mrs. H. had devoted the time and resources necessary to look good. Slender but curvy, she was a blonde (with a bit of artifice and assistance) and was known locally as an experienced dancer in old time and modern.

Little time passed before her name cropped up over dinner. "I think Mrs. H. has her eye on you," Vera said.

Dad glanced across the table, mildly curious. "You do? Can't say I've noticed."

She sniffed. "You're always eager to dance with her."

Dad sighed, probably exasperated. "Vera, I'm always eager to dance with anyone who wants to dance. I'd dance with you, but you keep refusing, so—"

I noticed Vera's posture stiffen.

"Well, I'm just saying, I would like it if you wouldn't dance with her so much."

"Right y'are." Dad left the table and headed for his chair and the evening paper.

Sometimes, I would drop in at the local dance. Several older gentlemen whose wives did not dance were delighted to escort a young woman around the floor. I was happy to oblige, and it gave me a chance to observe this person of interest who had entered their lives.

Mrs. H. was a good dancer with a cordial personality. I watched her partner Dad, teaching him new steps and routines. She recognized Dad's burning desire to learn and she was a methodical teacher. Dad was overjoyed; he had his own personal mentor.

At home one night, he pestered me with questions. "Did you see the last dance, the one where I danced with Mrs. H.?"

I was peeling vegetables but stopped and thought for a minute. "Yes, I think so. Why?"

"I have it down.' Dad started demonstrating the steps with precision that suggested he was ready to apply for a position with the Royal Ballet. "I know the steps. I know the routines. I just have to practice."

I looked over at him and grinned. "Okay."

His enthusiasm was irrepressible. "Did you see me ask your mother to dance?"

I hesitated, sensing a land mine. Was Dad using me to make a point with Vera? "Sorry. I can't recall."

"Well, she refused." Dad's punched the back of his chair. He turned and stared out the window, frowning.

"She did? Okay, so…." I kept peeling spuds as he walked into the dining room, snatched the paper from the table, and headed for the living room, closing the door behind him.

I had witnessed Vera's reluctance to dance, but preferred to remain neutral. Vera's lack of self-confidence and fear of failure remained. Dad would try to teach her at home but, as patience was not his forte, they often ended up in an argument.

As an adult observing their current struggles, I was relieved to be out of the loop. There was no way that Vera could blame me for any animosity between her and my father over dancing.

―――――

My divorce became final in July 1969, and I left England to work abroad. Later the following year, during my six-week vacation, I returned home for a two-week visit.

One night, over dinner, Vera dropped a bombshell. "Your Dad and I are no longer dancing."

I paused, a slice of roast chicken balanced on my fork, halfway to my mouth. I stared at her. "Really? Why?"

She stabbed angrily at a piece of broccoli. "Why? Ask your father."

I finished eating the bite of chicken, then turned to Dad. "What's going on here? Why are you and Mum no longer dancing? I don't get it. You love dancing."

Busy slicing the vegetables on his plate, Dad winked at me before answering.

"Not a clue. Ask your mother." He captured a cauliflower floret on his fork and put it in his mouth.

Vera set her knife and fork across her plate, placed both hands on the table, and leaned in, staring at my dad. "You know bloody well why we're not dancing any more. It's that hussy of yours, Mrs. H."

Convinced she had made her point and that was all that mattered, Vera picked up her knife and fork and continued to pick at her food.

Dad eased back in his chair and shook his head. "Oh, come on, you know that's not true. We're not dancing because you got your knickers in a twist, thinking that Mrs. H. fancied me." After another sly wink in my direction, Dad reached for his glass of water and took a sip.

I looked up at the sudden loud clattering of cutlery. Vera was pushed back against her chair, arms folded, face flushed. "Well, she kept asking you to dance, didn't she? There were other men in the room, but she always came up to you."

Vera wagged a finger at Dad. "Knowing that you were married and I was sitting right there beside you! That hussy always came up to you. And you always got up and danced with her. You egged her on. I suppose you fancied her over me.

I'm disgusted at your behavior, and I'll never enter that dance hall again."

She picked up her knife and fork and jabbed at the food on her plate.

Dad sighed. "I wanted to learn new dances. You obviously weren't interested. Mrs. H. needed a partner, and, frankly, I'm a good dancer. Of course she likes to dance with me." He sliced through the chicken breast on his plate, but I didn't miss the sly twinkle in his eye.

Vera's voice became louder. "If she needed a partner, why didn't she bring her husband along?"

Dad paused between bites. "Maybe because her husband isn't as interested in dancing as she is?"

"Oh, that's right. You have an explanation for everything, don't you?" Vera slammed the cutlery onto her plate. Tears brimming, she tossed aside her napkin, rose from the table, and stormed out of the room.

Perturbed, I turned to Dad. "What the hell is going on here?" I asked. "Why is she so upset?"

Dad sighed and shook his head. "It's your mother's fault. We've been dancing for years. I learn new dances. I try to teach your mother, but she's not interested. Mrs. H. needed a partner, and I was happy for the practice. I'm not interested in sitting and watching others, I want to get out there, and show people what I can do."

I sat back, folded my arms, and assumed a judicial expression. "Hmm.... Was there any hanky-panky going on between you and Mrs. H.?'

Dad chuckled. "Course not, but I'm letting your mother think that perhaps there was an attraction. Gotta keep her fired up."

Concerned, I leaned closer to my dad. "Why? You're just

creating a problem."

"Stay out of it, Glenda." His tone was sharp. "I know what I'm doing. Your Mum and me, well, we have a sort of ritual. I dig at her and she needles me. Now it's time for me to dig at her for her jealous nature—and I think I'm gliding into the final dance of the night."

At an anniversary celebration, 1988
Vera, Uncle Jack, Uncle Gordon (in bow tie),
Aunt Molly, and Uncle Len

37

ANGER
1973

M Y ANGER HAD BEEN IN SIMMER MODE for most of my life. It lurked just beneath the surface, like a circling shark, ready and waiting to lunge. I was certain the anger stemmed from my childhood. Feelings of abandonment by my biological mother had helped create pockets of sadness in my heart. Adding to that was an adoptive mother whose sensibilities were foreign to mine and who was physically and verbally abusive—so much so that I had threatened to kill her. That was who I was; that was who I saw when I looked in the mirror.

I had recently immigrated to the United States of America but could not shake off the anger. It had traveled with me, locked inside the personal luggage of my heart.

I never understood why I felt unloved by my adoptive mother. At night, alone in my room, only my teddy bear and the family cat knew of my heartache. I would bury my head under the sheets and blankets so that my parents, close by in the next room, could not hear me sobbing. I was convinced I must be to blame for how my mother treated me, but how or why, I never understood and the answers never came.

Who was this woman I had to call Mum?

In my teens, my sadness had morphed into defiance, and the pent-up anger gathered throughout childhood. It's not unusual for a teenager to be angry and rebellious, but I knew the origin of my anger. Unlike other teenagers, I was scared that it would not fade with time, and my fears became reality. The anger remained. For many years, its force propelled me forward and further away from Vera, as I tried to escape the cries of sorrow from within.

After that one and final, nearly violent confrontation with Vera, where my anger had grown cold and focused, I was shocked to realize that I was capable of harming someone. I feared and dreaded the consequences if my anger was ever unleashed and allowed full throttle.

By the time I reached my thirties, my suppressed anger had swelled, like an ocean gathering waves for a tsunami. I hated Vera, I felt guilty for hating Vera, and I hated myself. I was a complete emotional and psychological mess.

After I arrived in Phoenix in 1973 and had landed my first job as a legal secretary, for the first two months I spent every weekend in bed, buried under the covers, sleeping, and rarely eating. My energy was so low it was almost nonexistent. I could get through the workweek, but not the weekends. Many days, a black cloud would seem to enfold me, sapping any enthusiasm I had for life. It was a constant battle, fighting the demons of darkness while trying to appear normal to coworkers and neighbors as I went about my daily routine. I thanked God for my cat Monster. Somehow, he understood my pain, curled up beside me, and gave me warmth and unconditional love, something I needed but never received from my family.

Thus far, I had managed to diffuse potential explosions. I would walk away from someone who grated on my nerves, or cajole any perceived nitwit with a "plastic smile and vanilla words." Bluntly put, if the nitwit was my employer, I would need to kiss ass.

That was the rule. Ass-kissing was not only distasteful but degrading. I had done more than enough of that as a child, trying to win Vera's love and approval. I was not willing to grovel further—not for anything. However, in the 1970s ass-kissing for was a crucial part of economic survival for secretaries working in the legal field.

I ignored that rule twice, and twice I found myself fired and out on the street.

The first time, I was allegedly "rude to an attorney's wife" when she called him at the office. I had never met the woman but understood their marriage was a recent one. She would call three or four times a day. I found it interesting that she never called her husband on his private line. I always wondered about that. Did she even know he had a private line? Did he not want to be bothered at work with domestic chatter? Perhaps that's why her calls were bounced over to me.

My boss beckoned me into his office. "I've been informed by my associate that on several occasions you have been rude to his wife when she's called. We can't have that around here. I'm letting you go." After three months on the job, I was again unemployed.

I didn't even remember the woman. *Was I curt with her?* If faced with a ton of work and deadlines, very possibly I was. Most offices expected professional conduct from their employees and that they should abstain from making or receiving personal calls on the job, unless it was an emergency. It was a fair policy and one that I've always followed. Unfortunately, there was one rule for the employees and a different rule for the employers' families and friends.

The shark would begin to circle, tail thrashing. Not only did I have to suck up to the attorneys but also to their families. It was evident that employees were not considered equal to wives, children, friends, and relatives. That alone rankled.

Years later, I wondered whether my reaction to such employers was the product of my background and a lack of self-esteem. I had not felt loved or deemed important by Vera who, I believe, considered me competition for Dad's love and affection. Perhaps underneath, I was jealous that the attorney, unlike me, had a family who loved him. I was someone who moved forward and rarely looked back; I never took the time to evaluate my feelings and actions—perhaps I should have.

———

The second time I became involuntarily unemployed was because of a coffee dispute. I had refused to pour a cup of coffee for an attorney who happened to be standing next to the coffee pot, someone who had just loaded me with a stack of work.

"Glenda, could you please get me a cup of coffee?"

I stopped typing, mystified, and stared up at him. "Oh? You're standing right next to the coffee pot. It'd probably be faster if you poured your own."

Unlike my experience in San Francisco where, more often than not, attorneys poured their own coffee, I didn't realize that my employers in Phoenix had included the function of waitress within the job description of legal secretary. This was perplexing. Apparently, it was more important for the attorney that I pour him a cup of coffee than get to work, typing up voluminous interrogatory answers to meet a critical deadline.

I was summoned to the inner sanctum later that day, and once again my employment was terminated. Seated behind a massive mahogany desk that was piled high with case files, the senior partner puffed on a cigarette. "Glenda," he said. "I'm sorry but I have to let you go."

Seeing the blank expression on my face, he repeated, "I have to let you go. You know, terminate your services with my office."

I stared at him and frowned. "I'm being terminated? What on earth for?"

Coughing a little, he stubbed out his cigarette, stood, walked around to the front of his desk, and leaned back. "I've, well.... A complaint was brought to me that you were rude to my junior partner."

"Rude? How?"

"Well, let's say that... um... you refused to pour him a cup of coffee. Is that correct?"

Flabbergasted, I responded. "Really, from where I stand, I think I'm being terminated because your junior partner is inconsiderate to staff. He had just loaded me up with work, most of which had deadlines. He was the one standing next to the coffee pot—so why on earth should I stop working, get up, cross the room, and pour him a cup of coffee when it was quicker for him to pour his own?"

The senior partner smiled and nodded. "So you admit it?"

I took a deep breath to calm myself. "I admit only that your junior partner has issues when it comes to consideration of staff."

It appeared that my reasoning, interpreted as an admission of guilt, landed on ears attuned to the rhythm of a bygone era, unwilling or unable to evolve.

The battle, however, was not over. To be fair, the senior partner who had hired me was a nice older gentleman. He treated his secretary with respect; she was fully indoctrinated and willingly kissed the ring. The junior partner, all five foot seven inches of him, was a pompous Melvin Belli-wannabe.

"During the time I've worked for this firm, have you had problems with my work performance?" I asked.

"No, not at all," the senior partner said. "You're very efficient."

"In that case I believe I'm due severance pay."

He stepped away from his desk and wandered over to the window, extracting another cigarette from his pack. Turning to face me, he pulled out his lighter, lit the cigarette, and inhaled, then tapped the lighter against the window ledge. "We don't normally give severance pay."

"And I don't normally get fired because I refuse to provide waitress service to a junior partner in a law firm," I said in response.

I'd obviously hit a nerve. He glared at me for a moment, but pursed his lips and paced across his office for a moment.

I said nothing further: I had lobbed the ball over the net and was waiting.

He stopped and faced me. "Although you've been with us for only about six months, I'm willing to give you two weeks' severance pay. I think that's generous."

There's a time to fight and a time to fold. I considered the reason for my termination as frivolous, but two weeks' severance pay was an acceptable financial cushion. I would have enough money to pay my bills and, in two weeks, I would have secured another position.

During the 1970s apparently a sense of entitlement was typical of many employers. Secretaries were expected to pick up dry cleaning or gifts for the wife or kids and run numerous other errands for the boss or his wife on the lunch hour. Performing chores for my employer on my unpaid lunch hour—my time—did not sit well with me. Had I stepped back in time to the nineteenth century?

Thirty years later, I would occasionally watch certain TV reality shows. The twenty-first century has introduced the position of Personal Assistant. This individual is called upon to do anything and everything for the employer, his or her kids, the family, and their friends. Apart from certain TV reality shows, another example was the movie *The Devil Wears Prada*. I understand the need for such employees in today's society, but I wonder whether employers take advantage of these employees as they did in previous decades. A personal assistant, always accessible to the boss regardless of the day or hour, is today's extended version of a secretary. Unlike secretaries, many personal assistants receive generous salaries but they remain well-paid servants. Studies have shown that one of the most stressful positions in the workforce is a secretary, or, in today's vernacular, personal assistant.

When I was forced to interact with inconsiderate, demanding employers, there was an instant clash of wills. On some level, I must have viewed them as members of Vera's army. The shark would again rear up out of the water, ready to lunge. I was snapping back at employers when they made me feel as worthless as a cigar butt ground into the sidewalk. The fragile grip I had maintained on my temper was slipping. I needed help.

38
THERAPY
1975

MY DEFENSE MECHANISMS needed a reality check —and soon. I had mulled over the thought of professional help for several years, but always decided against it. I was reluctant to let someone else wander around in my head.

However, my predicament and my problems were not something I felt comfortable discussing with a neighbor while I lounged around the pool on the weekends. I finally succumbed and sought help from a psychiatrist.

I made an appointment at a local mental health clinic. I knew nothing about the doctor, other than my health insurance program covered his services.

The day of my appointment arrived. I had scheduled a vacation day from work because I didn't know how I was going to react to psychoanalysis. Would I burst into tears? I hated to cry, especially in front of others. Would I become angry? I hated to lose control in front of others about anything. Would I be able to drive home safely? I didn't know.

I was nervous at the thought of exposing myself to a

stranger but at the same time, hopeful that I might receive new tools to shore up the weaknesses in my defenses. I was naïve about how psychotherapy worked.

My appointment was at eleven in the morning. That day I wore a navy and white pinstriped shirtdress with full skirt, navy blue sandals, and silver hoop earrings, and I carried a scarlet red purse.

At 11:05, the receptionist showed me into the doctor's office.

A tall, thin man—probably in his mid-thirties—was standing behind a large, grey metal desk by a black metal bookcase. He had a receding hairline, angular features, and a haughty demeanor, and he peered at me over half-spectacles. He beckoned me to sit in the chair by his desk.

I sat and rested my handbag on my lap. There was silence. His back was turned away from me as he scanned the shelves. He selected a book at random and began flipping through the pages. I was becoming uncomfortable. Was he ever going to introduce himself? Was I supposed to introduce myself to him? Seconds that felt like hours ticked by.

I was feeling stressed. I needed a cigarette. I spotted an ashtray on the credenza behind his desk, about three feet from where he was standing.

I cleared my throat. "Excuse me. May I have the ashtray, please?" I gestured toward the credenza.

"Hmm... an ashtray?"

"Yes, please."

"Hmm...," he repeated as he handed me the ashtray. "Do you always get what you want when you ask for it?"

All possible words had frozen on my tongue. What was he getting at? I felt under attack: the shark's fin was breaking the surface of the water. Words returned and I snapped, "I rarely get what I want, but ashtrays don't usually fall into that category." I fumbled in my purse, found a lighter, my hand shaking as I lit the cigarette. I was dumbfounded: my only comfort in this clinical situation was tobacco. *How totally absurd.*

Closing the book and returning it to the shelf, the psychiatrist stepped away from the bookcase, leaned against his desk, and chewed on one earpiece of his glasses, studying me as if I was a microbe in a laboratory.

"Are you always this acerbic?" he asked.

I did not know the definition of "acerbic" which made me feel foolish. My hackles rose up like quills on a porcupine. "Are you always this rude?" I asked.

Lowering himself into the high-backed, black leather desk chair he asked, "Rude? You think I've been rude?"

"Yes, I do."

"And why is that?"

Is this guy playing some sort of game? I thought. *I've come to his office for help. Why is he giving me the third degree?*

"You've completely ignored me since I entered your office."

His eyes held mine as he put his elbows on the desk. His fingertips met in a neat arch over the desk blotter, and he pursed his lips. "That's a problem for you?"

"Yes, it is."

"How so?"

"At the very least, I expect a doctor to introduce himself. We had an appointment, remember? You've ignored me since I arrived. I call that rude."

"Okay. So would you say that you need a lot of attention?"

Stunned, I stared back at him. Was this guy for real? A conversation with him was like a game of tennis, but language had replaced the ball.

I felt tears sting my eyes; I stubbed out the cigarette in the ashtray. What was I thinking? Why would I share my pain with a stranger, even a psychiatrist? I was stupid to think that an outsider could help me. I was not up for emotional tennis.

It was time to leave. I stood, picked up my purse and brushed down my skirt. I was done: poached, sautéed, grilled, and roasted.

Facing the psychiatrist, I let loose. "I came to you seeking help. You've offered me nothing." My feelings of insecurity were building. "You've made me feel anxious and angry through your idiotic questions. It's obvious you don't even give a shit why I came here today." Tears threatened to spill onto my cheeks. "I should have known—how stupid of me. I can't rely on people like you for help. Despite your paper credentials, you're a first-class asshole."

As I turned to leave, the psychiatrist started up and out of his chair, "Well, well now," he was trying to say. "Just a minute...."

His protestations did nothing to deter my exit. As I slammed the door behind me, I knew I should have followed my instincts: find a way to work out my anger issues on my own. Later I would read that this is the pattern of many adopted children who have had less than successful experiences. We trust no one but ourselves. Sadly, I left with less than when I arrived.

39
PREPARING FOR MY FUTURE
1976–1986

I WAS DISAPPOINTED AND CONFUSED at the outcome of my meeting with the psychiatrist, but pushed aside my feelings and forged ahead. What other option did I have? Maybe I could have made an appointment with another psychiatrist, but my level of trust with this profession was low. Therefore I thought it best to concentrate on finding a more interesting position and compatible working environment. I could get lucky and the memory of the psychiatrist would vanish into a black hole.

The next decade bombarded me with valuable on-the-job training from three separate employers: an architect, a hospital, and a senior partner of a law firm that practiced "the dance of domestic relations." Thankfully, there was minimal drama in my personal life. In actuality I had no time for a personal life; I was always working.

The architectural field was going through a rough economic patch in the mid-1970s. To salvage his business, my boss sought architectural projects abroad. This entailed frequent travel. In his absence, his wife who was an interior designer and whose business had folded during the economic downturn, temporarily assumed running the company. The firm had few local projects so most of her time was devoted to the financial aspect of the company and keeping the bill collectors at bay. The change in circumstances considerably altered my duties and position. Instead of functioning as an executive administrative assistant to the president of a successful architectural firm and always kept in the loop, I now functioned merely as a secretary, which included regular coffee runs. I was bored.

Some employers continued to expect the help to perform personal chores, and my new temporary boss was a member of this group. When she asked me more than once to pick up her dry cleaning on my lunch hour, I decided it was time to go. I had the time, but not the inclination. The firm now needed a basic secretary, not an executive administrative assistant. I handed in my resignation a few weeks later.

The hospital administrator and senior law partner for whom I subsequently worked, never asked me to run personal errands for them on my lunch hour or even bring them coffee, although I did so willingly. In fact, they often brought *me* coffee when they saw that I was bogged down with work. What a difference that was. Perhaps there were other factors in play at the architectural firm.

———

During those ten years while I was expanding my skills and working my butt off, I was always able to meet my basic needs. I had a cozy apartment, a car that was in good condition, money to pay my bills, friends, and occasionally an interesting male would wander into my world. Was I happy? Since I didn't know how "happy" felt, I had no answer. I knew was that I was treading water, surviving, going through the motions of a life that lacked passion and purpose.

Little did I realize that those on-the-job skills would be invaluable in my future and picking up someone's dry cleaning during my lunch hour would merely be an irritating memory.

I became an expert in multitasking and preplanning; I excelled in organizational skills. I was always an industrious employee who had a good work ethic and would produce an excellent work product. I could also anticipate and meet the needs of the boss in a timely fashion. I maintained the agenda and minutes of monthly board meetings that I attended; I always made myself available when needed.

I think that I poured myself into my work because it validated my need to feel valued and appreciated. I was no longer the unwanted and unloved bastard.

In May of 1986, the door to new beginnings cracked open. I stepped inside, anticipating challenges, and ultimate success.

An advertisement in the local Phoenix newspaper encouraged people interested in learning mediation techniques to take a forty-hour class, free of charge, with the Civil Rights Division of the Arizona State Attorney General's Office. The basic concept of mediation was for both parties to meet with a neutral third party, discuss their issues, and work together to reach an amicable resolution. I signed up immediately.

For the next five months after work, I volunteered with the South Phoenix Justice Court every Monday night to mediate neighborhood disputes, small claims, and truancy issues: anything and everything that came before a judge who determined it would be appropriate for mediation.

The Civil Rights Chief Counsel had persuaded the State Attorney General to start a conflict resolution program within the Division. In October of that year, the Division advertised for a mediation coordinator. I applied, was interviewed, and several weeks later I was offered the position, which I accepted. After three years of working with lawyers and domestic relations clients going through a divorce, the idea of mediating instead of "cock fighting" a negotiated agreement was appealing.

My days were consumed with jostling priorities: phone mediations, interviewing people from the community who wanted to be trained as mediators, and attending training sessions. I also coordinated volunteers to mediate at numerous justice courts in the mornings, afternoons and evenings, and also created and wrote a monthly newsletter. My workweek was more than fifty hours and, for the first eighteen months, I worked on a contract. If I wanted to be paid, I worked all holidays.

My dedication paid off. In February 1988, the agency created a full-time position within the conflict resolution section. I competed and was hired for the position and became a permanent civil servant with health insurance benefits and participation in a retirement program. Later that year, I received a promotion to project manager. This position included supervising six staff members and assuming the training duties and public speaking engagements throughout Maricopa County.

I had been in survivor mode since early childhood, and that attitude was ingrained in my brain when I immigrated to America. Now it was time for me to thrive and excel. I'd gambled. I tossed the dice, scored a double-six, and finally landed a professional position that had purpose and ignited my passion for service. This was not work. This was something that absorbed every pore, every waking moment—and I loved it. And, that was just the beginning.

The Author, 1985

✐ 40
FAREWELL HEAT
1980

IN JANUARY 1990, at age forty-seven, after seventeen years of oppressive Phoenix summers, I leapt at the chance to pioneer a satellite civil rights office for the Arizona State Attorney General in Flagstaff. I would be investigating discrimination complaints in employment, housing, and public accommodations. I would also be responsible for establishing and managing a mediation program.

The Flagstaff compliance officer at the time, Vincent, spent three days a week in northern Arizona, taking complaints from local employees, and beginning the groundwork for a mediation program. When his wife received a promotion and a substantial increase in pay, their plan to relocate to Flagstaff was no longer feasible. I knew that my boss wanted someone full time in northern Arizona, so I asked him to consider me for the position.

It was at the end of a busy week and we were sitting in his office reviewing the status of each project. The topic of Flagstaff came up. "I've been thinking," I told him. "You know that I'm a certified paralegal through the Arizona State University program. I'm familiar with the legal system. I've worked in conflict resolution for four years, two of which were in management. I think I'm a perfect fit. All I need is a crash course in investigative techniques combined with studying the pertinent discrimination statutes—I could study at home on the weekends if necessary. What do you think?"

My boss raised his eyebrows and lowered his reading glasses. "You'd be willing to relocate to Flagstaff?"

"Absolutely. I could move to Flagstaff, and Vincent could take over my project manager position in Phoenix. He's a trained mediator and has management experience." I studied my boss's eyes; my proposal had lit a spark of interest.

"Let me think about it. I'll speak with Vincent and get back to you."

The following week the decision was announced: it was a done deal. Vincent and I were going to switch jobs. I would receive intensive training on discrimination statues and investigative techniques from the lead attorney in the office. This would be followed by meetings three days a week for a month in Flagstaff with Vince, who was an experienced investigator. He would gradually transition his files to me, and I would quiz the hell out of him on the best ways to investigate a variety of complaints.

Some of my coworkers were less than enthusiastic about my good fortune, even though none of them wanted to or could move their families to Flagstaff. I heard through the grapevine there were rumblings of discontent from other investigators: I got the job because I was the boss's favorite, that I was overpaid, and that I didn't deserve a Level Three investigator classification. All such complaints rolled off my back. Through hard work and long hours, I had earned this opportunity.

One miffed coworker claimed he was allergic to cigarette smoke. This was during a time when employees could smoke in the office. After hearing that I was again being promoted and also moving to the Flagstaff office, he spent twenty minutes standing in my "smoking" office telling me that smoke from my office had affected his breathing. I guess standing in a smoking office for twenty minutes, complaining about me smoking, didn't bother his respiratory system. He never once coughed.

I was determined to become an excellent investigator. My boss had put his faith in me to accomplish what he needed in northern Arizona, and conducting thorough investigations and reaching the correct conclusion seemed to come naturally: I was, as my female supervisor once commented, an "intuitive investigator."

By the end of 1993, I had reached my goal. The mediation program in Flagstaff was flourishing; the number of discrimination cases investigated and resolved was the highest throughout the entire Civil Rights Division that also encompassed Phoenix, Tucson and Flagstaff. I suppose the Arizona State Attorney General agreed: he pronounced me Investigator of the Year for 1993.

When it came time to move to Flagstaff, I was anticipating escape from the desert heat and embracing country living. For me, this was like sipping a fine wine and way beyond my budget.

In early March 1990, after selling my Phoenix home, I bought a house in Mountainaire, a small community six miles south of Flagstaff in the midst of the Coconino pine forest. Though rather small, this one-story house, located in a cul-de-sac at the edge of the forest, was perfect for me. A spacious master bedroom in the front offered an expansive view of towering pines, and there was a smaller bedroom and bath-room in the back. An adequate kitchen overlooked a large back yard where an unexpected bonus was a colossal doghouse, stuffed with clean straw, ideal for my fur kids, Molly the greyhound and Lady the Australian Shepherd.

My new home's creamy-colored interior walls and nutmeg-colored carpeting throughout complimented my autumn tone furnishings. Three large double-paned windows in the living area offered a cozy environment during the winter plus hours of natural light during the summer. There I could indulge my passion for painting wild life and Indian designs on ceramic pottery. On the west side of the living room, set securely on a crescent of red brick, was a sturdy black, wood-burning stove. It generated so much heat during the winter months that its warmth reached all the way to the back bathroom.

After two weeks of packing, discarding, and donating items gathered during the five years I'd lived in Phoenix, I backed my Honda hatchback out of my driveway one last time. The dogs were secure in the back seat, and my cat Monster was curled up on the passenger seat, and we followed the moving van, bound for cooler temperatures, fresh air, and country living.

By mid-afternoon, gray skies promising snow greeted our arrival in Mountainaire. I was impressed at how skillfully the movers executed several sharp turns before the van slowly climbed the steep path leading to my new mountain home.

Eager to escape their confinement, my dogs quickly found the back yard and started exploring and anointing to make it their own. They finally settled in their doghouse for a nap, leaving me free to supervise the movers. After three hours of lugging furniture and a great many boxes into the house, the movers wished me luck and left.

Anxious for order, I immediately started to unpack boxes, hang pictures, and arrange my clothes in the closets. However, I was ill prepared for the higher altitude that quickly sapped my energy. After a couple of hours, I reluctantly accepted defeat. The rest would have to wait until tomorrow.

Now dusk, the house was cold. I shivered as I switched on an assortment of lamps, realizing that it was time for an initiation into lighting the wood-burning stove. Shredding newspaper into loose balls, I tossed them into the stove and covered them with kindling. After several frustrating attempts, the kindling finally ignited, and I quickly fed the hungry flames with the cedar wood kindly donated by the previous owners. Soon, the house was warm and cozy. Exhausted, but pleased with my efforts, I called the dogs into the house, fed them, took a shower, and went to bed.

The next morning, I awoke early and chilled. Cold, gray ashes filled the wood burning stove, and my front yard was buried under three feet of snow. Over the next two months, my transition to living comfortably amidst snow and slush was swift. Thanks to the ongoing support from my new neighbors, I soon mastered the art of keeping the wood stove burning safely and continuously and learned to maneuver my car through Mountainaire's steep, irregular slopes leading to my home.

Spring arrived in early May, resplendent with wild flowers scattering the landscape. Before I left for work, I would enjoy the peace and quiet of hourly, early morning jogs through the forest with seven dogs. Many of my neighbors had to work more than one job to survive due to the low salaries in Flagstaff. Time was precious, especially if they also had children, so walking the dog for an hour every morning before work was unrealistic. Molly and Lady trotted behind me as I dashed across the street and into the forest and then gathered speed. Pathetic barks and whines could be heard from a Doberman, a cocker spaniel, two Béarnaise mountain dogs, and one golden retriever.

I was fortunate and grateful that my state salary covered my needs. I asked the five neighbors who owned the dogs, begging for freedom, whether they would let me take their fur companions on my hourly run through the forest, at least Monday through Friday. All were delighted that their dogs would get a chance to socialize with other dogs and an hour's exercise every morning. Henceforth I was dubbed the "dog lady." I also doggie sat occasionally on weekends when the owners were out of town. It's was amazing how fast all five dogs learned that doggie door.

During the winter of 1991, a devastating snowstorm flattened many of the wooden fences that surrounded our yards. After inching along I-17, occasionally grinding the gears of my Honda Hatchback and swerving into snow banks, I eventually arrived home around seven in the evening, clambered out of the car and immediately plugged the electric cord to the engine into an outside socket. The engine would stay warm during the night and the following morning the car would fire up at the first turn of the key.

With numbed fingers, I fumbled through my bunch of keys and eventually located the key to the front door. I opened the door, thankful to be out of the elements, anticipating thirty minutes on the couch with a glass of red wine before I prepared dinner.

I stepped into my living room and removed my coat. As I turned to go into my bedroom, I noticed that *six* dogs were lounging about or snoozing close to the wood stove. Six fur heads of assorted colors immediately lifted from the floor. I obviously passed inspection because their heads flopped back down on the carpet, all eyes closed. Molly and Lady had company.

I had recently rescued a woefully neglected tri-collie from a house way back in the woods, so my three had been joined by the Doberman, the golden retriever, and the cocker spaniel. I wished I'd had a camera. Monster, my grey tabby, was on the couch, overseeing a bunch of dogs littering the floor in front of the stove. I was thankful that my doggie door provided the necessary shelter for my jogging companions. The next day, all the neighbors pitched in and our collapsed fences were quickly repaired.

When I had to travel out of town on an investigation for a couple of days during the winter months, my next-door neighbor would feed my three dogs and check on the wood stove. Upon returning home, some kind soul would have shoveled the snow from my driveway. I never knew who, but always knew that I could rely on someone to help me out. Arriving home, often late at night, I could park my car in the driveway, totter into the house, take a hot shower, and hit the sheets.

This was my first and only experience living in a community where the residents looked out for each other: I felt blessed.

In mid-June, spring acquiesced to summer, the shortest season, but one that demanded relentless physical labor as houses and yards screamed for attention after the ravages of winter. Everyone was busy repairing fences and roofs damaged by the weight of snow and ice. Dead trees and kindling were sawed and hauled home. Gardens were raked and weeded, and chimneys were swept in readiness for the next winter.

Winter's first snow arrived in late October and continued to lambast Mountainaire through the following April. Winter brought with it the thrill of cross-country skiing. How I relished the crunch of packed snow under my skis as I forged uneven trails through the forest. After each tumble, and there were many, eight fur kids patiently waited for me to synchronize my energies and coordination and try again to navigate those sinuous slopes, the obstacles of which were invisible during the summer months.

I loved my life in Mountainaire.

Unfortunately, I discovered that the leash laws extended to Coconino Forest. One morning, toward the end of my run, I came across a deputy sheriff parked on my street, watching me and eight dogs clamber up the final hill. All the dogs were off leash, of course. The deputy approached me.

"Excuse me, miss. Are you aware there's a leash law in Coconino County?"

I stopped, hands on hips, panting, and stared at him. "Are you kidding? In the middle of the forest? There's a leash law?" All the dogs flopped down around me, staring up at the cop.

"Yes, there is, and you're violating it. I have to issue you a citation for loose K-9s. Are these all your dogs?"

"No, five of them belong to neighbors."

The deputy nodded. "Lucky dogs." He took out his citation

pad and started writing. He handed me the citation. "Have a good day."

Much as I wanted to tell him where to shove the citation, I had to remember I was a public servant, representing the State Attorney General's Office, so I swallowed my proposed response. I had jogged with eight dogs from six to seven in the morning, in this section of forest, for a couple of years. Apart from rabbits and deer, I believe I came upon a human twice. Who made up these ridiculous laws anyway?

I dutifully showed up for my court appearance on the loose K-9 charge. The judge called me up to the bench. Scanning the citation, he said, "So, you regularly roam the forest with eight dogs off leash, is that correct?"

"Yes, sir."

"And you work for.... Can't read—?"

"I work for the State Attorney General's Office."

"You do, huh? What do you do there?"

"I'm a Compliance Officer."

"Compliance Officer. Really, strange that a compliance officer can't comply with the local leash laws, eh?"

I hung my head briefly in fake remorse.

The judge chuckled. "What does a compliance officer do?"

I looked up and smiled. "I investigate complaints of discrimination in employment, housing, and public accommodation. I also manage a mediation program."

"Really. I've heard about mediation." He cocked his head to one side, brow furrowed and looked at me. "Didn't I see you on the local television news a few nights back?

"Yes, sir, you probably did."

"Mediation certainly sounds like a good option to litigation."

"We believe it is. I could make an appointment with your

secretary for us to meet so I can explain to you how it works."

The judge nodded. "Hmm…. Maybe later in the year." He glanced again at the citation. "So, what am I going to do with you?" He looked down at me and grinned.

I noticed the twinkle in his eyes. In my late forties, I was still a slim and good-looking gal with a flowing mass of auburn hair, green eyes, and quick humor. "Well, Your Honor, as you probably know, state employees don't make a lot of money, so a fine would be a hardship. What other options are there?"

"Well, I could sentence you to community service."

"That would be good. What would I have to do?"

"Can you cook?"

"Yes, I like to cook."

"Okay, good. I sentence you to work every Sunday for two months at the local soup kitchen. I'll notify the guy in charge that you will start serving your sentence this weekend. Okay with you?"

"Yep, fine with me."

His gavel hit the desk. "Next case."

I was free to leave and did so, quickly.

That Sunday, I reported for kitchen duty with the local soup kitchen. I was working alongside young men sentenced to community service after accusations of domestic violence, drug possession, and the like. It was an interesting experience.

Those sentenced for domestic violence were the most vocal. Not loud or obnoxious, but expressive, they didn't understand why they reacted violently when their wives started nagging. It reminded me of Vera, her words beating against my brain even after so many years. I understood their frustrations and could not condone their actions, but recognized that societal barriers could be stomped into the ground when the pressure became overwhelming.

After I'd completed my sentence, I continued to volunteer twice a month at the soup kitchen. I liked the person who ran the operation, and the community sure liked my turkey stuffing at Thanksgiving.

The week following one of my volunteer shifts, I checked my mailbox when I arrived home from work. Inside was a letter from Vera.

41
VERA'S VISIT
1991

VERA WANTED TO VISIT me in Flagstaff in July for three and a half weeks and wondered whether she could also bring her close friend Gwen. It frequently amused me that my Aunt Gwen and Mum's only close friend shared the same name. I had known Gwen since I was a child. Her sense of humor gelled with mine, so I was happy that she would be accompanying Mum.

I had not seen Vera since 1988, shortly after my dad died and just before she sold the family home and moved into the senior living complex of Chestnut Close. How would we get along?

We had a turbulent history, one that I did not want to revisit. I hoped that since Gwen would be with Mum, delving into the emotional family vault would be unnecessary. I wrote back and told her that she and Gwen would be welcome and asked about their dietary needs. What types of food would they enjoy and also digest without any ill effects, considering their age?

In July, the summer flowers were blooming in the forest and one of my favorites, the Indian Paintbrush, its color close to vermillion, was particularly abundant that year. It was illegal to pick wild flowers, and anyway they lasted only three days in a vase before dying, whereas in the forest they lasted much longer. I looked forward to showing them to Vera and Gwen on a morning walk with the dogs.

I poured a glass of Cabernet, sat at the kitchen table, and started to make a list of places my guests would enjoy visiting. It was important to me that their visit flowed perfectly, with no mishaps, missteps, heated arguments, and definitely no stress. Who was I kidding? I was already stressed knowing that Vera would be visiting me for nearly a month. I hoped she had mellowed; I knew I had.

Perhaps a ride in a helicopter up, over, and through the Grand Canyon, then shopping in Sedona for crystal or Native American jewelry, or checking out the art galleries in Jerome. Closer to home, they could view the beauty of the Painted Dessert, tour Flagstaff, and explore the forest early in the morning with me and the dogs.

For ladies in their mid-to late-seventies, I thought this would probably be sufficient, especially as my long-time girlfriend from Phoenix, Connie, planned on visiting for one day, and my neighbors, John and Holly, had invited us one night to their home for dinner.

From Vera's letter, I judged their journey would be grueling. She was seventy-eight and I was concerned that the trip might be overly exhausting for her. She and Gwen would take the train from Bristol Temple Meads to Paddington. They would change trains at Paddington, which would take them to Heathrow Airport. After boarding the plane at Heathrow, there was the air travel of nearly ten hours to Phoenix, where they hopped onto a small plane bound for Flagstaff. I would collect them in my Honda Civic and head for Mountainaire and a comfortable bed.

Vera would sleep in my room; Gwen would sleep in the second bedroom, and I would haul out the bed from the sleeper-sofa in the living room.

I had roasted a fifteen-pound turkey and made various side dishes in advance. Since Vera had suffered with severe digestive issues most of her life, certain foods could trigger an attack. One of these was mayonnaise, so I used a little cream cheese when making my potato salad. Then I sliced tomatoes and cucumbers while they were still at room temperature, so they would keep their flavor. For Gwen, I bought coleslaw, black olives, and dill pickles—things I knew she liked. I was thinking that a warm turkey sandwich, a nibble of veggies, and a cup or two of English tea might be all they could manage when they first arrived.

The plane from Phoenix to Flagstaff arrived at quarter to six, late afternoon and earlier than expected. Mum and Gwen were waiting for me: two elderly ladies sitting on a rickety bench with a suitcase on either side, waiting and nearly teetering with exhaustion. As I strode toward them, Gwen spotted me first and waved. Vera gave a wan but relieved smile.

"So, here you are! Wow! You two must have some stamina to make this journey," I joked.

I extended my hand toward Vera. She hesitated and then placed her hand in mine, and we shook hands. I turned to Gwen, hand outstretched. She met my gaze. I could see she was perplexed. Wouldn't a mother and daughter greet each other with at least some affection she probably was thinking. Then she beamed a smile, and we shook hands. Gwen had correctly summed up our mother-daughter relationship, and the realization had disturbed her.

It also troubled me that I hadn't held Vera's hands, gently help her up from the bench, hug her, or tell her how pleased I was to see her, like other daughters probably would do. However, warmth had never been part of our relationship, unless it was accompanied by flames of anger. The thought of hugging her had never entered my mind. That part I found disturbing, and it left me feeling empty.

———

I carried their heavier suitcases to the car, opened the trunk, and tossed them in. Vera and Gwen kept the smaller bags with them. They both heaved a heavy sigh of relief as they slid into the back seat.

"Oh, my God! I could do with a cup of tea," Vera said. "How about you, Gwen?"

"Probably two," Gwen responded.

"Don't worry," I said. "I'd anticipated tea would be the first thing on your mind. It won't take me but a minute to fix a pot."

"Oh, lovely," said Vera.

"I sliced the turkey breast before I left home for the airport. There are some side dishes that you both like. Wouldn't a turkey sandwich and a cup of tea fix you up nicely?"

Groans and sighs of appreciation flowed from the back seat. My visitors needed nourishment and sleep after what must have been one extremely exhausting day. The next morning, I awoke early as usual. I folded back the bedding, slipped on my robe, and tiptoed into my room to check on Vera. She was sound asleep. Next, I padded into the second bedroom to check on Gwen. She, too, was still asleep. I wandered into the kitchen, filled the kettle with water, and placed it on the stove. When these ladies awoke, I suspected the first thing on their minds would be a cup of tea. I tossed three scoops of English tea into my tea pot and laid out a tray next to the toaster with two cups and saucers, sugar and milk, a loaf of bread, butter, and marmalade. I also left a note telling them that I would be gone for an hour walking the dogs and that they were to help themselves. When I returned, I would cook them breakfast.

There was one minor point I had forgotten to mention. I was doggie sitting for the weekend. They were two well-behaved Béarnaise mountain dogs, Suta and Loma, and they would be arriving at my home in a couple of hours. Both were large dogs, weighing over eighty pounds.

Vera and Gwen were up when I returned from my morning walk, thirty minutes before Suta and Loma arrived. They had showered and dressed and wandered along Pawnee, the street where I lived, checking out the neighborhood. They were delighted when several neighbors waved and called out, "You must be Glenda's mum and her friend. Welcome to Mountainaire."

A knock on the door announced the arrival of Suta and Loma. I opened the door and in they bounded. Vera and Gwen were on the couch, sipping tea. Both ladies were surprised— perhaps a little alarmed—at these large, curly-haired fur balls who rushed straight to them, hoping to be petted.

"Good heavens!" Vera said. She held her cup of tea protectively out of the dogs' reach. "These dogs are huge."

"Yes, they are," their owner Barbara said in agreement. "But they're loveable and will settle down very quickly. They know their Aunt Glenda. We'll be picking them up early tomorrow evening. It's nice to meet you, Mrs. Taylor. I hope you have a lovely stay in northern Arizona."

"Thank you, dear. I'm sure we will." Gwen smiled and resumed sipping her tea.

"Here's their food, toys, and chewies. Are you sure this isn't too much, considering your mom and her friend are visiting?" Barbara asked.

"No, they'll be fine," I said and turned to Vera and Gwen. "Sorry guys, I completely forgot about Suta and Loma. They're good dogs, and they're used to the doggie door so we can do whatever we want. We don't have to worry about being home to let them out to potty."

Me, holding Suta, 1991

"Well, gotta go," Barbara said. "We want to make it to the Hopi reservation in an hour or so. See you tomorrow evening." She waved goodbye as she closed the door behind her.

Barbara and her husband, who both had Ph.Ds. in psychology, worked with the Hopi Native American community. They were wonderful people whom I loved and respected. When they first adopted Suta and we were introduced, Suta and I bonded immediately.

As Suta grew, which he did rapidly, he would stay with me some weekends, Barbara's husband was a generous guy, and he bought me a larger doggie door to accommodate Suta's girth. Molly, my greyhound, weighed only seventy pounds so a doggie door that could accommodate a dog weighing close to one hundred pounds must have seemed to her like she was entering and exiting the grand lobby of the Ritz Hotel.

The minute Barbara's SUV roared into gear and she drove away from my home, Vera's voice thundered at me across the living room. "Well, if you ask me, that's a right state of affairs. She drops off her dogs for two days, knowing you have company, and doesn't offer to pay. She's playing you for a fool, my girl. She wouldn't do that to me. I wouldn't stand for it."

Gwen stared open mouthed at Vera, her teacup poised in midair.

I too stared at Vera. *Oh my God, she's been here only one night, and she's already come unglued,* I thought. *What the hell was her problem?*

I had to make a decision. This was my home and my rules. I took a deep breath and turned to Vera. "Mum, where are the dogs?" I kept my voice cool and level.

"Well...." She gestured toward the fireplace. "They're sitting in front of the wood stove."

"And are they bothering you?"

"No, but that's not the point.... You have company and that woman is putting on you. I don't know why you stand for it."

"No, that is the point. Barbara and I had an agreement. I know these dogs. I knew they would not bother you and Gwen. My God, they're only here until tomorrow evening—and you're here for nearly a month. Barbara is not putting on me, as you say. I'm just helping her out at no inconvenience to you."

Vera raised her nose and sniffed. "Well, at least she should pay you, but if you want to be treated that way...." Her head wobbled in a way that resembled her all too familiar spates of righteous indignation.

I had made my stand. "Let's get one thing straight right now. This is my home. If I want to help someone who has been a good neighbor to me, that's my decision. And you will live with it. Do I make myself clear?"

I left the living room, headed to the kitchen, and started making breakfast, revved up enough to throw Vera's ass into the doghouse in the back yard. While I scrambled eggs and fried bacon, I could hear Vera's sobs and protestations in the background.

"We're family. I should be able to say anything to family."

I ignored her.

Gwen was trying to calm Vera down, "Now, Vera, don't upset yourself over such a little thing."

A few seconds later, Gwen sidled around the wall between the kitchen and living room. "Your mum's upset."

"Gwen, she's always upset when she doesn't get her own way. I lived with this for eighteen years—and I'm not falling for her shenanigans at this stage in my life. Please tell Mum that breakfast will be ready in about five minutes."

Gwen bit down on her lip, nodded, and returned to the living room.

I set the table for three, put warm toast in the rack, and set out a platter of scrambled eggs and bacon and a dish of sautéed onions and yellow peppers on the side. "Ladies, breakfast is served."

I retired to the back yard for a smoke and a silent scream, wondering whether Vera was going to act up during the entire visit and whether I would have to walk on eggshells or broken glass for the next three weeks. I could have used a Bloody Mary right then.

When I returned to the kitchen, Vera and Gwen were enjoying their breakfast and tea.

"Is everything okay here?" I asked. "More tea, perhaps?"

"Glenda, sit down and eat your breakfast while it's still hot," Gwen ordered. I did as she suggested.

"Breakfast was fine," Vera said. She sniffed and blew her nose, in a manner I strongly suspected was for affect. "What are we going to do today?"

"I thought we'd explore Flagstaff and the Painted Desert. Get you acclimated to Flagstaff and the surrounding area. How does that sound?"

"That sounds marvelous to me," Gwen said. "What do you think, Vera?"

"Yes, I'm looking forward to touring Flagstaff." She turned to me. "I'll be able to imagine you in this environment when I return home to England."

"Okay, let me take care of the dogs, grab a quick shower, get dressed, and we'll be on our way."

Five dogs were fed, and plenty of doggie toys were scattered around the living room. I checked that the doggie door was working properly for them to access the garden and play or anoint a weed or two. They certainly had a variety from which to choose.

———————

For three weeks, everything went swimmingly, and I began to relax. We spent two days in Sedona and Gwen fell in love with Red Rock country, the jewelry stores, and southwestern cuisine. She seemed awed by the luxurious homes scattered throughout the area.

Vera enjoyed puttering around the stores and especially liked the ones that sold Western clothing, crystal, jewelry, tableware, and kitchen novelties. When I admired some tableware, she insisted on buying me a set for six. I was taken aback: this was unlike Vera. However, she had never been known for her generosity. At Christmas or on my birthday, she would send a card, occasionally enclosing $20.00 as a gift. I still have and treasure the tableware and often think back on our Sedona trip and Vera's spurt of generosity.

She also had a penchant for second-hand stores, so when we drove back to Flagstaff, I took her to the two I knew about. She browsed there for over an hour. I was trying on a pair of gloves when Vera tapped me on the shoulder. She was holding a pair of salmon-pink cowboy boots, never worn, marked at $20.00.

"Look at these! They're brand new," she said. "Never been worn by the looks of it. Do you like them?" Vera always loved a bargain.

"Yes, I love them." I took them from her. The leather was soft and supple; I tried them on and they fit me perfectly.

"Twenty bucks! Boy, that's a bargain. I suspect someone tossed them because of the color, but I love 'em!"

"All right then," Mum said, "I'm glad you like them because I want to buy them for you." She waved to the sales clerk. "We'll take these boots, please."

I wore those salmon-pink cowboy boots regularly for more than five years before they fell apart. Every time I pulled them on, I remembered Mum's joy in finding a bargain and giving it as a gift to daughter, a memory that warmed my heart.

When they wore out, I was so attached to those boots that I seriously considered holding a wake.

———

We visited the Grand Canyon and a helicopter pilot friend of mine persuaded Vera and Gwen to view the canyon from the air. At the end of the flight, while getting out of the helicopter, both ladies were so overwhelmed by the beauty of the canyon, they kept talking over each other.

"Did you see—?" Gwen asked.

"Yes, wonderful. And what about—" Vera said.

"Beautiful, Vera, just beautiful," Gwen said. "I must buy some cards from the gift shop for my grandkids."

I thought it best not to mention that a month or so previously a helicopter had plunged into the canyon and the pilot and passengers were killed. Why spoil their sense of adventure with facts?

The Painted Desert captivated Vera. She was amazed at the color palette and dubious whether the colors of the earth were authentic and not painted on by the City of Flagstaff employees. I had to drag her away because we were due for dinner with my neighbors John and Holly.

Watching Vera and Gwen dress for dinner with people whom they had never met was a sweet and charming experience. I sat on the couch, wearing shorts, sandals, and a tee shirt, smoking a cigarette and sipping wine.

First, Vera appeared from my bedroom parading a turquoise dress, a cream wrap, and Navaho silver drop earrings and a clasp bracelet that she'd bought in Sedona. What did I think? Was it too much, too little? Did the jewelry go with the outfit? Who would have imagined that after thirty years, Vera would be consulting with her tomboy daughter on fashion?

Next, Gwen stepped forward and the scenario repeated itself. "Do you think this is suitable for dinner with your friends?"

"Ladies, we're going next door for dinner with John and Holly. Don't sweat it. Dress comfortably."

"But, Glenda, we've never met them," Gwen persisted. "We want to make a good impression. After all, they're your neighbors and friends. We don't want them to think that me and your mum are street urchins now do we?" Her shoulders shook as she giggled. Mum and Gwen were from an older generation where appearances were important. When Gwen asked, "Do you think this bracelet goes with this skirt?" I steered her toward a bracelet that she'd bought in Sedona. "The color's a better contrast with your red skirt," I said.

After several outfit and jewelry changes, the ladies were comfortable that they looked their best. I happily escorted them to our dinner engagement—next door.

Holly, an excellent cook, had prepared a chicken dish lightly spiced so that Vera's temperamental tummy wouldn't misbehave, and for dessert, she'd made a delectable fruit pie with whipped cream.

After dinner, we sat outside on the deck, chatting, sipping wine, and watching the occasional falling star in the night sky. Mountainaire at night was entrancing. Apart from a few barking dogs, it was quiet and peaceful, and the night sky was ablaze with stars. The conversation flowed, as did the wine, and when we arrived home, Vera and Gwen were content, tired, and ready for bed.

———

Our next trip was to Jerome, but it was too hippy and reminiscent of the 1960s for the ladies; there was also the number of hills they had to climb. Sedona was more their style.

The next week, my girlfriend from Phoenix, Connie, came to visit.

Connie and I had met early on a cold winter morning. There was a knock on my front door. I opened the door, and there stood this shivering woman dressed only in a light blue, flimsy nightgown. I immediately asked her to come in and have coffee: Connie had locked herself out of her house. She went outside to water the plants in her front yard, and the door clicked closed behind her. Unfortunately, the lock was on and the keys were secure in the house on her kitchen counter! That was in 1985, and we'd been friends ever since.

At the time of her Flagstaff visit, Connie was in the workforce and an excellent hairdresser. She had cut my hair on several occasions and the results had been outstanding. Cutting naturally curly-wavy hair takes a special skill, and Connie had it in spades.

I was fixing lunch when Connie asked, "Are you going to do your mum's hair?"

I hesitated. "Well, if she would like her hair done, I'll make an appointment with my hairdresser. She's very good. She's Navajo, but she understands European hair like mine nearly as well as you do."

"No." Connie rolled her eyes. "I mean, here, at the house. Do you have rollers?"

"Sure, somewhere I think. Not sure where they are—you know, I don't use rollers. I wash my hair, pat it dry with a towel, run my fingers through it, and when it dries, I brush it."

"Yes, well, we're not all blessed with hair like yours. So can you look for the rollers? Then I'll do your mum's hair." Connie winked at Vera. "Can you believe that, she didn't ask you if you wanted your hair done?"

Vera dimpled a smile.

Connie walked up to me and whispered, "I can't believe you didn't think to do your Mom's hair."

"No, I didn't think of it." *Oh my God*, I thought. *How embarrassing! I'm a terrible daughter!*

I did as Connie directed, searching and finally finding the rollers. I gave them to her, and watched her escort Vera to the kitchen sink. Once her hair was washed, Vera sat in the breakfast nook, a towel draped over her shoulders, and Connie began rolling her hair around small curlers. She had taken care of her mom before she needed to move into a nursing home, so she was used to dealing with elderly ladies.

She and Vera were laughing. When I asked what was funny, Connie said, "Your mum asked me to make 'a little look a lot'."

Vera had fine, sparse hair. Twenty years ago, when I would do her hair, like Connie, I had to use loads of small rollers to achieve the effect of making "a little look a lot." Another fond memory had popped up unexpectedly.

The following day, Connie returned to Phoenix, leaving behind one happy client sporting a new hairstyle.

———

It was four days before Vera and Gwen would again board the small plane that would return them to Phoenix en route to England and home.

Around five in the morning, Gwen woke me up.

"I don't feel so good." Hunched over in pain, she was holding her tummy.

I swung my legs out of bed and put on my robe. "What's wrong?"

"Well, I have something wrong with my digestive system. I went to the doctor before I came over here, and he gave me some tablets—told me they would tide me over until I returned home. But the way I feel, I think I need to see a doctor. Go to the emergency room. Do you have a hospital close by?"

"Sure we do, don't worry. Get dressed and we'll head on over to the hospital."

Gwen returned to her room to dress. By this time, Vera was up, dressed, and wanting to know what was going on. She went into Gwen's room. I was pulling on jeans and a tee shirt, when I heard Gwen telling her that she needed to see a doctor and get some medication.

"Did you know you were sick when you agreed to make this trip?" Vera demanded.

"Well, yes, I did," Gwen said. "But my doctor put me on medication and told me I would probably be okay until I returned home. If not, I was to go to the emergency room immediately. Glenda's going to take me."

I walked into Gwen's room. "You about ready to go?"

Before Gwen could answer, Vera interrupted. "So now we have to run around dealing with your health situation while we're on holiday. I can't believe it. If I'd known you were sick, I certainly wouldn't have bought you a plane ticket. Why didn't you tell me you were sick? I would have told you not to come."

"Exactly. That's why I didn't tell you. Vera, don't you understand? I was so looking forward to this trip. It was a trip of a lifetime, something I would remember until the day I die." Gwen looked in my direction, beseeching. "Sorry, Glenda if I'm putting you out, didn't mean for this to happen, I—"

"No problem, Gwen. Don't you worry. You're not putting me out. Let's get in the car and go to the E.R. We have this handled." As I helped Gwen into the car, I could hear Vera muttering in the background.

Would I ever understand this woman? Her good friend Gwen was doubled over in pain. She and Mum were going home in four days. They'd had a fabulous time and medical care was immediately available: I didn't get it—and still don't. So what if Mum paid for Gwen's plane ticket. I suspected she was using her as a buffer between her and me. Frankly, I was thankful that Gwen had come: I, too, had needed a buffer.

From my perspective, Gwen had earned her plane ticket. I had been glad to see her and now my immediate concern was her health. Mentally, I shut Vera down, anticipating that later, sure as hell, she would explode.

We arrived at Flagstaff's hospital emergency room close to six thirty in the morning. There was only one other patient ahead of Gwen so she was able to see a doctor quickly. Vera and I sat in the waiting room. I immediately picked up a magazine and buried my head in an article about trains, something in which I had little interest despite liking to ride them, but the magazine was a useful barrier against Vera.

"I'm going to give her what for when we get home," Vera declared.

I stole a side-glance at her: she was sitting erect in a high back chair, lips pinched, and one foot tapping. The trains were looking better all the time.

Soon, Gwen returned with the doctor who assured us that she would be fine. He had given her medication that would control her digestive condition for a while. However, he did stress that Gwen must see her own doctor as soon as possible after she returned to England.

Gwen shook the doctor's hand. "Thank you so much for the medication, doctor. I will do exactly as you say and phone my doctor the day after I arrive home."

I linked arms with Gwen and led her back to the car; Vera was bringing up the rear. "Are you ready for a nice cup of tea?" I asked.

"Yes, I certainly am." She looked at me and grinned. "Some toast and marmite might also hit the spot. Whatever the doctor gave me has settled my tummy."

"Okay, we can definitely do that for you." Settling Gwen and Vera in the car, I slid into the driver's seat, hit the accelerator, and headed for home. The twenty-minute trip, filled with awkward silence, seemed to last for hours

To my surprise and relief, Vera didn't press Gwen further on her health issues. Their last four days were spent amicably browsing the local mall, second-hand stores, lunching at local restaurants, and napping. The one exception was the time Vera wanted to accompany me and eight dogs on my daily morning walk.

I told her our route was over two miles and involved climbing up a couple of hills, but she was adamant that she could do it. I said, "Okay. Let's go."

The following morning, Vera and I were up and dressed by six thirty in the morning. My three dogs, tails thudding against the back of the couch, were standing by the front door. Slipping on their leashes, I opened the door and we set off.

A path ran behind the houses that faced the forest. I walked with Vera to the middle of the path and told her to stay put while I collected several other dogs.

The first dog released from its yard was Luca, a red Doberman. It always amazed me that every dog that I walked knew when I was going to open my front door because all of them would be lined up by their respective gates for the "dog lady" to set them free.

Luca was a gentle dog but a little rambunctious. As I opened her gate, I could see her gaze focused on Vera: here was someone new to sniff. I reached for her collar and started to place the leash around her neck, then with one quick twist of her head she was off, running free, and charging right at Vera. I was dashing after her.

I yelled to Vera, "Stand still! Don't move! Don't shout. She won't hurt you, but she will sniff you." Luca reached Vera several seconds before me. Thankfully, she behaved as I'd predicted: she circled Vera, thoroughly sniffed her, circled her again, and then discarded her as if she'd been an old leather shoe that had lost its musky smell.

Inside, I was frantic but tried to stay calm for Vera. "I'm

sorry about that. She was so fast that I couldn't stop her. Are you okay?"

Vera was unflappable. "I was a little taken aback at first, but she didn't act aggressive or growl at me. So I told her, 'You can sniff, but biting is out.'"

There were moments when Vera could impress me, and this was one of them.

"Well, we have four more dogs to pick up. Let's try this. Why don't you walk beside me, then they'll know we're a team and you're not a stranger. We don't want a repeat performance, right?"

"Right!"

In five minutes, we had collected a cocker spaniel, the two Béarnaise dogs that Vera had already met, and a golden retriever. Again, Vera underwent the sniffing ritual before all eight dogs dashed into the forest, around trees, back to us, and off again.

It took us more than two hours to complete the walk. Sapped, Vera's legs were dragging slowly up the last hill. She suddenly stopped and stood still, looking all around her.

We were surrounded by tall pines, patches of shade on the forest floor, with the sun glinting through the trees and leaving slashes of sunlight on the trails. She said, "I understand why this environment brings you peace, contentment, and joy."

On this, we were on the same page.

During our absence, Gwen had set out cups and saucers, milk and sugar; the only thing missing was a pot of steaming hot, English tea. When Vera and I walked through the front door, Gwen turned on the knob for the burner under the kettle. Soon it would be breakfast time.

If I recall correctly, Vera went to bed early that night.

With Vera in Flagstaff, 1991

Unfortunately, Vera remained true to her nature. It was during one of our Sunday morning chats after she and Gwen had returned to England, Vera told me: "I ripped Gwen up one side and down the other for not disclosing before the trip that she was sick. She lied to me. I paid her fare, and she lied to me. Had us upset, running to a hospital because she didn't feel well. Humph! Completely disregarded her doctor's orders!"

Their friendship was over. Vera wanted nothing more to do with Gwen.

I was shocked, but remained silent. I had been happy to host Gwen. For her, it was a trip of a lifetime. We have continued to stay in touch. It continues to amaze me that she remembers my birthday and Christmas; her cards are always beautiful and elegant.

I also kept quiet on the subject of Gwen. After all, Vera did not need to know everything.

42

FINDING MY BIOLOGICAL FAMILY 1995

BEING AWARDED INVESTIGATOR OF THE YEAR for 1993 did not protect me from unwelcome political changes within Arizona. Following the election of 1991, some of the Division Chiefs at the Attorney General's Office were replaced, and my boss was one of the casualties. However, I also liked the Chief Counsel who was my new boss. He was very smart and a strong advocate for employees who suffered from employment discrimination.

I discovered that being good at my job had unanticipated consequences. During my time in Flagstaff, I had resolved more cases annually than the Phoenix and Tucson offices combined. This resulted in the new Chief Counsel's decision to close the Flagstaff office and transfer the jurisdiction to the Federal Agency. He wanted my closure skills elsewhere. It was my choice: Phoenix or Tucson.

I decided on Tucson. Phoenix was an expanding metropolis that was attracting new businesses and a swell of people from other states. It had morphed almost into another Los Angeles.

Tucson was also was expanding, but more slowly. Its culturally diverse population and less stressful energy made it the better town for me. Four magnificent, soaring mountain ranges surrounded this southern Arizona city and stood guard like Roman sentries: the Santa Catalinas, the Santa Ritas, the Tucson Mountains, and the Rincons.

With Molly my greyhound secure in the back seat, on December 31, 1993, I backed out of the driveway to begin my trip to Tucson. A few weeks earlier, Lady, my Aussie shepherd had had a seizure during one of our morning walks and lost the use of her back legs. Based on the vet's recommendation that Lady would never recover the use of her legs, I had her put to sleep. A week later, it was evident that my darling nineteen-year-old cat, Monster, needed to be released from life due to health issues brought on by old age. Now, it was only Molly and me, returning to the desert.

When I packed my belongings and bid farewell to people that I had come to know and love during my four years in Flagstaff, emotions emerged, far deeper than I had imagined. I realized that for the first time in my life I was content and not driven to strive for something better. I was professionally successful, creatively alive, physically active, and living in the woods, a truly spiritual environment. I had found peace and contentment in Mountainaire and finally knew how happy felt. Due to circumstances over which I had no control, I was being dragged back to city life. I stuffed my clothes into suitcases, wishing they were the officials that had wrenched me from a lifestyle that my soul had yearned for, for so many years.

Despairing at the loss of my life and home in Flagstaff, I sobbed as I drove from Mountainaire through the Verde Valley. I ended up with lousy headache. As I steered the car through the winding hills and dales of the Valley and moved ever closer to Phoenix, I had cried out all my tears.

I stomped angrily on the accelerator and thrust my Honda to over 90 mph down the freeway, zooming through the busy outskirts of Phoenix, and we reached Tucson in four hours. I was lucky I was not stopped by law enforcement. Driving angry and sad isn't a safe combination.

Molly and I moved into our new home on January 1, 1994. The following week, I reported for work. Exchanging cool mountain air for the blistering heat of the desert during the summer months sapped my energy and left me depressed for over four years. I tried to shake off my depression by doing something that I had put on hold for many years: tracking down my biological family.

By 1995, I had calculated that if my biological mother Norah was still alive, she would be in her eighties. It seemed the perfect age for skeletons to pop out of the closet and start up a conversation. In all probability, her parents would not be living, and she would be free to share information without hesitation.

In the fall of 1996, I wrote to George Moore, my former boss in England, and asked him whether he could do a little research for me. I enclosed a copy of my original birth certificate that I'd found at the Mormon Genealogical Library in Tucson. The document showed my name as Anna Townsend and my mother's name as Norah Townsend. To my astonishment, one month later, my office phone rang. It was George. He and his wife had traveled to Devon and located a branch of my biological family, my mother's cousin, Bill, and his wife, Wynn.

"When I received your letter," George said, "I told Brenda, 'Get in the car love, we're going to Devon.' It was easy. I stopped by the registrar's office and asked the fellow if he knew of any family in the area by the name of Townsend. He said, 'Yes, there's a branch of the Townsend family that lives about two miles from here, Bill and Wynne Chaffe.'"

George drove to the location, and my cousin invited him and Brenda in for tea.

"The first question out of Bill's mouth," George said, "was 'Does she have red hair?'" George reassured him I definitely had a mop of auburn hair, fair skin and freckles, and was quite feisty. "Bill grinned when I told him that." He told me, 'I understand that her father had red hair, but I know from experience that her mother was definitely feisty!'"

A year later, I sent Bill a photograph of me taken in 1990, and he wrote back: "You look a lot like your mother."

During their conversation, George learned that Bill had been upset that I was "put up for adoption." In 1943, society was not ready to accept an unwed mother and her bastard child. George told me that my biological family, who were country folk, lived in a very conservative village in the south of England. My grandfather, Sydney, worked all his life fitting out ships for the Royal Navy.

"He was a very well-read man and an intellectual with a dry humor and ready wit," Bill told George. "The entire family shared a love of animals, country living, creative and intellectual pursuits, sports, and all were avid readers."

According to Bill, my grandmother Susan enjoyed doing "Bullets" and often won prizes. Bullets were competitions with words and pithy sayings in the magazine *John Bull*.

Maternal biological grandparents, Susan and Sydney, with my biological mother, Norah Townsend

My great-grandparents Thomas Boon and Elizabeth Hannah had five children. One was my grandmother Susan and another was my cousin Bill's father, John. Grandfather Sydney had tried to help Bill with his homework when Bill was in high school, but gave up. He told him, "Your lights went out years ago." Despite my grandfather's low assessment of Bill's intellect, Bill became an engineer and worked for local government most of his life.

His eyes were misting when Bill told George: "Sydney insisted that Norah leave the village and enter a home for unwed mothers until her baby was born. Then she could return home. I always felt that was the wrong decision. Norah and her baby should have stayed with the family. But Sydney was adamant."

Anxious to hear from me, Bill told George that I would have to initiate any calls. "If she does, I will be delighted to speak with her."

"So there you have it," George said. "The next step is up to you."

I thanked him profusely for his help, we said goodbye, and I hung up the phone. The first thing Saturday morning I would make a call to a member of my family who had been previously inaccessible to me.

Saturday finally arrived. With some trepidation, I called Bill. I could hear in his voice that he was pleased to hear from me. We had a lengthy conversation. He suggested that I write him with all my questions and he would try to answer them.

When the call ended, I sat at my computer and poured out fifty-two years of unanswered questions about my beginnings and connections. The next day, I popped a lengthy letter into the mail on its way to England.

———

Norah Townsend on her wedding day with David Preston
January 16, 1954

Three weeks later, I received news from Bill who was able to answer most of my questions, although not all of them. The most important answer was: "Your mother Norah Townsend was a natural blonde with blue eyes. She was a very attractive woman with a strong character who was always immaculately dressed and who loved to dance. She fell in love with a red-headed fighter pilot and test pilot in 1942. She told my sister, Marie, that she and her pilot beau planned to be married. Unfortunately, he was on a mission and was killed before their union received formal church blessing."

The war had interrupted their plans, but not my arrival.

Bill's letter continued: "Once the adoption was concluded, Norah left Plymouth and traveled to London to work as a secretary. She was a civil servant, but in which branch, I have no idea. Later, she moved back to Plymouth. Her last position was secretary to David Preston, a County Hospital Administrator with the Cornwall Health Authority. She eventually married him in 1954, when she was thirty-five. Norah was a crackerjack secretary with extremely fast shorthand and typing speeds."

I was thrilled to read this, because I was no longer a nobody—I was a somebody. My biological mother had passed on to me her secretarial skills and her love of dancing. We had a bond.

Bill's letter went on: "In 1969 Norah died in her sleep of a massive heart attack. She was only fifty-three, but she had been a chain-smoker." He'd previously written me that Norah's father had been a heavy smoker too and had died from cancer of the tongue. Norah died the same year I left England to work abroad and start a new life.

"Norah had no other children," he continued. I was sad to read this as I'd hoped for siblings. "Following Norah's death, her husband immigrated to Canada."

I have never tried to trace his whereabouts.

My original birth certificate showed my birth name as Anna Townsend. I was disappointed to discover Norah had omitted the name of my father on the birth certificate. Why would she do that? Was it because my father died in the war? Was she thinking of his family who probably was unaware of her relationship with their son and was certainly unaware that she had given birth to their granddaughter? The absence of my father's name on that document was irksome and caused me speculation for many years. However, I would later learn that unwed mothers would frequently omit the father's name for many reasons.

Considering the information from my cousin Bill, a couple of scenarios made the most sense. England was at war with Germany. My country was under nightly attack from bombs, especially in Plymouth where the navy yard continued building ships throughout the war. Buildings crumbled, people perished. Come morning, none of them knew whether they would still be alive. Norah was no exception. Her expiration date could have been any time.

I speculated. Norah might have been a country girl, for the moment stepping out as party girl. Such a girl in her mid-twenties, living through the nightly hell of World War II, might want to kick up her heels, dance, have a drink or two, meet a guy, fall in love, and have sex. The normal rules of courtship no longer applied. Entwined in her lover's arms, Norah could feel safe, at least for an hour or two. In 1942, that was a gift.

Norah met a man, possibly Richard Brian Dunsmuir. They had fun, he made her laugh and feel special, and she fell in love. Her womb offered his sperm the warm hospitality of Southern England, and she was soon pregnant. Condoms must have seemed as necessary as a fur coat would be in Florida in the month of August.

Norah and her beau obviously failed to use birth control. I don't know how easy it was in 1942 to access condoms, but I suspect that the couple was cocooned in their passion, away from the shadow of pending doom. Was it possible that, unbeknownst to Norah, there was a wife, fiancée, or girlfriend somewhere in the background? If my biological parents had planned to marry, wouldn't my father's name have been on the birth certificate? Wouldn't the couple have told my maternal and paternal grandparents the good news?

Norah was a country lass, not a sophisticated city girl, and she may have believed—or wished—that she and the handsome pilot were going to tie the knot. Perhaps my father was not convinced, already spoken for, or not the marrying kind.

There's another possibility. It was late 1942, around the holidays when Norah became pregnant. My presumed biological father died February 15, 1943. I was born in August 1943. Norah may not have known that she was pregnant until after his death.

He was twenty-two, and Norah was twenty-three, the year my biological father died. It's hard to imagine that in the early 1940s that her beau Richard would have been married and possibly had other kids at age twenty-two. However, there's no way I'll never know the absolute truth.

Research showed me that if the name of the father was missing from the birth certificate, their child was probably born out of wedlock. It seems that Norah followed the rules of her time. After all these years, I can live with that.

———

Unwed mothers in 1943 were a blight on the family name; therefore, it would not be unusual for Norah's father to have hustled her off to a home for unwed mothers in one of the nearest cities, either Plymouth or Yelverton, to await delivery. Six weeks after my birth, the adoption agency transferred me to a hospital in Bath to await a new family. I couldn't know it then, but Bath was only ten miles from Bristol, the town where I would spend the first eighteen years of life.

Vera never told me how long she and my Dad waited to adopt a child. The years passed and I speculated that in 1943 it was probably not a lengthy process. Newborn infants were more readily available as "accidents" occurred more frequently. In those days, for people who followed Catholic teachings, I understand that the preferred method of birth control was withdrawal or the rhythm method. I have no idea whether Norah was Catholic, but whatever birth control method Norah used—if any—obviously failed because she ended up pregnant with me.

———

As an only child, I had always found adult conversation fascinating and would linger in the kitchen and eavesdrop when Vera was gossiping with the neighbors over the backyard fence. One day, Vera was nattering with Mrs. Miles, the mother of a family of four that lived next door to us. Apparently, a neighbor across the street had delivered her fourth baby and refused to breast feed the infant.

Mrs. Miles was horrified. "Any good mother knows that *babies* need their mother's milk to grow up healthy. Trouble with 'er is that she 'as too many kids. I told my 'usband, just you watch. She'll neglect this young 'un like she did the rest, and it'll grow up to be another juvenile delinquent." The family across the street had one or two sons that had a close relationship with the law—at least, that was what I'd heard.

Vera was quick to agree. "Yes, she certainly keeps 'em coming. I wish I could have had a second child but, you know, I adopted, so that's it. I wanted another one, but Alf wouldn't hear of it. He says one's enough."

I often wondered whether my birth mother breastfed me and whispered "I love you" as she rocked me to sleep. It's possible that my wonderings never materialized. In England in the 1940s and up until the early1950s, bottle feeding formula was encouraged over breast feeding, especially in planned adoption cases. Therefore, I suspect that I was not breastfed during my first six weeks of life, during the time before I was transferred to my new family.

Vera was not an affectionate person. I never recall her holding me, hugging me, kissing me, or telling me that she loved me and, of course, since she was not my birth mother, she couldn't breast feed me. I suppose I clung to a bottle for nourishment.

I needed warmth, like a sunflower, to unfurl my petals and allow my heart to blossom. Under Vera's "maternal guidance," I found it difficult to develop, let alone mature, as an individual. Any attempts to deviate from *her* status quo were met with corporal punishment or emotional blackmail. Occasionally she would pout for days. The only affection I received was from my dad. That was in the early years, before

Vera announced during an argument that she came first and Dad had better not forget it.

Alone with my thoughts in bed at night, I would stare at the ceiling, wondering whether Norah had ever held me close and told me that she loved me. Did she tearfully try to explain why she had to leave me to the arms of strangers? Did she even see me after giving birth and before releasing me to face an unknown future? While growing up in my adoptive home I dragged around all this raw sadness within me.

43
VERA'S PASSING
2007

MUM DIED ON FEBRUARY 7, 2007; she was ninety-two. From our weekly phone chats I gathered that she was ready for the transition, but I also sensed that she was a little fearful of death. For several years, home health care professionals had regularly intruded on Mum's privacy because she was incapable of caring for herself. Due to the disabilities of age, the joy she derived from sewing, crocheting, knitting, and embroidery had faded in tandem with her vision.

On February 19, 2007, she was cremated; coincidentally, it was my Dad's birthday too. Her ashes were scattered in the February Garden of the cemetery. I like to imagine that Dad was waiting for his wife, there in the February Garden. Vera, confused, alone, and scared, suddenly spotted him. Overjoyed, she rushed to his arms, her eyelashes glistening with tears. Dad would give her a lengthy hug, one arm around her waist, and escort her toward the light of new beginnings, obliterating any desire that Vera might have had to glance back.

The news of Mum's death traveled through the Internet and arrived via email from my cousin Robert, the co-executor of Vera's estate. Robert later told me that he had tried to contact me by phone, but I had already left for work. Since he did not have my work phone number, email was the only option.

My first thought, upon reading the email was: *I'm an orphan, again.* For a brief moment, I panicked; I was all alone now. Tears unexpectedly welled up in my eyes at the next thought: *I won't be able to chat with Mum again on Sunday mornings.* The realization tugged at my heart. I had grown comfortable with our Sunday morning phone ritual and was thankful that, finally, Mum and I had reached some sort of peace. My final thought, over which I felt slightly guilty, was that I would inherit a portion of my parents' hard-earned savings and could pay off my car. I had lived paycheck-to-paycheck all my working life. To have some financial breathing space would be a blessing.

When I opened Robert's email, I was not alone. My friend Michael was staying with me while he was searching for his next computer consultant gig. We were sitting at the computer, debating the narrative for my next greyhound grant application, when I saw Robert's name pop up in my email in-box.

Instantly, I knew that Mum was dead. "Robert never contacts me, so I'm sure Mum's died," I said.

Michael had lost his mother to cancer a few years earlier. "Oh, come on. Are you kidding? Why do you think that? He's probably just sending you news from the family."

He was not emotionally prepared to hear about another death, I suppose. I said nothing because I knew better. I stared at the screen for a few seconds before clicking on Robert's message.

The email read that the ambulance had taken Mum to the hospital's triage unit. The medical staff had stabilized her, and Mum was waiting for a vacant bed in one of the wards. Overcome by what was probably a massive heart attack, she passed away quickly but totally alone.

A few weeks later, I received a phone call from Barbara, Mum's former next door neighbor and friend. Barbara was quite a bit younger than Mum. She was living in an assisted living facility because her husband had severe health problems that required round-the-clock care.

According to Barbara, when she had stopped by to see whether Mum wanted anything from the grocery store, Mum said she was feeling queasy. Barbara, a retired registered nurse, instantly recognized that Mum was in trouble and promptly called for an ambulance.

"When the paramedics were loading your mum into the ambulance, I was waving to her." She paused a moment, trying to control her emotions. "Never thought for a minute that it'd be the last time I'd see her. I don't know who's going to move into your mum's flat. I'm not ready for anyone new to move in. I hate passing your mum's front door and not knocking and calling out, 'Vera, do you need anything? I'm going to the shops.'"

Barbara was upset; she missed Vera. She had grown attached to a frail, feisty, older woman whose quick, deft movements could produce exquisite items through knitting, embroidering, crocheting, or sewing. It was in Barbara's nature to care for others. Over the years, Mum had told me that she and Barbara had developed a comfortable and somewhat symbiotic relationship. Barbara shopped for Mum and checked in on her, while Mum would sew and bake for Barbara.

At the age of seventy-five, Mum had invested the proceeds from the sale of her home into an annuity plan. For many years, she received a monthly check. Then the stock market took a tumble, and the checks stopped. This infuriated Mum. Later, at age ninety-two, when her investment matured and there was no withdrawal penalty, Mum decided to transfer her money into her local bank account. She told me that I was the beneficiary in her will and whatever money was left at the time of her death would pass to me. The only exception was that should she need to move into a long-term care facility, her entire savings would be paid directly to the facility at the time she moved in and there would be no refunds.

We had gone back and forth on the phone for about a month, discussing how to transfer the funds. Mum was overwhelmed with anxiety, unable to comprehend the wire transfer of money after she signed and mailed back the authorization form to the financial institution.

I was not surprised that Mum could not grasp this concept. After all, her brain cells were ninety-two years old. Additionally, she was paranoid that the money might get lost. How did it *really* get there? What would she do if the money did not arrive in her bank account? Would she be tossed out of her flat onto the street? What would happen to her? Financial security was always a concern for Vera.

To set her mind at ease, I wrote to the directors of the financial institution and asked how the money would be transferred into Mum's bank account. The financial institution was very cooperative. They sent me the requisite form and a brochure explaining the procedure for a transfer of funds; I mailed this on to Mum. My speculation was correct. The money would be wired straight into Mum's local bank account once the authorization form was received by the financial institution.

I encouraged Mum to review the form and the brochure with Barbara. Once Mum received the "thumbs up" from Barbara, she understood how the transaction would occur and was "shakily" confident that the wire transfer of money would safely arrive in her bank account in Bristol. Then she was able to proceed. With Barbara's help, Mum completed and mailed the authorization form to the financial institution, ten days before she died.

On February 6, 2007, the money was wired and deposited into Mum's bank account in Bristol. On the morning of February 7, 2007, Mum died.

Dad had distanced himself from the ongoing conflict between Mum and me years earlier. Shortly after he died, I recall Mum telling me that Dad had made her promise to make sure there was some money left for me in my later years. Mum was getting close to where she needed long-term care. Had she been admitted into a long-term care facility, my inheritance would have immediately helped purchase physical therapy equipment, a whirlpool, or other such needed services for the elderly.

The timing of mailing in the authorization form and the subsequent wire transfer of funds had been executed flawlessly. Dad got his wish, and I inherited some of their hard-earned savings, for which I was grateful. The drama played out like an inspired, well-directed movie. Thinking back, Mum's death and my financial survival must have been orchestrated by divine intervention.

Two months after Mum died, my heat pump/air conditioner and kitchen refrigerator spluttered and expired after twenty years of faithful service. The replacement cost for them was $8,000. Thanks to providence and my inheritance, I am grateful that I had the funds to replace both items.

In May 2007, I was delighted to receive another call from Mum's friend Barbara.

"Well, I still miss your Mum," she said, "but I'm gradually adjusting. Someone has moved into your Mum's flat, but I don't socialize with her. Frankly, I don't want to go in there now that your Mum's not there. Too sad."

I told Barbara how serendipitous I considered my inheritance. It had arrived at a time when my home began to fall apart and I was thankful I could pay off my car loan. There was silence on the other end of the phone.

"Barbara, are you still there?"

"It was the money that killed her."

I gasped. "What do you mean?"

"Your Mum was fretting something awful over that damned money. I told her, 'Vera, don't worry about the money. It'll be transferred to your bank account in a couple of days once they receive the authorization.' Couldn't get through to her—she couldn't sleep—worried herself to death literally."

"But she knew that the money had arrived safely, right? I thought it was in her account the day before she died."

"It was and she knew it was. But she was so flustered the whole time she was waiting for it I think her heart just gave out. I told her a couple of years ago 'You should send your daughter money to pay off her car. That would be a real help to her.'"

Now it was my time to remain silent for a long moment. "What did she say?"

"She said, 'No. I need this money in case I have to go into long-term care.' Well, I told her, 'Vera, the government will help pay for long-term care if you don't have enough to put down.'"

I interrupted her. "What do you mean? 'Enough to put down'?"

"Well, when you go into long-term care, the facility wants a certain amount of money up front. However, if Vera had only part of it, the government would pick up the rest. That's why I couldn't understand why she never sent you money to pay off your car."

I knew. Mum and Dad were proud, hardworking people. As Dad would often say, "pay as you go" and Mum supported this fiscally conservative philosophy. Mum had sufficient money saved to pay for long-term care. She didn't want to be in a position where she needed to ask for financial assistance, which might have occurred if long-term care was in her immediate future and if she had she given me £7,000.00 (approximately $14,0000) to pay off my car.

Barbara had tried to educate Mum on how long-term care facilities would work, but Mum, always stubborn, closed her ears, held to her beliefs, and kept her money "under her mattress."

By 1969, my adoptive parents had been debt free: the mortgage on their home was paid in full. Their value system, while commendable, became an issue of frustration for Vera later in life. She frequently complained that she was paying rent every month while several of her neighbors were living off the government.

"They can afford to go on holiday, drink and smoke, but they can't pay their rent." Her reaction to people that she perceived as deadbeats or free loaders was fierce. She couldn't forgive that kind of behavior.

Despite being told by the local financial aid authorities that if she spent some of her money she, too, would be eligible for government assistance toward the rent, Mum refused. She preferred to retain her pride, and I continued to make monthly car payments.

I am thankful that the need never arose where I had to ask my adoptive parents for money. I always knew that if a financial emergency loomed, I would need to fend for myself because I did not believe I could not rely on them for help or support. Dad would have been sympathetic but no doubt would have acquiesced to Vera when it came to parting with money.

I was not sad at Mum's passing. At ninety-two, her quality of life had deteriorated, but I was filled with an unexpected sadness that she had to die alone on a cold, steel gurney amongst strangers in the Emergency Room.

Vera's parenting skills as a mother had left me emotionally and psychologically bruised and battered. However, as the years passed and we maintained distance between us, we had both mellowed and matured. We had finally achieved a cautious truce.

44
THE CELESTIAL VISIT
2005

WHERE WAS I?

My mind felt sharp as a blade but absent a physical body. I was in a room without windows. I didn't see burning torches or candles but the room was dimly illuminated somehow. Was it a dungeon? I couldn't tell.

Without a physical body, the sense of freedom was as exhilarating as the environment was intimidating. Movement was easy and swift. I just thought of the place where I wanted to be and I was there instantly. The ceiling was my first experiment. In a second, I shot up, way up, amidst soaring arched stone vaults and looked down, way down, on a portion of the room.

Eager to explore my surroundings, I quickly discovered that my ability to move freely was limited. I sensed this limitation was imposed by whoever or whatever was in charge of my visit. My impression was of a large, stark room, perhaps some type of hall. It seemed to exist within a massive stone structure with ceilings that soared upward, more than a thousand feet. Cold and uninviting, the floor, walls, and ceiling were an unrelieved, clay-colored grey. It could have been in a Norman castle in England or Wales.

This was not my first experience with soul travel, far from it. Freedom to travel backward or forward in time, visiting far away destinations or dimensions—all the while snuggled and asleep in my bed—seemed perfectly natural to me. This time, I felt anxious and didn't understand why.

The restrictions had suddenly eased. The room appeared lighter, and my view of the surroundings broadened. In the center of the space was a vast, cream-colored marble chair with heavily carved, wide arms. The chair rested on a raised dais, five feet above the floor. For some reason, my view of the scene was from behind, at the top of the chair and several feet to its right.

I sensed an imposing presence seated in the chair. There was a click, followed by a brief flash of light. A figure who was wearing a white robe and appearing to be over seven feet tall was in the chair.

My mind groped back in time and recognition seeped to the forefront. Although the figure in the chair appeared to be androgynous, I knew the person was female. Where or when I'd met her, I couldn't recall. She reminded me of a statue outside the United States Supreme Court building in Washington, D.C., called "Contemplation of Justice."

What was going on here? What did all this mean? I had no idea.

A brilliant shaft of light suddenly burst from above, shining an inverted V and casting a six-foot-wide pool of light onto the floor directly before the chair. Alarmed, I felt mental prodding from someone or *something*. I was free to move, observe, and hear what was about to happen but from only one of two positions: either behind the eyes of the mysterious figure seated in the chair or hovering above her head. My mind zipped to a place above the head of the figure in the chair.

Caught in the light and standing in front of the dais were my dad and Vera, side-by-side, but not touching. Shocked at seeing my long dead, adoptive parents in these strange surroundings, I froze and then started to panic. I bounced around like a renegade tennis ball—in, out, and about the head of the woman in the chair.

Again, I felt the mental prodding, but now it helped to calm me.

Dad was wearing a dark grey suit, a light grey shirt, and a charcoal-grey tie. Vera was wearing a slate grey dress that blended in with her surroundings; there was a black belt at her waist. She wore no makeup, not even lipstick. Something was amiss. Vera never left home without lipstick. I remember thinking that she looked like a matron in an orphanage or a mental institution or perhaps even at Auschwitz. I felt chilled.

Dad pulled back his shoulders and took a deep breath. "May I speak?"

A few seconds passed. The woman in the chair nodded and raised her right hand, signaling her approval.

Dad cleared his throat. "I'm here to apologize."

The woman waved a second time.

Dad continued. "When I first saw you at the hospital, I knew that I knew you. I knew I had to adopt you. I wanted you for my daughter. If I'd known how Vera would treat you, how mean she would be to you, please believe me, I never would have agreed to the adoption. Will you forgive me?"

Everything seemed to freeze, except my mind, which was in frantic overdrive. After all these years, Dad was confessing that he knew Vera had been a mean, bullying mother. I noticed he never mentioned his failure to intercede when Vera was out of control and physically and psychologically abusive. Was he cleaning his karmic slate by seeking my forgiveness? I couldn't help but coldly speculate on this.

Most confusing was that Dad had just addressed the figure in the marble chair as if she and I were somehow one. That made no sense whatsoever. How could *she* possibly be *me?* Why would my dad speak to the woman in the chair as though she were his adopted daughter?

I wondered whether Dad and Vera had stepped off the elevator on the wrong floor. As I tried to collect my troubled thoughts, the scene started to shift again.

Dad shuffled his feet, looked down at the floor, and then directed his gaze at the person in the chair. I looked to Vera for her reaction. There was none. Like a statue, erect and motionless, she stared straight ahead and remained silent. That was so unlike Vera. She never let an opportunity pass where she could express her opinions. It seemed to me that Vera had not attended this meeting voluntarily—it was more like she'd been summoned.

Will I forgive him? I hesitated a moment, continuing to stare at my dad. *Did he realize how damaged I was because of Vera?* Then I realized that, at this point, he was no longer my dad, but a soul who was seeking redemption. I remember thinking, thoughts which were more like prayers: *I love my dad and I forgive him, but please, please don't make me relive this life.*

Seconds that seemed like hours ticked by. Eventually, the person in the chair slowly and deliberately nodded toward my dad and then waved her hand in dismissal. I heard another click: the chair and the figure had disappeared.

Alone in these strange surroundings, after what I had just witnessed, I was grateful that my Dad and Vera could not see me. Dad bowed his head and began to weep. His tears soothed my heart and washed away some of my pain. All I felt was compassion for the person who used to be my father.

Vera remained motionless, detached, and unemotional. She looked like a cutout cardboard figure in a movie foyer.

I awoke abruptly at 3:30 a.m. *Where was I?* Everything looked foreign to me. When I heard that all-too familiar click my awareness seemed to slot back into my present life.

I hugged the pillow and tears trickled down my cheeks. If only Dad had supported me against Vera's tirades when I was growing up instead of burying his head in the sand like an ostrich, perhaps my childhood would have been different.

As I passed from teenager to young adult and beyond, I developed a hard, practical streak in which tears were not allowed to flow freely. They accomplished nothing.

Tears had proven to be a luxury, wasted on "if only." Such dreaming is a threat to survival. Life moves forward, not backward. The unfinished business with my dad was complete. He had asked for and received, somewhat begrudgingly, my forgiveness. Our slate was clean.

As far as Vera, well....

45
REFLECTIONS
2014

MUM AND I NEVER SPOKE OF THE DAY I threatened to push her down the stairs. She lived another seventy-four years, nineteen of them alone after her husband, my dad, passed away. However, she never once raised the topic. It was as if the day had never happened, that it had magically been erased from her memory. I believe that shock and fear thrust the events of that day into crevasses far at the back of her mind. She had not wanted to relive the horror that the child she had adopted and lived with for eighteen years had once confronted her with enough cold rage to kill her. Whether she ever pondered the reasons for my anger and actions, I'll never know.

For me, the day has continued to linger in the back of my mind. I did not feel apologetic about striking out for survival or wanting to escape the claws of an abusive, maternal bully, especially one who had chosen to adopt a baby given up by her biological mother due to circumstances and societal pressure. Yet I found it disturbing to realize that, within me, I could access such a dark space.

Sometimes I hear people say, somewhat dismissively: "You need to get over it." My initial thoughts are always these: *We never get over it. It's part of us. It's helped shape us into who we are. Don't you get it? We've struggled to map a route around or through the pain, knowing that whatever pierced our hearts still exists and will forever invade our peace of mind if we let our guards down and remember.*

Others have viewed us as pathetic victims. To them I say: Walk in *my* shoes for a few years. All abused children are victims. Our characters will shine through despite our early years, when we survive and thrive. The lucky ones, like me, are strong enough to map that route, move around or through the pain inside, and carve out a productive life. We're always hoping the walls we've built won't crumble down. Others fall by the wayside. Pain, from whatever source, makes people fragile and vulnerable. Some become addicted to drugs, sex, or alcohol. Others commit suicide.

When I recall my work history and volunteer activities over the last thirty-five years, I believe my painful childhood cultivated within me a deep compassion for others, and a desire to be of service. When I left home at eighteen, the physical, psychological, and emotional baggage were weighing me down. Over the years, much of that baggage has become tattered and worn; I've eventually allowed most to slip from my shoulders while I forged new paths. However, some baggage remains; it's determined to stick around until the day I quit breathing.

For two decades, I had tried to sidestep conflict by turning away when I encountered someone whom I perceived as abusive or a bully. When I was in my forties, I was involved in two separate and very special circumstances, both of which helped change my way of dealing with bullies. During 1984 and

1985, two of my former coworkers who were trying to escape spousal abuse, lived with me for a while, waiting for their husbands' tempers to cool.

At work one morning, my friend Elsa, a petite and attractive young woman, followed me into the ladies' room.

"What's up?" I asked as I checked my makeup in the mirror.

"Not much."

"How's that new personal injury case shaping up?" She did not respond. I glanced aside. Tears were trickling down her face; she was slumped against the wall. Alarmed, I went over to her and put my arm around her shoulders.

"What's wrong? Talk to me."

"I don't know what to do."

"About what?"

Elsa started to sob.

I hugged her close. "It's okay, cry it out." I handed her some tissues. "Take these to mop up the mascara. Can't have beautiful you looking like a raccoon now, can we?" The sobbing stopped. She shuddered slightly and giggled. I dropped my arm. The worst was over. Elsa mopped the tears running down her cheeks and wiped away the mascara under her eyes.

"Is it the job? Is the pressure here getting to you?"

"No, the job's fine. It's, well… it's John, my husband." One forlorn tear slid down her left cheek.

"Your husband? What's going on with your husband?" I had seen bruises on Elsa's arms and, more recently, she came to work nursing a black eye. I had suspected her husband was responsible.

She took a deep breath and looked me square in the eyes. "I know you saw the bruises and the black eye. Hell, the whole office saw them." She shook her head and stared down at her feet. "When Jeff asked me what had happened, I told him that I'd walked into a door. But that wasn't true. John and I had a terrible fight a week ago. He got so mad that he slammed his fist into my face. He busted my eardrum and gave me a black eye."

Elsa crossed her arms over her chest, hugging herself, and the tears again spilled onto her cheeks. "I'm scared of him. I don't know what he'll do next. What if he hits my son? Richard's only eight. I can't complain to John's bosses; it would jeopardize his career."

I put my arms around her and held her tight. I knew that Elsa's boss, Jeff, also suspected that her husband was responsible for the injuries, and now Elsa had confirmed our suspicions.

I recalled seeing Elsa's husband occasionally stop by the office to pick her up at the end of the workday. I had heard him bark orders and his attitude toward Elsa showed me that he expected her immediate compliance. Perhaps his manner was due to his training in the military. I understood from Elsa that he held a command position.

I could feel Elsa calming down and I loosened my grip. "We'll figure something out. Don't worry. Do you have any vacation time?"

She blew her nose. "No, I can't take any yet because I haven't worked here for a year."

"What about your family?"

"They all live in California."

"Can you go visit them? Under the circumstances, I'm sure Jeff would give you a week off."

She shook her head. "I'd rather not. Mom didn't like John. She didn't want me to marry him. Said he wasn't good enough.

She would just gloat, telling me that she was right and I was wrong. I don't want to deal with that right now."

Elsa straightened her shoulders, wiped her eyes, and examined her face in the mirror, checking to see where repair work was necessary.

"What about friends in Phoenix?" I asked. Elsa turned away from the mirror and looked at me. "John and I have a few, but he would track me down. Things would get worse if I stayed with any of them. I can't risk that."

At that moment, there seemed only one solution. "Well, he doesn't know me or where I live," I said. "So why don't you and Richard move in with me. I have a second bedroom and a comfortable couch for your son. We'd have to share the bathroom, but you guys would be safe and that's what counts."

Elsa mouth gaped; her hands flew to her cheeks. "Do you mean it?"

"Of course. Just be sure to tell Richard that, well... because I'm not really a kid person, I don't know how to talk to kids. I've never been around them much, but he's welcome in my home."

"Oh, my son's easy. You two will get along fine."

She was right. Richard and I did get along fine. It turned out that, like me, Richard loved animals. At that time, I had a Great Dane and a German Shepherd. I walked the dogs in the mornings for forty minutes at a nearby park before I went to work. During the months that Richard and his mom lived with me, he always tagged along whenever I walked the dogs.

Around five in the morning, every weekend, Richard and I would stop at the Jack in the Box for breakfast. Then we would drive to Lake Pleasant and swim across the narrow part of the lake, with the Great Dane paddling beside us. The German

Shepherd was content to sit on the shore and watch. The dogs loved Richard, and he loved the dogs. To my surprise, those weekend mornings with Richard were great. I enjoyed his company and quick wit. Apparently I did like *some* kids.

Elsa stayed home, giving her a chance for some private space. Everyone was happy and John never found us.

One night after work, Elsa told me that she was intending to reunite with her husband. "I miss him, but I told him, 'I will not put up with any more of your bullshit.' He wants to come here tomorrow evening, pick us up, and take us back home with him."

"Are you sure you want to do this?"

"Yes, I'm stronger now. He knows; I've told him, I won't put up with any more crap. If he lays a hand on me again, I'll leave for good."

The following evening her husband knocked on my door. I let him in and studied the man. He was muscular man, six feet tall and still in uniform.

He introduced himself. "I am so grateful to you for taking such good care of my wife during our difficult period. She says you've been great to her and Richard."

I was unimpressed. A bully and a wife beater is a bully and a wife beater.

I walked up close to this man who was quite a bit taller than me. Standing within his personal space, I stared up at him. "Just remember this. If I hear from *anyone* that you've laid a hand on her, I will immediately drive to the base and lodge a complaint with your commander." I gestured toward Elsa. "She does not want to soil your career with complaints of spousal abuse. I have no such allegiance. Are we clear?"

Her husband raised both hands, palms out, defensively. "Absolutely, absolutely. I will keep my temper in check, I promise. Honest to God, I will not touch her."

I believed he would try, but would he succeed? Elsa told me that when her husband was on duty, people catered to his every whim and followed his orders without question. Unfortunately for Elsa, when he was off duty and at home, it seemed that those same expectations were carried into his personal life.

I had known Elsa and worked with her for six months before she moved in with me. I knew her as a kind, usually quiet, but sometimes opinionated and willful young woman. According to Elsa, when she was growing up, her mother had constantly told her that she was beautiful, just like a princess, and no man was good enough for her.

Considering the personalities of both parties, whether future incidents of domestic violence could erupt was anyone's guess.

This was my first major step toward confronting bullies—not including Vera—whether they were trying to bully me or someone else.

There were times when employers, coworkers, and boyfriends tried to bully me. At least, that was my perception, and instantly, they became opponents, just like Vera had been. Words became my primary weapon to smite and vanquish any enemy, with a few hand gestures thrown in for necessary emphasis.

When I heard from a dear friend that her father had molested her sister when they were kids, I was shocked. I'd known this woman for ten years, so this revelation was unexpected. "Oh, my God! How bloody awful! Did your mother know?"

"Yeah, I think so, but she pretended she didn't. Life was easier that way. Dad could be a bastard, especially when he was drunk. There were six of us kids, and we felt the belt all too often."

"Did he molest you too?"

"Are you kidding?" She laughed. "He would never have tried that with me. I'd've kneed that filthy bastard in the balls and he knew it."

Like me, my friend was a survivor. Our anger from childhood memories had shoved us forward, protected us from future abuse, and kept us alive, but it also gnawed at our innards. We had both toyed with the idea of seeing a therapist, but were reluctant to relive the misery.

"There's no way I'm gonna sit across from a guy and spill my guts," my friend said. "What's done is done. Can't change it. Let's have a drink."

During one of our weekly phone chats when Mum was close to ninety, she said, "I was probably hard on you when you were growing up."

Her remark came totally out of the blue. For several long moments, silence hung in the air like Arizona monsoon humidity. I took a sip of Jack Daniels, a long drag on my cigarette, and then made a decision. This was my opportunity to hurt the bitch, let her know the depth of pain she had inflicted on me and the damage she had caused. I took a deep breath and decided to remain silent.

To unwrap the pain of those first eighteen years and bombard my elderly mother with a barrage of anger and resentments, which she probably would not remember, was not an option. I'd always lived with sadness at feelings of abandonment, and pain that grew into anger as a teenager, because of how Vera bullied and abused me. Still, I did not wish to hurt her intentionally. Vera had little to do with my life after I left home at age eighteen, although I had plenty of Vera to unravel for the next fifty years.

———

It was a few weeks after my mother's death when my cousin forwarded me a letter that Mum had written shortly before she died, but had never posted. She wrote, in part: "I was not always the mother I should have been. I am very proud of her." That was the closest she came to apologizing to her adopted daughter.

Now in my seventies, I have a better grasp of Mum's possible insecurities and the reasons why she acted and reacted in certain ways when we lived under the same roof. This I can forgive. From what I learned about her family background, I suspect she too acted out of pain.

She was not a perfect mother; I was not a perfect child.

What I cannot understand is why a woman who so desperately wanted a child sought to destroy her daughter's self-esteem. How could she not see that I was in such pain for lack of love that I wanted to die?

Adoption may be a good option for many, but it didn't work well for me. But then, what would have happened to me, placed in an orphanage and then into service? Who knows? Those who are considering adoption need to educate themselves on the difficulties of raising someone else's child. Children who are adopted will frequently feel a deep sadness, wondering why they were given up by their biological mothers for adoption. That feeling may never heal. Even if children are adopted by exceptional individuals, questions about why their biological mothers chose to give them up for adoption will probably always litter the backs of their minds, regardless of whatever level of success and happiness they achieve.

Have I forgiven Mum for her verbal and physical abuse, the years of bullying, and her inability to show love and affection to the bastard child she and Dad adopted? Let's say that I no longer harbor anger toward my adoptive mother. Mum gave me what she knew: practical training to earn a living and be independent, which she learned from her mother, and for that I will always be grateful. As I evolved as a person, my life became richer and more fulfilling, and the pain has diminished. I survived and thrived.

No wonder Vera's last note said she was proud.

Ends

Acknowledgments

A Tarot Card reader in San Francisco once told me that I would write a book. That was in 1970. I wondered if she'd been smoking those "funny" cigarettes and gave no more thought to the idea. Sixty-seven years later, I started writing a creative non-fiction book about my life as an adoptive child. I spent eighteen years in a home where my adoptive mother was a bully; she followed the dictates of society when it came to raising children in the 1940s and 1950s. The book has taken me four years to complete.

When I read several chapters of my book before members of my writers' critique group, tears of repressed pain, locked away in my heart for many years, flowed uncontrollably. I hate crying in public so the experience was embarrassing. Thank you to the members of my critique group who were always supportive and provided the necessary feedback for me to improve my manuscript.

I believe in Angels, people that come into our lives at certain times to help and guide us. The following is a list of some of those angels who are mentioned in the book. I would like to thank:

Nellie Miles. Her back door was always open to me when my adoptive mother's anger was out of control and I needed to escape.

Anne and her mother, who offered me sanctuary when I left my parents' home and had no place to go.

Eleanor Clark and George Moore. Miss Clark gave me the opportunity to improve my work skills and retain my job. George Moore mentored me to ensure that I met Miss Clark's expectations.

Phillip Austin, Esq., Chief Counsel, Arizona Civil Rights Division. He gave me numerous opportunities and encouragement to expand my skills in mediation, training, public speaking, and investigations.

Heather Sigworth, Esq., and Judy Drickey-Prohow, Esq., former Assistant Attorneys General with the Arizona Civil Rights Division. Their training in civil rights laws, report writing, and investigative techniques for employment, housing, and public accommodation cases was invaluable.

Michaele Lockhart, my editor. Her skillful guidance and expertise as a teacher, author, and editor helped me create a book that I am proud to say is mine.

Glenda Taylor
May 2015
bobcatroja@comcast.net

Made in the USA
San Bernardino, CA
11 October 2015